MW00586508

Oh, Do I Remember!

NON-RETURNABLE

SUNY series,

Theory, Research, and Practice in Social Education

Peter H. Martorella, editor

ANNA VICTORIA WILSON
AND WILLIAM E. SEGALL

Oh, Do I Remember!

EXPERIENCES OF TEACHERS
DURING THE DESEGREGATION
OF AUSTIN'S SCHOOLS, 1964–1971

STATE UNIVERSITY OF NEW YORK PRESS

Published by
STATE UNIVERSITY OF NEW YORK PRESS
Albany

© 2001 State University of New York

All rights reserved

Printed in the United States of America

No part of this book may be used or reproduced in any manner whatsoever without written permission. No part of this book may be stored in a retrieval system or transmitted in any form or by any means including electronic, electrostatic, magnetic tape, mechanical, photocopying, recording, or otherwise without the prior permission in writing of the publisher.

For information, address
State University of New York Press,
90 State Street, Suite 700, Albany, NY 12207

Production, Laurie Searl
Marketing, Patrick Durocher

Library of Congress Cataloging-in-Publication Data

Wilson, Anna Victoria.
    Oh, do I remember! : experiences of teachers during the desegregation of
Austin's schools, 1964–1971 / Anna Victoria Wilson and William E. Segall.
    p. cm.—(SUNY series, theory, research, and practice in social education)
    Includes bibliographical references and index.
    ISBN 0-7914-5037-6 (alk. paper)—ISBN 0-7914-5038-4 (pbk. : alk. paper)
    1. School integration—Texas—Austin.   2. African American teachers—
Texas—Austin—Interviews.   I. Segall, William E. (William Edwin), 1938–
II. Title.   III. Series

LC214.23.A95 W55 2001
379.2'63'0976431—dc21   00-054908

10 9 8 7 6 5 4 3 2 1

This book is dedicated to all the teachers who saw the visions of equality in education and in particular to the teachers who willingly shared their stories with us

Charles Aikins
Iola Taylor
Vernice Smith
Ann Stoll
Herbert Brown
James Dorsett
Tom Allen
Melvin Chambers
Alvin Patterson
Clifford McPherson

Lastly, this book is a special dedication to

DR. PETER H. MARTORELLA,

editor of this series, who died prior to the
publication of this book.

Like the teachers in this book, Peter saw the visions of equality in schools and shared his passion to have others understand through writing and editing. He was a leader in the field of social studies education and believed that good teaching was about "the heart, the hand, and the head." He always challenged his students, colleagues, and friends to achieve what they thought was beyond their grasp. We remember and honor Dr. Peter Martorella for his relentless pursuit of excellence and his passion for knowledge.

We will miss you, Peter.

Contents

Foreword

Most Americans do not remember official segregation. Across almost a half century, the nation has disassembled many of that segregation's most egregious and obvious signs and symbols. For example, the offensive "For Negroes Only" and "For Whites Only" placards over public drinking fountains and restrooms long ago disappeared from view. Millions of African Americans could not freely vote in elections and could not participate actively in the political process. Notably, public schools legally separated both students and teachers by race. Segregation policies and practices were raw, inflexible, and widespread. They held the entire nation, not just the South, in bondage.

These chains were loosened and broken through massive public efforts and little known acts of real women and men. Laboring in this Civil Rights struggle were Black and White Americans, government and business elites who attempted to frame positions of public policy in private, as well as others who negotiated in the halls and back rooms of power. They included blue-collar "no-names" who marched on the Main Streets of cities across the nation under the leadership of Martin Luther King, our brother, and others no less our sisters and brothers, but less well known. Many of these persons who sought too long delayed justice faced scorn and ridicule and shaming in the quiet venues of their existence; others endured the highly publicized physical insults characterized by Bull Conner's Birmingham police who used fire hose streams and bludgeons on peaceful demonstrators and by the picketers at Little Rock's Center High School who shouted insults at the quiet African American youth who sought simply to attend the school. Casualties of the struggle included the deaths of real people, children and adults, the loss of institutions, both churches and schools, and personal relationships. Still, as the years wore on, official segregation gave way.

The 1954 Supreme Court decision in *Brown v. Board of Education* required desegregation of American schools " . . . with all deliberate speed." Remarkably, few ably researched and narrated stories of school desegregation exist. Most of these extant stories are not pretty and few are happy. The mandated "speed," for the most

part, was known in everyday life "as slow as possible—if ever." Court orders, busing plans, new magnet schools, redistricting efforts, even the development of middle schools became approximations or temporal responses to the general school
desegregation concern. Moreover, Americans remember most of these activities,
especially the local engagements of public controversy, mainly in personal fragments. Even these private recollections are fading and disappearing from possible
public memory as the major participants age and die. School desegregation remains one of the defining episodes of the American portion of the twentieth century. Therefore, it should be understood as completely as possible, in all its variety,
and through its tortured politics and the ruined lives and careers of thousands of
individual Americans, Black and White. It also should be understood for its contributions to the continued nurturance of the American dream and the enhanced
lives of millions of American citizens. The need to deepen the vessel of public
memory about school desegregation should be transparent.

Most stories of the desegregation of American public schools are imbedded
in local circumstances. They began and continued and, to be sure, ended as local
responses to more general concern or to adversarial confrontation. That they differ from community to community does not devalue them. Indeed, that very difference emphasizes their importance. This variety elevates awareness about the
political efforts to frustrate as well as to dismantle school desegregation. It also
renders visible the real individuals, Blacks and Whites, adults and children and
youth, who were the human agents of desegregation. The stories of school desegregation may focus on plans, but they are about persons. Some received national
publicity; others, perhaps most, occurred outside the spotlight.

One of the little known efforts was a plan to desegregate schools by beginning
with the desegregation of school faculties. It was called "cross-over teaching." Apparently, the number of school districts across the nation that participated in such
plans is unknown; maybe only a few districts implemented this notion. For those
districts that did, ones like the Austin (TX) Independent School District, courts
subsequently ruled the plans to be evasive and not in compliance with the Supreme
Court's basic ruling. Still, the human stories that attended this abortive plan include
a panoply of near heroic as well as sordid accounts of human interaction.

I resided in Austin during the several years of our district's engagement with
cross-over teaching. I followed the stories of some of the first cross-over teachers, a
few of whom were my students. These stories passed along an informal, person-to-
person, almost "underground" network. In large measure, the public news media
were silent in description and candid appraisal of this practice. Only sometimes
did notice appear about this plan and it conventionally took the form of "official"
news. The cross-over teachers and their students existed invisible between the lines
in these public reports. Efforts to formulate and implement realistic desegregation
plans, each that involved both students and teachers, further obscured the cross-

over plan, its operations, and its teachers and students. Meanwhile, enlargement of the cross-over plan to include increasingly more teachers ground mainly silently through the bureaucracy of the schools and within the community. Throughout the interval of the plan's existence, I always felt uncomfortable about it. I also opposed the scheme in those few forums of which I was a party. Nevertheless, all of us Austin's citizens never knew enough about the cross-over plan. I confess that I did too little. However, legal action finally accomplished what much public sentiment could not obtain. The plan disappeared.

Only now, as a result of the diligent efforts of Anna Wilson, is a first serious account of cross-over teaching in the Austin schools available. This book began as a doctoral dissertation. As Professor Wilson's supervisor, I followed her research and writing almost every step of its way. Subsequently, Professor William Segall joined the enterprise and this book is the result of their collaboration.

Properly, the book focuses on the stories of Austin's few African American teachers who "crossed over" from their professional assignments in the still-segregated schools for African American youth to schools that, at the time, continued to enroll mainly White, including Mexican American, students. For this account, Wilson located and interviewed at length all but a few of the living African American teachers who were transferred from Anderson High School to previously all-White schools. These teachers clearly were major pioneers of school desegregation in Austin. This book opens this episode in the history of the city's schools for review and understanding as well as for wonderment. Although the district's policy temporized and postponed realistic desegregation initiatives, these teachers' journeys across Austin's political and social divides constituted significant movement in the city's Civil Rights movement. Their teaching and their lives, as portrayed in this study, manifest strong teaching practices as well as personal anxieties, hostilities, and joys. When cross-over teaching ended in Austin, the entire school system's teachers and administrators knew that the cross-over teachers had not only survived and endured, they had contributed mightily to the ongoing transformation of Austin's schools. Other African American teachers and students followed in their footsteps to enriched and educational and professional opportunities. A few positive legacies of this frustrating plan continue to be visible, although scarcely recognized. For example, Austin's newest high school carries the name of Charles M. Aiken, the city's first African American teacher to cross over to a formerly all-white school.

This book emphasizes the lived experiences of Austin's African American secondary school cross-over teachers. In this portrayal, however, it does not obscure the experiences of the district's White teachers who crossed over to Anderson High School. It is evenhanded even as it exhibits its emphasis.

Wilson and Segall's book is a story of beginnings, not of endings. Its focus on the African American high school teachers who crossed over to formerly all-White secondary schools constitutes an important prelude to subsequent research, to the development of a more encompassing account of this Austin desegregation plan. Indeed, it serves as a partial but an essential element of an unwritten and larger account of the closure of Austin's original L. C. Anderson High School, itself a victim of desegregation. This book also contributes impressively to the much-needed comprehensive story of desegregation in Austin. Much remains to be uncovered. Still, scholars who will seek to penetrate additional elements of this story must begin their inquiry with this book.

Although most Americans don't remember official racial segregation of schools as personal experience, none of us can remain ignorant of it. Moreover, as the resegregation of the nation's schools continues, we Americans must be aware of the means that individuals of the Civil Rights generation and, specifically, the teachers portrayed in this book, undertook to dismantle segregated schooling. This knowledge truly is power.

O. L. DAVIS JR.
Professor of Curriculum and Instruction
The University of Texas at Austin

Acknowledgments

This text would not be complete if we did not acknowledge those who took note of our work. First and foremost, we are deeply indebted to the teachers who willingly gave of their time and experience as they shared their memories and experiences during the tumultuous times of desegregation. Without them, this book would not exist. At the University of Texas at Austin, we would like to thank Drs. Mary Black, Ann Brooks, Don E. Carlton, O. L. Davis Jr., Diane Schallert, and the late JoAnne Sweeney for their professional comments and criticisms, especially of the Austin interviews. Their interest and support resulted in the completion of this text.

A very special thank you is given to Dr. Peter Martorella, friend, colleague, and mentor, at North Carolina State University. He supported, as well as critiqued, our writing throughout the preparation of this book. His friendship was invaluable. Dr. Terrence O'Brien, interim head of the Department of Curriculum and Instruction at North Carolina State University, understood the importance of this text as it related to curriculum and teaching. Dean Kay Moore, College of Education and Psychology, recognized the importance of the text's treatment of school desegregation and offered continuing encouragement in its completion. At Oklahoma State University we would like to thank Dean Ann Candler Lotven who supported the completion of the text and its significance as a continuing exploration of schools and teaching in a diverse society. Dr. Martin Burlingame, head of the School of Educational Studies, who supported the text by actively involving himself in its progress, asking constructive questions, and encouraging its completion. Their support is greatly appreciated.

We want to thank our graduate students and colleagues who read drafts of chapters, engaged in critical discussions immersed in the multiple voices of desegregation, and supported our goal of honoring those who taught during that turbulent time. Lastly, we commend each other for the willingness to write with one voice.

CHAPTER ONE

Introduction

THE AMERICAN SCHOOLHOUSE, like so many other elements of history's capricious choices of time and place, hardly looks the part of a last stand. New or old, painted or peeling, the schoolhouse seems more suited to its own world of pencils, papers, maps, and books. Yet, American schools were the site at which more than two hundred years of racial segregation in the United States ceased to exist. Here, also, a new generation of Whites and Blacks[1] learned together, played together, and some wondered later "what the fuss was all about." Blacks living in segregated communities definitely understood the difficulties surrounding public school desegregation. Iola Taylor, for example, remembered the simple act of buying candy as a Black child in Hearne, Texas.

> It was . . . so segregated in terms of racial treatment that I can remember several of the real negative kinds of experiences. For example, the experience of not being treated in the same fashion [as Whites]. . . . If I went to the store to buy a bar of candy, the storekeeper would hand me the candy, but he would never hand me the change. He would always put the change on the table. I would pick up the change from the table. It was a no-no for him to touch me and for me to touch him . . . When I would pay him, I would put the money on the counter and he would pick it up. There was never any touching between Blacks and Whites. You just didn't do that![2]

Although such incidents were the norm for Blacks during segregation in the South, most Whites seemed oblivious to the consequences for Blacks. The social implications of superiority and inferiority based on racial identification emerged during simple tasks such as buying candy in a store or attending school or working in a factory or walking down a sidewalk.

In many ways, the future of Black children was formed by the varying and conflicting White and Black institutions. Of course, White institutions excluded Blacks from general interactions, but of all the institutions, except the family, the one that touched children the most was the school. For Whites, schools were thought of as extensions of the American social and economic infrastructure. Beyond learning how to read and write, along with other fundamentals, White children learned how to compete in a society imbued with individualism. In many ways, schools taught White children they were exclusive. That is, they were made to believe that, depending on their own abilities, they could be anything they wanted to be in a meritocratic society.

On the other hand, Black children learned the opposite. Black children knew that, as slaves, it had been illegal for their grandparents to learn. They also knew Jim Crow[3] laws later relegated their parents to schools that had fewer accouterments than public White schools. Left to their own devices, Blacks, in their own communities, developed schools for their children. Although the curriculum in Black schools taught children how to read and write, other fundamentals were different. Because Blacks were not allowed to compete in a society that rewarded competition, their children were taught that education should act as a shield against corruption and slavery. Success in school was marked by the knowledge that Blacks could defend themselves in a society in which they had few legal rights. In short, American Blacks, like European Jews, believed schools and the knowledge they dispensed were the bricks and mortar of a community that would protect its citizens.

How did these communities work? Whites, looking from without, thought they seemed to be without an essence. They thought those who lived in the communities were unable to look beyond the community to the outside world. That is, they confused the Black communities with slums and gladly placed them outside the White neighborhoods. For those within the Black communities, the essence was visible to all who participated. In fact, the Black communities acted as families of community interests in defense of their futures. Beyond the natural families of fathers, mothers, grandparents, and siblings, the Black community enveloped everyone within its borders. Bluntly, the Black community was the awareness that each person was part of the all, and the all was responsible for each. To make the Black community a reality, it was important that children receive an education.

In many ways, Black children went to school like their White contemporaries. Most of the curriculum was the same as in White schools. Just as White teachers taught and gave homework assignments, so did Black teachers. Just as

White children tried to find ways to lighten their academic loads by hoping for less homework and fewer assignments, so did Black children. However, as White children saw themselves entering a society that would encourage their success, Black children saw themselves held within the loving arms of a family and community.

In 1954 the social disequilibrium called segregation came to an end. Striking to the heart of segregation, *Brown v. Board of Education Topeka, Kansas* ruled that *Plessy v. Ferguson* (1896) was wrong. As a consequence, the *Brown* decision became controversial. It was popular and unpopular for the same reasons at the same time. In fact, this decision generated more conflict over a longer period of time than its authors anticipated. No other Supreme Court decision likely has fostered as much fundamental social change, or has touched as many families and institutions in so many communities as this judicial decision. While the primarily focus of the decision dealt with the education of children and where they would be schooled, it ultimately changed what schools would teach. That is, White children would learn about other elements of American society they did not recognize. It would eventually take Black children from their safe havens and leave them by themselves, defenseless and alone in a world they did not understand nor wish to live in.

The Southern drama of *Brown* differed from community to community. Yet, while local conditions created different circumstances, in the broadest sense, each community came to terms with desegregation along a similar path. First, among Blacks, a sense of relief was expressed that their children's future would be better. Then came the realization that Whites did not want their dreams to become realities. For Whites, the inference of *Brown* was at first misunderstood. Many community leaders believed that if nothing was done, desegregation would simply go away. But, as it became clear that the old social order was disappearing, most White community leaders, for their own reasons, wanted that change to take place at a snail's pace. For example, delay for White school board members meant devising various plans, that, although on the surface they appeared to foster desegregation, simply delayed racial intermixing and heighten racial tensions. Some school boards developed plans that put the onus of desegregation on the shoulders of White parents who were publicly opposed to their children studying with Blacks. Other plans that gave the appearance of desegregation simply reshuffled teachers from school to school. Like other plans, these actions simply delayed the inevitable. It was this inevitability that the Austin, Texas, district school board fought so long to avoid.

In the final analyses, *Brown v. Board of Education* changed the lives of all Americans. For some Americans of both races, the changes were welcomed because the United States Supreme Court recognized and attempted to correct a basic evil within the nation's social fabric. But it forced others of both races to look at themselves from within, and sometimes what they saw they did not like. Regardless, *Brown* caused White Americans to change in ways they resisted. That is, parents feared that their children would somehow become different if they attended integrated schools. Families were afraid they would become different if they lived in integrated neighborhoods or worked with Blacks. *Brown* forced Black Americans to change beyond the buoyed emotions of completing a long struggle for equality. Most did not realize their lives would change in ways they did not totally understand. For some Blacks, inequality had been equated with "opportunities lost." Now, they were to discover that equality could also mean the loss of neighborhoods, schools, and families. Those that looked saw their communities decline.

Our original idea of this project focused on the untold story of cross-over teaching in Austin, Texas, as part of the process of desegregation. Using teachers' narratives, this book explores the many and diverse ways of interpreting school desegregation. The teachers' willingness to share their experiences through their stories allows us to unravel a major historical event that affected all of society. The teachers' stories encapsulate the personal (social/professional) histories of people who reflected the great changes of that time, and paints a picture about how individuals, with their very own specific lives to live, were caught in a web of social change. However, we soon learned this project was more than a story about desegregation. It was a story of people attempting to control their lives while changes swirled around them.

The public desegregation history of Austin provided the framework for understanding the private histories of Black teachers juxtaposed with White teachers. While this study [4] is important in the overarching history of civil rights and Southern public school education, the significance of the teachers' narratives is paramount. The teachers' narratives transport us back some thirty years to segregated high school classrooms, and the process of desegregating those classrooms. Revealed through their narratives was the dominant culture's exclusive control over the political, cultural, and social institutions. In many ways, this study demonstrated the dominant culture's overwhelming need to continue the sociopolitical controls limiting the discourse of Blacks regarding an important period in the history of schools. Within the framework of this study, Black teachers constructed remembered experiences of realities that were meaningful and empowering in their lives.

The seeds for this study of cross-over teaching were first planted in a curriculum seminar at The University of Texas at Austin. Our participating in the gathering of teachers' stories who taught during World War II [5] opened the door to another area of education that has remained closed until recently. In this case, the door opened to the history of school desegregation through the memories of classroom teachers. [6] Classroom teachers possess an intimate knowledge of the experienced policies and practices of schools. Therefore, we concluded that classroom teachers' memories of school desegregation would provide an opportunity to more fully understand the policies as they were practiced in the classroom.

Given this context, as we uncovered the largely unknown component of teachers in classrooms during school desegregation, an informed understanding about this unique, yet hidden, time in American educational history slowly emerged. Our interest in cross-over teaching led us in search of those teachers who, as a result of collective struggles and community support, changed the process of desegregation in Austin, Texas.

Untangling the web of cross-over teaching in Austin proved to be a more difficult task than we first imagined. Many of the participating teachers were deceased, had moved from Austin, or could not be located. Of those interviewed the majority had retired from teaching and many of them were in their mid-seventies. Even though the teachers' ages and the distance in time from the actual events potentially contribute to disjointed recollections, their remembered experiences were complementary of one another and with the few documents still available.

FINDING THE PIECES

Between 1964 and 1971, thirty-three Black and fifty-two White teachers participated in Austin's cross-over teaching plan at the high school level.[7] Of those teachers, eighteen were located and interviewed. All oral history interviews of the eighteen cross-over teachers were recorded on audio tapes.[8]

Apart from the remembered experiences of the teachers, few traces of Austin's history of school desegregation exist. The Austin school board minutes yielded minimal information about cross-over teaching. Newspaper articles of the time conveyed the public story of cross-over teaching; but, many teachers recalled, the newspapers glossed over the actual events in Austin. Unfortunately, when L. C. Anderson High School was permanently closed during the summer of 1971, its files were largely destroyed. Scattered through Austin school district's archives were some snippets of general information but little documentary evidence specific to school desegregation and cross-over teaching existed. We were forewarned by Marius's comment that

> all historians confront an essential problem: the past is dissolving under our feet all the time . . . time is the devourer of all things. Time destroys. The evidence for past events is always incomplete and fragmentary, like a jigsaw puzzle washed out of a shipwreck and cast upon a rocky beach by the waves. Many pieces are lost. Those that remain are often faded and warped.[9]

Something other than "time" destroyed the history of L. C. Anderson High School. We believe it was the insidious and continued marginalization of the Black high school that resulted in so few public documents.

Sadly, few primary sources, other than the oral histories, could be located. In fact, potential sources identified by the teachers, such as television videotapes

(KLRU), Anderson High School archives, the University of Texas-sponsored program for school desegregation assistance (TEDTAC) files, and the school district archives, were found to be less than adequate. The records, when available, were spotty and disappointing. Despite local television documentaries about school desegregation, the videotapes were not preserved by the television station. The school district archives contained a multitude of materials, of which some related to school desegregation while others had no bearing on school desegregation or the decision to use cross-over teachers as an integral component of school desegregation. Although we easily located boxes of materials about each school in the school district archives, we soon noted an exception—minimal historical materials were located specific to the Black schools, from the elementary schools through to L. C. Anderson High School. Finally, no major documents could be found specific to the cross-over teaching policies as articulated by the Austin school board or its central administration.

As in all great social movements, desegregation was advanced by individuals who were willing to risk living on the edge of revolution. Usually, these individuals were not thought of as "leaders" or "decision makers" by their friends or those that knew them. Mostly, these individuals were neighbors or family members or co-workers or others, who, after the task had been completed returned to anonymity. Thus, Black teachers such as Charles Aikens, Iola Taylor, and Vernice Smith, for their own personal reasons, were willing to become leaders by "crossing over" to White Austin schools. As teachers, their purpose was to teach White students. As learners, they discovered what it was like to be a part of society searching for stability. White teachers Herbert Brown, E. Ann Stoll, James Dorsett, and Tom Allen learned the same lessons when they "crossed over" to teach Black children at L. C. Anderson High School.

While the history of the desegregation of Austin schools was played out by individual teachers, students, and school administrators of both races, the educational environment in which they lived was, in many ways, equally important. Of the high schools that taught Austin's youth, only Anderson High School was reserved for the Blacks. It was located at 900 Thompson Street, in the heart of East Austin. Anderson High was originally built in 1889 by Austin's Black community. Because the school board had budgeted existing finances for White students, Black parents "double taxed" themselves so their school could exist. Its first principal was Professor H. T. Kealing. After several rebuilding and expansions, the Austin School board employed Mr. E. H. Anderson as principal. In 1909, the high school for Negroes was named Anderson High School in honor of E. H. Anderson's pioneering educational leadership. His younger brother, Mr. Laurine Cecil Anderson became principal in 1896. L. C. Anderson's administrative career lasted thirty-four years. In 1929 he resigned as principal but remained on the faculty as a Latin teacher until 1932. Two days after his death on January 8, 1938, the Austin School

Board renamed the school L. C. Anderson in his honor. Even though many people who do not know its history referred to the school as simply Anderson, it was appropriate because the high school exemplified the ideals of the two brothers.

In 1971, L. C. Anderson High School was closed by a District Court order in which East Austin's Black teachers were reassigned to other high schools within the district. Much against their parents wishes, Anderson's students were bused to White schools. In 1973, Anderson High School would "cross over" to northwest Austin in the form of a new facility. Now located at 8403 Mesa Drive, the school is the home of White and some Black students. For those who were part of the early desegregation years in Austin, Anderson High School may be viewed as a metaphor for those years of struggle.

VISIONS CHANGE

Are we more interested in image or substance? Which is more important—how we are seen or who we are? When we speak our history, what is the history that we want to remember?

—Lorenzo Thomas,
quoted in *A Short Guide to Writing About History*

For many years, the narratives of Black teachers have been ignored by educational historians. To deal openly and honestly with the teachers' narratives as lived past lives, we had to confront the White community's power and control over the public and private lives of the teachers. Until recently, much of the documented experiences of teachers focused on White teachers and ignored the experiences of Black teachers. Thus, using Black and White teachers' memories of historical events in order to render an interpretation of the event itself remained a unique undertaking. The teachers' individual histories were inextricably linked to their collective history. Enriching the Black teachers' narratives was their willingness to share their childhood experiences during segregation.

The teachers' willingness to share their experiences opened the door to a unique and no longer hidden part of Austin's history. For this, we must thank each teacher who was a pioneer in desegregation. The cost to Austin Independent School District was more than money. The real cost came in the school administrators' deliberate inability to recognize that a person's worth is not based on the color of her/his skin. Resistance to desegregation continued the educational inequity experienced by Blacks in Texas. In reality, Austin paid dearly as it postponed the inevitable, full desegregation of its public schools.

We have special memories of the great stories shared with us by these wonderful teachers in their openness and desire to make a difference. Their reflections transcended cultural borders based on the color of one's skin. Their voices from within engaged and challenged us as we wrestled with the social constructions of race, gender, and class. This project presented opportunities for the construction of alternative realities embedded within stories within other stories. We constructed alternative realities by engaging in thoughtful deliberations concerning the realities of everyday lives through the complex intertwining of self and work and through our learning to value the silence in the teachers' texts. The teachers invited us to share their life as they lived it—for this experience we are profoundly and eternally grateful.

Finally, a word about how this book is constructed. Chapter two, *Social Construction of Race*, discusses the text and subtext of racism in America. Using United States Supreme Court and state court decisions as examples of how White America constructed definitions of racism and segregation, this chapter identifies many of those who were willing players in marginalizing African Americans and the rewards they felt were their due. Identifying the Ku Klux Klan, Southern Protestant fundamentalism, the military, state, and federal governments, and individuals as players in the drama of "othering," the chapter frames the futures both Blacks and Whites envisioned in the mid-1950s.

Chapter three, *Oh, I Do Remember!*, introduces the reader to Iola Taylor, Charles Akins, and Vernice Smith. Meeting them in the mid-1950s when they are young, the reader is attracted to the youthful spirit they demonstrate as each evaluates how her and his personal future could change because of *Brown v. Board of Education*. It is not until the chapter outlines the political and social reactions to the Supreme Court decision that it is made clear that the lives of these teachers will be influenced by the polarization of Texas opinion. Each of the young Black teachers is unaware of the influence social change will have on his or her life.

Chapter four, *Moving from the Shadows into the Sunlight*, addresses the problems school desegregation was causing Texas school boards. Much more than a context, the chapter brings to light some of the options the Austin school board was aware of as it faced similar issues. It could attempt appeasement policies such as those used by the Goose Creek school board at McNair's Harlem Elementary close to Houston. Or, it could risk the wrath of the NAACP, as Mansfield's school board discovered when their only concession to Black high school students was to issue them free Trailways bus tickets to Fort Worth's Black schools. Or, worst of all, it could create a political nightmare such as that generated by the Big Springs school board when their attempts to forestall school integration would be fought in the courts and public media by Texas politicians whose interests were self-serving. Unfortunately for the Austin school board it chose what would later be called "freedom of choice."

Chapter five, *With All Deliberate Slowness*, portrays the Austin school board and its central administrators, committed to segregation, developing policies intended to delude the Austin community of their real intent. Picturing these policy makers, who were unable to resolve the conflict between their personal values and the children they were legally bound to serve, the chapter concentrates on the abilities and professionalism of Black cross-over teachers who were forced into unique, interracial classroom conflicts with minimal assistance from those who were charged to help.

Chapter six, *No White Missionaries Need Apply,* narrates how the Austin school board continued its ill-fated attempts to delude Austinites by expanding its teacher cross-over policy to include White teachers. First asking White teachers who believed in integration to volunteer, and then assigning new, inexperienced White teachers to the city's only Black high school, the board felt it had succeeded. Like their Black colleagues, the White teachers discovered that their interactions with professional teachers and students inspired their own growth as teachers and human beings.

Chapter seven, *Death of a School,* describes the consequences to east Austin caused by the closure of L. C. Anderson High School. This chapter traces the organizational and political processes of school closings during this period through the lenses of Black and White classroom teachers who were committed to their Black students. It pictures the destructive elements of the "I" to students and their parents who had historically thought of themselves within the social structure of "We."

Chapter eight, *Reflections and Memories,* recounts the agonizing conflicts within Austin's White community, torn by rural values and White provincialism, regarding school integration. The chapter focuses on their failure to understand their urban environment and, examining why Whites fled to small rural communities outside the city, helps the reader form social parameters about questions of equality, opportunity, and assimilation.

Chapter nine, *Creating Places of Engaged Listening,* locates the experiences of Austin's cross-over teachers within the parameters of an exposed segregationist society. Using materials with which the reader is familiar, the chapter brings the text to a close by allowing the reader to engage in reflection about today's pluralistic classrooms and teachers' attempts to mold them into places of engaged listening.

CHAPTER TWO

Social Construction of Race

Lucy was watching television the other day when she saw a news clip on CNN. It was a short story about some little old lady[1] in a wheelchair who was escorted into the White House by several well-dressed men. They were taking her through a door when the commentator mentioned that the little old lady had been a housekeeper there during the Eisenhower administration. "Because she is Black," said the television voice about the little old lady, "this is the first time she has come through the front door rather than the side door she used when she worked in the White House." "How nice," thought Lucy sarcastically "Why is it those TV people always try to make such big deals about such unimportant things. I don't see them coming to interview me about my life."[2]

OF COURSE, LUCY IS NOT an actual person, but in many ways she really exists. Lucy is that specific something that dwells within many of us that forces us to gild our experiences with our own brand of knowledge or feelings. For Lucy, CNN's newsclip was important for three reasons. The first was the story about a little old lady in a wheelchair, and the second was that she had worked at the White House. The third reason was the most important, however. The news clip was about Color—a little old Black lady and a little old White lady.[3] This commentary demonstrates the confusion expressed by many about the need for conversations about race.

Lucy's comments are important to understand because they come to us from another time and space. They represent a world that is difficult for us to remember, but lurks with us still. For the Lucys of the world, it was that time when certain things always happened to everyone—without exception. It was a world in which everyone had the same experiences and understood the same things and agreed on the main points of living. Lucy was that person in many of us who subconsciously remembered the time when everyone came from a special place or neighborhood that signaled others who you were. Lucy wanted to know who you were before you told her. Lucy was that type of person who could comprehend the problems bemoaned by Mrs. Emerson 143 years earlier.

DRED SCOTT: SEEKING THE RIGHT TO BE FREE

A reserved lady, Mrs. Emerson was the wife of Dr. John Emerson, a United States Army surgeon. Not long before the Civil War, in 1843, Dr. Emerson died, and Mrs. Emerson found herself confused by her new responsibilities and freedoms. At the same time, she couldn't understand why her husband's slave, Dred Scott, came to her and demanded something that she believed was not her right to give. He kept alluding to his right to be free. Mrs. Emerson was confused, and without reason refused Dred's application. Three years later, in 1846, Scott sued Mrs. Emerson for his freedom. His lawyers argued his case before the Missouri Circuit Court, contending that when Dr. Emerson had taken Dred to Illinois, a slave free state, and Wisconsin, a slave free territory, Scott had gained the right to demand his freedom. Shortly after the Missouri Circuit Court ruled in Dred Scott's favor, Mrs. Emerson appealed to the Missouri Supreme Court.

While the Missouri Supreme Court was hearing the case (the lower court's decision was reversed on the argument that Blacks are property and therefore cannot be citizens), Dred Scott's life was further complicated. He was placed under the authority of Mrs. Emerson's brother, John Sanford of New York.[4] The case was again tried, this time in New York State, and once more Dred Scott lost. In 1857, Dred's legal journey ended in Washington at the Supreme Court. The seven to two ruling was simple and straightforward—slaves could not bring suit in a federal court because they were not citizens of the United States. In the meantime, Mrs. Emerson was exhausted by the confusion of the times. "Thank goodness," she may have thought, "At least the ruling came out all right." Not long after the Supreme Court ruling, Mr. Sanford sold Dred. Within two months, his owners gave him his freedom, ending his fourteen-year quest.

"GLORIOUS LOST CAUSES": CIVIL WAR AND RECONSTRUCTION

As Dred Scott quietly left the stage of history, his was the first significant discussion of race relations in the United States, in which Blacks defied slavery in a White forum.[5] That defiance was demonstrated three years later during the Civil

War. With most of the war taking place in the Southern states, many slaves ran away to join the Union army. It was not so much that the Union army solicited Black slaves to join up, nor were all Northern soldiers always happy to have Blacks join them. Rather, some soldiers felt Blacks were simply one more body that could carry a gun and shoot at the enemy. It would be interesting to know the thoughts of these soldiers. Like most Whites at that time they were interested to know if these Blacks were really human. Did they have feelings about freedom? And, could they take on leadership roles? Would they become dangerous if they were not supervised by Whites? Undoubtedly, some soldiers sympathized with the runaways and were happy to have Blacks join them. Some may also have been happy because now there were others who could be sent into the heat of battle. If a soldier was to die, would it not be better if that person was an uneducated Black, rather than a young White male whose life lay before him? At the same time, what were the feelings of Black runaway slaves and Confederate slave owners who, in the midst of battle, recognized each other and knew that one of them would have to die?[6]

Southern Whites generally did not consider the military conflict between 1861 and 1865 as a Civil War. Rather, in their minds it was a "War Between the States" or, as others would call it "The War of Northern Aggression." Some White Southerners thought of the war was a revolution for freedom from oppression in the same spirit as the American Revolution. Southern Whites romanticized the War as a "Glorious Lost Cause." Some Southern Whites were bewildered when Blacks were unwilling to accept this "reality." The truth of the matter was that most White Southerners did not know the feelings of Blacks about the War. It had never come to their mind to ask.

At the end of the Civil War the politics of race relations eventually was distilled into a Northern Abolitionist experiment to see if Southern ex-slaves could shoulder the responsibilities of governing the states their past "masters" thought to be their responsibility. Beset with conflicting plans to bring the rebelling states back into the Union, Congress, with its Radical Republican majority, chose to develop its own model.[7] As Northern "Carpetbaggers"[8] came to help Blacks govern, Southern Whites resented the continuing efforts to force them into "submission."

This White Southern recognition of Blacks entering the power structure was shocking to them.[9] It was difficult for Whites to express, but for most of them Blacks had, through the decades, become an invisible segment of Southern society. Beyond White awareness that menial social and economic tasks had to be done by someone, Blacks did not really exist. They had, in the eyes of Whites, become those others who had been pushed to the edges of the Southern social order. It is for that reason Texas Whites were horrified when Northerners and Blacks controlled the legislature in Austin, the capital city. They seethed with anger at rumors of Black Union soldiers rampaging in Victoria, close to Houston, destroying private property and threatening White civilians. Other communities[10] were also torched. Worst of all, White Texans discovered that the Black slave population had increased from 35,000 before the War to more than 200,000 at the end.[11]

In the same fashion, Blacks were becoming aware of the damaging impact of marginalization caused by slavery and White hatred. While "free" by Northern standards, the truth was that many Black Texans and most "banked" Louisiana and Arkansas Blacks did not know where to go.[12] As slaves, few had traveled, so their understanding of geography was limited. Family members had been sold and resold during slavery, which compelled many husbands, wives, fathers, mothers, and children to search for each other. Casting about from place to place, not knowing exactly how to find someone, looking for work to keep hunger at bay, resulted in many seeking any type of work and shelter available. Like liquid in a wide, shallow bowl held in the hands of an unsteady child, the tides of ex-slaves sloshed from place to place. Many times, traveling in groups, they passed each other trying to make sense of their freedom. Regardless of their personal circumstances, Blacks knew certain basic truths. Beyond religion and the knowledge of God, beyond the knowledge of hunger, thirst and cold, Blacks knew that Whites feared and hated them and would lie for any purpose to keep them from living a worthy life.

While most ex-slaves had personal experiences with White lies, perhaps the most bizarre lie that was passed from Whites to Blacks was that which was discovered on June 19, 1865. Union navy ships had berthed in Galveston harbor to off-load Federal troops under the command of General Gordon Granger. The troops were to march to Houston and other locations to maintain a Union military presence. During General Granger's opening remarks he mentioned Lincoln's Emancipation Proclamation. Ex-slaves were, for the first time, aware they had been free for years. Their masters had told them President Lincoln would never grant liberty. To express their feelings of exaltation of the Emancipation and, at the same time, keep as a remembrance the White lie, Black ex-slaves labeled that date as "Juneteenth." White Texans never understood the meaning of the term, and responding through their labeling spoke about how childish the ex-slaves were in celebrating Emancipation beginning on June 19,1866, and not January 1, 1863.[13]

Lately Known as Slaves

In 1866, the Eleventh Legislative Session of the Texas Legislature, dreading what might happen if large numbers of unemployed ex-slaves roamed the Texas byways, passed legislation entitled an *"Act to Define and Declare the Rights of Persons Lately Known as Slaves, and Free Persons of Color."*[14] This was the legislature's attempt to regulate Black behavior. In fact, the bill was intended to be a one-two punch against ex-slaves, and was referred to as the Black Codes.

The first "punch" the act delivered was a White directive ordering Blacks to comport themselves in specific, ordered behavior patterns. Therefore, regardless of gender or age, Blacks were required to remove their hats as a deferential gesture when meeting a White. They would, with gestures of deference, step off the sidewalk and recognize by a motion of the head (such as a nod) the presence of the White person.

Black men would remove their caps and stand next to the sidewalk waiting for the White person to pass. Usually, with a nod of the head and a salutation such as "Good morning sir" by the Black, the White would walk by without the pretense of recognizing the existence of the individual standing in a subservient position. Of course, few Whites recognized the rebelliousness of some ex-slaves by the way they pronounced words or formed gestures. If and when that happened, Whites lamented the passing of a gracious society now populated by "uppity" Blacks.[15]

Mostly, this was the masquerade between men. Black women were expected to be working as domestics, and their children were supposed to be working in factories or fields. However, if a Black woman met a White, that deference was also demanded.

Beyond the element of race, the second "punch" was concerned with class. The act defined Blacks as workers or laborers. This bottom class of people was not expected to give orders to Whites or have sufficient capital for economic investments or to trade with Whites. Rather, the working class would labor for others (Whites). From that, Blacks were to learn to obey specific White hallmarks of labor-management relations. To illustrate, vagrancy was taught by Whites to mean the opposite of work. As a negative economic value, Whites taught that vagrants were lazy, immoral persons who wanted to live off the fruits of others. Good workers, on the other hand, were those Blacks who were loyal, obedient, hard working laborers who wanted to produce for society and their White employers. Therefore, the act required Blacks to be part of an apprenticeship system in which they learned specific tasks and skills while they produced for White employers. In retrospect, loyalty, or social stability, perhaps was the most important value Whites wanted Black workers to learn. Loyalty meant that Black workers could not quit their jobs if they didn't like their employers or try to better themselves by working for other Whites who paid higher salaries. Black laborers learned what loyalty was when they signed a labor contract written and enforced by the White employer. Most Black workers quickly learned the similarity between a labor contract with a White employer and slavery with a White master.[16]

If Whites had been confronted with Black workers' thoughts about slavery and employment, they would have registered surprise. White employers saw absolutely no relationship between employment and servitude. In fact, many White Texans thought Black employment was an appropriate method of giving ex-slaves an opportunity to build a future "good life." In other words, it just seemed logical at the same time to make certain that Texas was filled with law-abiding Blacks. It was this conflict of perception and remembrance that framed White Texans' judgment of Blacks. Not being able to see, hear, or value them and their environment, White Texans thought of Blacks as the "other" race. That is, Blacks were colored and Whites were not. Illogical as it became, White Texans visualized themselves as Anglo-Saxons. In their collective memory they saw themselves as representatives of those non-colored Europeans who formed the dawning of English society. White Texans valued their culture and believed it was sophisticated and complex. Anyone who worked hard had the opportunity to succeed. Because individual Blacks legally were not allowed to succeed, White Texans assumed they were representatives of a more primitive culture in which immaturity and childishness was valued.[17]

ONE DROP OF BLACK BLOOD: SEPARATE RAIL CARS

It is from this perspective that the 1896 United States Supreme Court case *Plessy v. Ferguson* should be understood. Like *Dred Scott v. Sanford*, this Supreme Court case was also a culmination of Black legal resistance to White assumptions of race and class.[18] It resulted from the actions of a young, twenty-three-year-old racially mixed cobbler by the name of Homer Plessy. The Louisiana legislature had developed Black Codes like those in Texas and other Southern states. In 1890, that state's legislature passed the *Separate Car Act* mandating that Whites and "colored persons" travel separately. Because train travel was cheap and accessible at the end of the nineteenth century, most people, rich and poor, found this form of transportation to their liking. Besides, most Southern states had poor road systems so it was sometimes difficult to arrive at a destination in a horse-drawn stage or private carriage.

Within the ballet called segregation, the act mandated that Blacks accept their social position while traveling.[19] Homer Plessy, on the other hand, contended that the Fourteenth Amendment gave him specific rights, privileges, immunities, and equal protection under the law regardless of the *Separate Car Act*. After discussion with others who were involved, he decided he would test the legality of the *Separate Car Act*. He and his friends knew he would be arrested and fined. But those events had to first occur so that the Louisiana legislation could be decided in a federal court of law. After buying his rail ticket and waiting in a waiting room marked "Coloreds Only," Homer boarded a passenger train in New Orleans for the short trip to Covington, Louisiana, on the north shore of Lake Pontchartrain. He entered a passenger car marked "Whites Only," sat in a seat, and waited. Not long after, the train conductor noticed he was not a servant or person closely connected with any of the White passengers and asked him to return to the Colored car.[20] Homer refused and and was arrested. He appeared before Judge Ferguson, who after hearing the case found Plessy guilty and fined him twenty-five dollars. Appealing the decision, the case moved through the legal system to be argued in 1896 before the United States Supreme Court.[21] The Court found Homer Plessy guilty and ordered him to pay the twenty-five dollar fine.

In part, the Supreme Court's decision was correct by White logic. Whites had rhetorically asked Blacks the question, "When a train pulls into the station, why should it matter to a person what passenger car he sits in, when all the cars arrive at the same time?" The question was illogical to Blacks who responded, "If it doesn't matter to you which passenger car people sit in, why do you have the cars labeled "Colored Only'?" Of course, Blacks knew it did matter to Whites and this ruling would impact every area of their lives. *Plessy v. Ferguson* gave credence to *de jure* segregation, that is, segregation sanctified by law. *Plessy v. Ferguson* voiced the White logic that discrimination could not occur if facilities, institutions, and racial interactions were "separate but equal." That meant the lives of every person in both races changed both dramatically and subtly. Segregation of waiting rooms, water fountains, churches, schools, and neighborhoods, among other things, was to become easily recognizable by both races. The subtlety was that Blacks experienced "separate but equal" to mean separate only. Because Whites chose to view Blacks as the "other" race, they had no interest in the lives of Black citizens.

The *Dred Scott v. Sanford* and *Plessy v. Ferguson* decisions affirmed and reaffirmed a fundamental axiom of American society—you can be judged by the color of your skin. Rightly or wrongly, that fact has acted as a legal, political, and economic foundation of the American society for centuries. It became for most Whites an assumed margin from which fellow citizens responded to each other. This margin, acting both as a wall and moat, separated Blacks from Whites. Most Whites assumed the separation of races was inherently moral and justified segregation as benign in the halls of government, the competitive market place, schools, and neighborhood churches. Without influence in government, commerce, or churches, poorly educated Blacks were defined as White society's scraps. Most Blacks knew that their present lives were destined to be their children's future. At the same time, if Whites thought of Blacks' circumstances (which they did not), it was they (Blacks) whom the Whites blamed. These were not empty thoughts.

FIRST CLASS WAR AND SECOND CLASS CITIZENSHIP

In 1918, twenty-two years after *Plessy v. Ferguson*, as American soldiers returned home from war-torn Europe, Black veterans soon realized that the freedoms they had fought for in Europe had been purposely denied them at home. In other words, they had fought a White man's war. Black veterans realized that both the Fourteenth and Fifteenth Amendment's constitutional guarantees given to ex- slaves had been restricted from them for decades.[22] For example, after Reconstruction, the United States Supreme Court, in *United States v. Reece* (1876), had reaffirmed the Fifteenth Amendment's meaning that states could not disenfranchise Blacks, although states could legally decrease the number of Blacks from voting by issuing literacy tests and instituting poll taxes. Thus, Texas had immediately developed legislation excluding Blacks from voting while grandfathering Whites into the system so that they could vote.[23]

As individuals, the veterans had fought in a war undreamed of in horror and magnitude. The "War to End All Wars," as it was popularly called, outclassed the technological and industrial military machines of the Civil War. Soldiers quickly learned that death was ever present, regardless whether the enemy was engaged or not. Just as some would die quickly on the battlefield, many more would die slow, painful deaths caused by influenza, mustard gas, unattended wounds, and the many curable diseases that were exacerbated by trench warfare.

The geographic hugeness of the war itself and the battlefields were incomprehensible to many Black soldiers who lived in the rural South. Black Texans who had never attended school, or who had gained only a rudimentary education from separate "colored" schools, did not know where they were. To live beyond the boundaries of the county in which they were born was confusing. The fear of being lost in a violent world gave them little hope of ever seeing their loved ones again. Yet, young Black men served in great numbers, often with distinction.[24]

Although the military was segregated, many young Black Texans still wanted to join. They were entranced by the glamor of the "Buffalo Soldiers" of the Ninth and Tenth Calvary, as well as the Twenty Fourth and Twenty Fifth Black regiments. Even though these regiments were commanded by White officers, there was a feeling of satisfaction they knew they never would have as workers on a West Texas ranch or farm.[25] In particular, Black Texans admired the Tenth Regiment. Commanded by General "Black Jack" Pershing, the Tenth had played a distinguished role in the Mexican-American War.[26] Black Texas soldiers felt that affinity with Pershing during World War I when he became commander of both White and Black regiments. The Twenty Fourth was also known as the Texas Blacks. It had been stationed on the Rio Grande during the Indian Wars in the last decades of the nineteenth century.

While the soldier's life undoubtedly appealed to young Black Texans, they soon found that military life was boring, dirty, and dusty. New recruits also discovered that the segregation of civilian life followed them into the military. In fact, they quickly discovered that the Jim Crowism of military policy mirrored the legislated and social policies of civilian life.[27] When not on active assignment, they were kept busy building roads, clearing sagebrush, and the like. Military life for the young Black recruit was dangerous at best. At its worst it was a lonely life, far from friends and family.

FLAMING CROSSES: WHITE ROBES AND PROTESTANT FUNDAMENTALIST JUSTICE

Civilian life after *Plessy v. Ferguson* was also difficult for Blacks. An increase in the number of Ku Klux Klan chapters during this period made Blacks aware they were strangers in their own communities. The Ku Klux Klan was reborn in 1915. This was not the same Klan that ran amuck in the years directly after the Civil War. The original Klan focused its hatred on Northern carpetbaggers and their "military and governing occupation" during Reconstruction. The "new" Klan focused on establishing and maintaining a religiously devout South fortified with the religious morals held by fundamentalist Christians and European social values.[28] The Klan forced its way into national prominence during the 1920s, actively campaigning against Catholics, Jews, southern and eastern Europeans, and Whites who acted "different." However, they reserved their deepest hate for Blacks. In many ways, the Klan had to prioritize its hatred because Catholics, Jews, and southern and eastern Europeans generally lived in Northern states. Of course, Whites who acted "different" learned quickly to hide that difference. Consequently, Blacks felt the brunt of Klan hatred.

The Klan's power was twofold. One was to act as moral policemen. As defenders of White Protestant fundamentalism, it was not unusual in small Texas communities for Klan members to meet secretly at an undisclosed location on Sunday mornings. Then, dressed in robes and hoods, and sometimes after a prayer, the Klan would march in regimental order to a White Protestant fundamentalist church. Opening the door to the sanctuary, preferably when the preacher was delivering the sermon, the Klan would enter in single file. Without a word, and with as much dignity their robes would allow, they would march down the aisle to the podium in front of the congregation. The Klan would then, with much gravity, deposit a large amount of money, perhaps two hundred dollars, in the collection plates. Turning, and without looking at the members of the congregation, in quiet order, the Klan would then march to the rear of the church and quietly close the door as they left. These quiet comic operas were designed to leave impressions on White citizens. The Klan wanted Whites to think they were staunch allies of the "common" person who wanted White, Protestant justice. There was a message for Blacks as well. Regardless of their Protestant religion, the Klan was telling Blacks that if they visited their churches or homes it would be at night with a flaming cross.

The Klan arrived in east Texas in 1921. The Texas Klan in many ways was like Klan chapters in other Southern states. It attracted Whites who feared social change and poor Whites who knew that if Blacks improved themselves, they would be at the bottom of the social and economic ladder. Like Klan chapters throughout the South, Texas Klan chapters hated Blacks. They also despised Catholics, Jews, and people who were different than they. Yet, Texas Klansmen differed somewhat from other Southern chapters. While they voiced individual adherence to Protestant fundamentalist values, their focus was on political corruption. Perhaps this had to happen, for few Klansmen had met a Catholic Texan and would not recognize a Jew on the street. In states located in the Old South, the Ku Klux Klan chapters focused their violence on individual Blacks who were believed to have challenged the status quo. These Blacks already lived in segregated communities. In cities such as East St Louis (1917), East Chicago (1917–1919), and Tulsa (1921), Whites instigated riots to physically force Blacks to live in segregated neighborhoods. Therefore, Texas Klan violence was obvious to Blacks, as they were the direct recipients of it. Perhaps one reason communities such as Houston, Brownsville, and San Antonio suffered at the hands of the Klan was because 60 percent of Black Texans lived in urban areas.[29]

Even so, there were a few urban "safe havens." A case in point is Austin. Seventy miles north of San Antonio, Austin seemed in another world. It was, by San Antonio standards, a small city. In part, it was a city of contradictions, within itself and Texas. It was the state capital and therefore had witnessed firsthand much of Texas' history. For a brief period it had thought of itself as the capital of a Republic, and had experienced the sophistication of "international" diplomacy and society, which ambassadors representing Mexico, United States, and England could bring.[30] Later, Austin was the capital of a state within another country, the Confederate States of America, and lastly, again as a state capital within the United States. Austin was also unique in that it housed the state university. Becoming a cultural center close to the state's political hub, the university allowed the community to experience the interactions between academics and politics. As in other southern cities, Austin's Black community was segregated. Located to the east of "down town," the Black quarter or "East Austin" as it later would be called, developed its own community with its own businesses, churches, and schools. Never to enjoy the riches of some Black communities, East Austin never represented an economic challenge to White Austinites, nor had its population reached a threatening peak as it had in other communities that experienced the horror of White violence.[31]

The Klan's second power was in the image it presented to Texas communities. It valued its power of intimidation over public officials, Blacks, and Whites with little social or economic influence. Sometimes, the Klan forcefully abducted "uppity" Blacks or White prostitutes or others who were "different," to Klan courts to try them for their "crimes." Some "offenders" were simply admonished never to speak of their experiences during that evening. Others were tortured. Blacks were lynched.[32] A lynching was different than other forms of Klan "justice" because it demanded a large White audience, the majority of whom did not know the "defendant." Lynchings were grisly, violent events intended to strike fear into Blacks who knew that if they lived too close to the "line between the races," this could happen to them. It notified Whites, especially those who feared Blacks, that their religious and cultural beliefs were being defended.

PEEKING OVER THE COLOR LINE

Still, at that time before World War II there were attempts by Blacks and Whites to cross the "color line."[33] A few Blacks, because of their extraordinary sports or musical abilities were able to distinguish themselves to such a degree that Whites could not minimize their achievements. And there were Whites who, with full knowledge of what they were doing, wanted to experience, even briefly, the other culture in America. Few Black Texans[34] risked the consequence of achievement, however. Jackie Robinson, who briefly was a player-coach at Huston-Tillotson College, "crossed the line" in 1948, when he became the first Black to play major league baseball. Others became role models for young Black Texans, such as Satchel Page who also had played in the Negro leagues.[35]

While crossing the "color line" appealed to few Whites, some were willing to live on the edge of segregation and White social acceptance. Young sophisticates would, for an evening's thrill, visit Black music halls and clubs such as Harlem's Cotton Club to listen to the new music called jazz. Captivated by the brilliance of Louis Armstrong, Jelly Roll Morton, and King Oliver, and others, Whites made them national icons.[36] In the same fashion, young "sophisticated" White Texans quietly escorted their dates to Black clubs to listen and dance and applaud local performers who were bringing to them the Black music of Armstrong and others. For example, an area of Dallas known as Elm Street[37] was lined with Black-owned bars, honky-tonks, clubs, and night clubs. Most of the clubs were on the professional circuit, so Black entertainers such as Blind Lemon Jefferson, Sam "Lightnin'" Hopkins, Huddie "Leadbelly" Ledbetter appeared.

There were others who crossed the "color line" in unique ways. In 1942, when Elmer Henderson, a Black federal employee, was traveling on government business from Washington to Atlanta, Georgia, discovered he could not eat dinner at the tables reserved for Blacks in the dining car because Whites were using them, he complained to the Interstate Commerce Commission. The ICC complaint forced railway companies to guarantee that Whites could not sit at reserved Black tables in dining cars, Henderson was unsatisfied and took his case to the Supreme Court. Because he was a federal employee, the case was passed to Philip Elman, an assistant to the Solicitor General who wrote a legal brief on Elmer Henderson's behalf. Basically, the brief contended that segregated tables in railway dinning cars violated the Interstate Commerce Act. In a unanimous decision, the Supreme Court agreed, ruling that in this situation calling attention to passengers' race was inappropriate.[38]

As Black Texans, like Blacks throughout the United States, continued to expand their education and social experiences, Whites reacted in various ways. While some White Texans continued to actively express their repugnance of Blacks, most were able to accept Black visibility within some type of perspective. In Austin, for example, Whites *knew* Blacks were happy with their social role in the community. After all, White Austinites *knew* Blacks had no interest in improving their lives beyond what they now had. White Austinites *knew* Austin's Black community would remain in "East Austin" along Thompson Street where they were happy.

Although not a Texan, perhaps Mary McLeod Bethune was the most notable Black who successfully crossed the "color line." Known mostly among politicians, educators, and women's groups, she was able to focus on removing federal exclusionary legislation that barred Blacks from participating in American society. Instrumental in desegregating the army during the Truman administration, she quietly helped thousands of Black Texas men have successful military careers.[39] Founding various professional education women's groups, she was able to quietly open the doors of study for uncounted numbers of Black Texas women who wanted to improve their education. Although segregated, these educational experiences gave educated Black women opportunities to mentor young Black women.[40]

OTHERING: NEW AND DIFFERENT DEFINITIONS

But by 1945, at the end of World War II, life had changed beyond what White Texans and Austinites were willing to accept. Again, young Black soldiers, returning from war recognized the social invisibility into which they had been schooled. Many of the disturbing gaps between Blacks and Whites were still the same their fathers and grandfathers had recognized at their homecoming from Europe in 1918. In the mid 1940s, Blacks were still unable to pass over that invisible line between the races Whites had drawn. Black attention turned to education. There had been some troubles when some "uppity" Blacks wanted to attend the University of Texas in Austin. Austinites, along with many university administrators, faculty, and students, had difficulty understanding Black insistence. After all, there were Black colleges in Houston and other areas in the state.[41] Shouldn't they go there?[42]

Looking back with the perception of time, White Texans' attitudes seem so insular. Their inability to look beyond themselves and their history of categorizing Blacks as the "other" race seems so ludicrous. It is this social irrationality Blacks were able to articulate, if not to White Texans, at least to themselves and federal courts. On Monday, May 17, 1954, the United States Supreme Court declared segregation to be unconstitutional. The Warren Court contextualized its ruling within a broad framework of racial relations. Recalling Homer Plessy, the Court dramatically rejected its 1896 decision, *Plessy v. Ferguson.* By focusing on the historic controversy, the Supreme Court acknowledged the unique history of an invisible group of Americans who had been brought to these shores against their will to live lives not of their choosing.

It should not come as a surprise, it seems now, that the 1954 United States Supreme Court ruling known as *Brown v. Board of Education* was the crowning achievement of those who, through the centuries, had envisioned racial justice and were willing to fight to make those dreams a reality. Nonetheless, in mid-twentieth century, as the United States prepared to change its perception of the "other" race, Blacks knew racial justice was not a gift freely given to them.

> Does segregation of children in public schools solely on the basis of race, even though the physical facilities and other "tangible" factors may be equal, deprive the children of the minority group of equal educational opportunities? We believe it does. We cannot turn the clock back to 1868 when the Fourteenth

Amendment was adopted, or even to 1896 when Plessey versus Ferguson was written. . . . We conclude that in the field of public education the doctrine of "separate but equal" has no place.[43]

In the same fashion, it was naive of those who lived then to believe that social wrongs could quickly be rectified with a stroke of a pen. Neither Texas Blacks or Whites thought of the decision as one would think of a letter of apology written when a friend recognizes another has been wronged. But Black Texans understood *Brown v. Board of Education* for what it meant to them. Now, they, and in particular Austin Blacks, had a chance to help White Texans learn they were not the "other" race.

CHAPTER THREE

Oh, I Do Remember!

Oh, do I remember! I was at home and that was in May of fifty-four. My son, Edward, was born May the thirteenth [1954] and then I heard about *Brown versus Topeka*. We sat down and cried. We were so happy over that decision and the reason we were so happy was because in a lot of small communities they had little small test cases. And Hearne was one of the communities where they had a test case. Oh, you wouldn't believe how many people paid the price for that decision. What the NAACP was asking Blacks to do all over [the South] was to take their children to the Anglo school for enrollment. This was testing the system as far as desegregated schools was concerned. I do remember *Brown versus Topeka!*[1]

IN THE SMALL AGRICULTURAL COMMUNITY of Hearne, Texas, a young widow, her newborn son, and her parents rejoiced when they heard the announcement that the United States Supreme Court had declared segregation in public schools unconstitutional. Iola Taylor, and her family, understood the high price Southern Blacks paid to secure public education for their children.[2] Having only known segregated education, Taylor yearned fervently for her son, Edward, to attend a nonsegregated public school. Segregation in education, as in other spheres of life for Blacks, meant poorly paid teachers, ragged books handed down from White schools, inadequate buildings, and large classes. On the other hand, segregated schooling also meant that the Black teachers saw themselves as caretakers for their students beyond their teaching in the classroom. That is, if students got in trouble in the classroom, the teacher would stop by and visit with the parents that same evening. Disruptive behavior was quickly resolved. Indeed, teachers were valued and trusted members of the Black community. Nonetheless, Taylor, like hundreds of thousands of American Blacks, wanted the best schooling for her son and believed that his educational opportunities expanded greatly with the *Brown* decision.[3]

As Charles Akins walked across the campus at Austin's Huston-Tillotson College on May 17, 1954, he too learned of the United States Supreme Court ruling that the "separate but equal" doctrine was unconstitutional. He wondered how the *Brown* decision would be implemented. Because he had one year left before he would graduate with a degree in education, Akins thought about what it would be like if his first teaching position was in a desegregated school. Still, he found it difficult to imagine how life for him and other Blacks would change as a result of the Supreme Court's decision. Much later in his life he reflected how little had changed during that next decade.[4]

Sacrifice was part and parcel of Vernice Smith's life. Despite her excellent teaching credentials, she had been unable to obtain a teaching position with the Austin Independent School District. In fact, Smith was concerned that the *Brown* decision would mean fewer teaching positions for Blacks. At the time of the Supreme Court's decision, she was working part time as a nurse as well as teaching part time at Huston-Tillotson College. Smith knew full well that most Whites would resist desegregation of the public schools. However, she treated Whites and Blacks the same, because, as she said, "people were people." Smith, like Akins and Taylor, had attended segregated schools all her life. As a very young child, she wanted to make something of her life and knew a good education was her only escape from poverty.

The lives of Akins, Taylor, and Smith would be changed forever by the United States Supreme Court decision that struck down racially segregated schools. In the midst of a community that did not want to desegregate its schools, they were willing to risk being the first Black teachers in formerly White schools. Akins, Taylor, and Smith later crossed over from the only Black high school faculty to White high school faculties. They were on the front line when tensions ran high in the city of Austin, Texas. Their remembered experiences illuminate a long-forgotten school desegregation plan in Austin's history. However, Black teachers' willingness to cross over into formerly White schools was complemented by White teachers' willingness to cross over into the formerly all-Black schools. Their remembered experiences reveal a contextual setting in which each of these teachers understood their role as a teacher committed to equality of education for all students, regardless of their skin color. The teachers' commitment to equality in education facilitated the death, however slowly, of segregation in Austin, Texas.

The day after the United States Supreme Court's opinion struck down segregation, residents of Austin voiced deeply divided opinions.[5] Opinions of adult

Whites ranged from thoughtful acceptance to outrage. Texas Supreme Court Justice W. St. John Garwood believed the decision would afford the United States a "solid base from which to defend against totalitarianism." An opposite opinion was given by Wallace Griffin, a bakery employee, "There'll be social mingling—even intermarriage—of the races!" Other Whites agreed with the State Civil Defense and Disaster Relief coordinator William L. McGill: "It's the law of the land, isn't it? That's all there is to it."[6]

In East Austin, the adult Black community celebrated. Dr. Everett Givens, a physician, labeled the decision, "the best news since the Emancipation." Religious overtones shaded many responses such as that of florist Bernie Hillen, "We are all made in the image and likeness of God and possess an immortal soul, regardless of color. If the Lord makes no distinction, why should the Constitution of the United States?"[7] Austin's residents were no different from people nationwide. Some were indifferent, but the majority held diverse beliefs about the implications of the *Brown* decision, both for themselves and for the nation.

Austin had another side, however. Government and school officials, responsible for carrying out the Supreme Court's decision, were less than enthusiastic. Governor Allan Shivers concurred with State Education Commissioner J. W. Edgar's statement that, "[t]here [was] a legal furrow to be ploughed. Compliance [although] necessary [would] take a long time." Shivers expressed hope that recommendations regarding compliance would be ready for the next legislative session. Commissioner Edgar recommended creation of a statewide citizens and educators task force to cope with the "inevitable problems arising from this decision."[8]

Not one to look a gift horse in the mouth, politicians used this time to voice their opinions. Senator Lyndon Johnson, noting the writing of the final decree would not be issued until the fall, said, "Texas has an opportunity to figure it [school desegregation] out." Senator Price Daniel hoped, "When the final decree is entered, it will take our problems into consideration and give greater consideration to them [Texas' problems] than the decision has done." Representative Homer Thornberry agreed with Senator Daniel: "We ought to be allowed to work out the problems among ourselves."[9] In fact, the concept of states solving their "own problems" was not new. This concept, known as *interposition*, was a seldom-used legal maneuver that challenged federal authority in connection with states' rights. The most notable case of interposition occurred when the Southern states seceded from the union over slavery. Despite Texas officials' cry for "time to solve problems" caused by segregation, their plea was never pursued.[10]

How Austin's role as the state capital impacted the district school board's response to school desegregation can only be imagined. That it played a role is certain; the extent of the role is less than clear. Certainly, as evidenced by the politicians' comments, the political climate invited resistance to school desegregation. The Austin City and Travis County school superintendents were even less certain of the immediate impact of the *Brown* decision. Superintendent Irby Carruth, when questioned about the implications of the decision for the Austin schools, replied, "I have no idea. In fact, I imagine that no one, anywhere, knows yet."[11] County Superintendent I. W. Popham concurred with Carruth, adding, "Local boards [will] wait for a cue to further actions from state school authorities."[12]

What did Austin's high school students think of the *Brown* decision? After all, they were the ones, apart from the teachers, most likely to feel the immediate impact of the Supreme Court's declaration. Despite Austin's veneer of liberalism, students had always been educated in a segregated system, with one system for Blacks and one system for Whites. In fact, another system housing Mexican Americans was also developing at this time although the Texas legislature, in the 1930s, identified them as White for purposes of segregation. Anderson was the designated high school for Blacks, and Travis and Austin were the designated high schools for Whites. Not surprisingly, Black high school students enthusiastically supported the Supreme Court's decision. For example, senior students at Anderson believed that desegregated schools would provide greater educational opportunities for them and all Blacks. Reminiscent of Taylor's hope for her newborn son, Anderson senior Hugh Ella Walker supported the decision saying, "We hope that it will bring greater opportunity to students in their educational pursuits in future years." Another senior, Edith Davis, agreed with Walker: "I think this [decision] perhaps will enable our children to attain a better education, and will give them a real feeling of belonging without fear." Classmate Robbie Burleson gave a slightly different perspective about the decision: "With everybody together, maybe world-wide peace will be much easier to accomplish." Several seniors believed the decision would have an economic impact as well. Eugene Toynes responded, "I've always thought it [segregation] was unlawful—and expensive, too. We can save more money this way. The other way, we had to build two of everything." Interestingly, Robert Norwood credited the Geneva Conference on solving postwar problems as playing a role: "I believe the outcome of the Geneva Conference played a great part in the decision of the Supreme Court. I think it was a wise decision, and a very economical one for our country."[13]

White students at Travis and Austin High Schools expressed mixed sentiments. Some claimed uncertainty about what the ruling actually meant. Others supported the ruling, but most opposed school desegregation. Nancy Mosteller, a freshman at Travis High, expressed mixed emotions about the decision: "I don't really know what to think. It doesn't make too much difference one way or the other." Randi Henriksen, a junior at Travis agreed with Nancy, "It doesn't make any difference to me. I think everybody should go to school together." Nance Franke, an Austin High School junior, approved of the decision: "Sure I'm for it. It's only fair. They fight and die for our country. They're good enough to go to our school, then. This is a democracy, isn't it?" But these students were in the minority. The majority of Austin's White students adamantly opposed desegregated schools. A Travis high freshman Bobby Craig said, "I'm one hundred percent for segregated schools." Cecil Shropshire, a senior at Travis, agreed with Craig, "I don't think much of it [the Supreme Court ruling]. I don't think Negroes and Whites should be mixed in the public schools." James Turner, a freshman at Travis, was even more adamant in voicing his disapproval: "I don't like it at all. Negroes have their own schools and we have ours. Let's keep it that way." Jack Teaff, an Austin high sophomore opposed the decision: "I don't want them cutting in on us. They'll be coming over here, joining the football team, attending our dances and getting in the plays. We'd be knocked out of a lot of fun." Pat Dingler, a junior at Austin high didn't like the decision at all: "I don't think it's right and I don't like it one bit. I don't know why—I just don't like it!"[14] Likely, these students and others voiced their parents' values as much as their own.[15] Teachers, when questioned about their responses, refused to comment. In Austin, as in other cities across the South, resistance to school desegregation figured prominently just one day after the Supreme Court's ruling.

Blacks, such as Akins, Taylor, and Smith, could easily recall where they were when the *Brown* decision was announced. But for most Whites, particularly young Whites, the Supreme Court decision created barely a ripple in their personal histories in the 1950s. Yet, for several young White students, such as Ann Stoll, Tom Allen, Herb Brown, and James Dorsett, this decision would have long-lasting repercussions, because they would come together as teachers and take an active part in the overall school desegregation plan in Austin. Nevertheless, more than a decade would ultimately pass before the *Brown* decision would affect those White teachers as much as it impacted Black teachers. The law changed immediately but the practice of segregation changed very slowly.

Notwithstanding the official illegality of public school segregation, issues about how schools could eliminate racial segregation were resolved only slowly. Public school *de jure* segregation, to be sure, was predominantly a phenomenon of Southern states.[16] Most officials appeared to take at face value the Supreme Court's ruling that desegregation of public schools was to proceed "with all deliberate speed" and that they must include "a good faith effort" toward compliance. In reality, government policy maintaining racial segregation of public schools was to be eliminated as slowly as local situations allowed.[17]

First attempts by individuals to desegregate public schools in the Southern states typically were met by official passive resistance. A later form of resistance was tokenism, a type of desegregation in which a few Black students were reluctantly assigned to schools such as Travis and Austin.[18] These responses often were followed by "freedom of choice" plans in conjunction with neighborhood schools.[19] When federal courts ruled school districts that used those plans were out of compliance with federal standards, local officials developed yet other avenues of resistance. One such avenue was cross-over teaching: The assignment of some Black teachers to White schools and a few White teachers to Black schools. Federal courts subsequently determined the cross-over teaching policy was insufficient. The failed effort of cross-over teaching has been forgotten in the overall history of the school desegregation movement. For the most part, scholarly attention to school desegregation has focused either on the legal framework of school desegregation or on some students who participated in the school desegregation process. Teachers, particularly cross-over teachers, have received minimal attention. The silence of their voices leaves a gaping hole in the history of school desegregation. In this book, voices of cross-over teachers in formerly segregated schools illuminate their remembered experiences in the very slow dismantling of segregation in Austin, Texas.

SEPARATE BUT EQUAL

The origins of the debate over school desegregation evolved from the United States' legacy of slavery. The complexities of school desegregation grew out of the cultural history of how the races would relate to each other. Telling the story of cross-over teaching flows naturally in and out of the history of school desegregation.[20] But, to understand more fully the complexities of cross-over teaching requires an understanding of segregation. Its ideology, as discussed in the previous chapter, was born and nurtured during the period when slavery was legal in the United States.[21] Segregation, many times referred to as the American caste system, implied that something touched by a Black was "unclean." Therefore, this was the message associated with every "colored" water fountain, waiting room, and courtroom Bible.[22] Segregation was a way of obeying specific rules for mingling between the separated peoples. The rules were numerous and had the sole purpose of maintaining the superiority of the White race. The policy of segregation resulted in unusually severe restraints for Blacks. It took the form of multiple legal exclusions, limited and highly unequal economic living standards, minimal political power, and many forms of legal and illegal coercion. This caused reduced social respect, restricted social mobility, and accepted invidious discrimination as normal social behavior. In short, Blacks were submitted to the authority of White people in the most important spheres of life, including occupation, residence, politics, and schooling.[23]

During slavery, education in any form for Blacks was illegal. By the time of the Emancipation Proclamation, formal public education in the South was established only for White students.[24] Certainly, public education was viewed as a viable means of perpetuating Blacks' subordinate position to Whites. Lincoln intended the Emancipation Proclamation to be a sweeping political declaration but it only freed slaves in the rebel states, and did not apply to slaves in either the border states or the remaining Union states.[25] In fact, freedom for Black Texans did not officially occur until June 19, 1865, some two and one-half years later when federal troops landed in Galveston, Texas.[26] That same year, 1865, the Thirteenth Amendment to the United States Constitution abolished slavery.[27] Thus began a brief attempt by the United States government to incorporate Blacks into full participation as first-class citizens. Three years later, the Fourteenth Amendment to the United States Constitution, ratified July 21, 1868, granted citizenship to former slaves and mandated equal protection for all citizens.[28] In 1870, the Fifteenth Amendment to the United States Constitution further delineated the rights of all male citizens, including Black Texans, to vote.[29]

Not long after the ratification of the Fifteenth Amendment, the active pursuit of separation between the races surfaced.[30] Although slavery was illegal after 1863, the South actively pursued entrenchment of its racial caste system. In the late 1890s, the stage was set for the first challenge to mandatory segregation. By the close of the nineteenth century, the United States Supreme Court had nullified the federal protection first offered Blacks upon their release from bondage.[31] In fact, the Court's opinion in *Plessy v. Ferguson* (1896) justified a flood of discriminatory state legislation enacted legally to segregate Whites from Blacks throughout the states' political and social institutions.[32] All of the Southern states enacted laws that separated Whites and Blacks in public schools, transportation, hotels and restaurants, and residential areas. Jim Crow, through *de jure* segregation, took over where slavery left off.[33] In other words, for Blacks, much of their freedom was gained or lost through the legal system.

At the turn of the century, *de jure* segregation existed in seventeen states and the District of Columbia.[34] In these states, including Texas, legal statutes mandated separate schooling facilities for White and Black children. In 1876, for example, the Texas Constitution mandated:

> Separate schools shall be provided for the White and colored children, and impartial provisions shall be made for both.[35]

In 1905, twenty-nine years later, Texas mandated separation of public funds for schooling of White and Black children:

> All available public school funds of this State shall be appropriated in each county for the education alike of White and colored children, and impartial provisions shall be made for both races. No White children shall attend schools supported for colored children, nor shall colored children attend schools supported for White children. The terms "colored race" and "colored children," as used in this title, include all persons of mixed blood descended from Negro ancestry.[36]

For Blacks, literacy was a fundamental contradiction of oppression. In other words, literacy and formal education were Blacks' means to liberation and freedom.[37] Clearly, education was a safeguard against fraud and manipulation. However, during this period White schools received three times greater funding than did Black schools. The separation of public school funds at the state and local levels enabled White school administrators to allocate less monies to Black schools.[38] Minimal funding ensured that Black schools would more likely be of poorer quality, thus meeting the Southern need for maintenance of the caste system of segregation.[39]

From the end of the Civil War to the beginning of the twentieth century, Blacks had relentlessly pursued schooling for both their children as well as themselves.[40] Black teachers were hired by Southern Whites with the belief that "colored" schools would amount to little or nothing. They were mistaken as many of the best schools in the South were for Black children who were taught by "colored teachers."[41] Nonetheless, the Southern planters' heavy use of child labor forced Black schools to have extremely short and irregular school terms. As a result, Horace Mann Bond concluded that

> [a]t the beginning of the 20th century, the condition of the schools for Negro children in the South was but slightly improved over their condition in 1875.[42]

In the Southern states, many Black children's school experience was influenced by vocational education. In this case, Black youth were taught certain industrial skills which were based on Booker T. Washington's "Hampton-Tuskegee Idea."[43] Washington's idea embodied the "ethic of hard toil" and "dignity of labor" as the core of his curriculum. But his emphasis on industrial education created an underemphasis for secondary education for Black children that continued past World War II.[44]

In concert with the emphasis on the Hampton-Tuskegee educational model, a second obstacle loomed in the Blacks' pursuit of formal education. Few teachers were available to teach Black children. Coupled with a critical shortage of Black teachers, Southern White teachers refused to teach in Black schools. Complicating the problems of teacher shortages, it was also during this period that Northern White missionary teachers were returning to their Northern homes. For example, during the early 1900s, there was only one teacher for every ninety-three Black students in the Southern states. Although the teacher shortage declined each year thereafter, it remained a major problem for Southern Blacks until the late 1930s.[45]

As teacher preparatory programs, nationwide, were transformed in the early twentieth century, intense struggles over the control and training of Black teachers developed. In fact, the struggle to control Black teacher training institutions rested on the assumption that Black teachers had the ability to influence Black students in their classrooms.[46] In other words, it was assumed that Black teachers would socialize their students into particular ideologies of Black education, such as vocational or the liberal arts.

An emerging struggle occurred therefore between White philanthropists and Black educators about the best curricula for Black teacher education students. Northern White philanthropists sought to impose Booker T. Washington's

Hampton-Tuskegee model on the Black teacher education curriculum, which many believed would relegate their students to academically second class citizenship. However, the majority of Black educators actively resisted the adoption of the industrial education model. The philanthropic foundations notably were unable to convince Black private colleges that were supported by various denominations to abandon the liberal arts curriculum in favor of the industrial arts education.[47] In fact, they inspired their students with the feeling that a traditional, academic education, reserved for Whites, was also appropriate for them.[48] Not surprisingly, high academic expectations continued in the Black schools well after the *Brown* decision.

As the Northern philanthropic foundations withdrew their financial support, Blacks faced other challenges in their pursuit of education—double taxation, hard work, and time. Despite the fact that Blacks paid taxes supporting the local White and Black public schools, Southern school administrators cried financial insolvency when Black parents requested new buildings or improvements to old buildings. Not to be deterred, in most areas, Black communities raised money and gave of their time and labor to erect school buildings, and purchase supplies and materials to be used by their children.[49]

In Texas and throughout the South, Blacks pursued public education for their children with a tenacity and determination that put to shame the majority of Southern Whites. For this tenacity, they were "double taxed."

> It was terribly unjust. Black southerners paid their taxes as citizens, and while White taxpayers got a system of free public education, [B]lack taxpayers got virtually nothing except when they taxed themselves again.[50]

Blacks submitted to the double taxation because it was the only way they knew of giving their children an adequate education. Little wonder parents expected their children to go to college and do well there. As Taylor said, "It was a given!"[51]

Notwithstanding their pursuit of a quality education, Black teachers and students continually experienced ideological contradictions every day as a direct result of segregation. Regardless, a basic tenet of the American Black culture was a deep and abiding faith in the power of education. With the public school as a symbol of American democracy and equal opportunity, many Black teachers questioned

> if democratic behavior [wa]s one goal of our educational program . . . in the public school our youth must be indoctrinated with democratic ideals. . . . C[ould] this be done in a segregated system? Does the segregation of the Black present a situation inconsistent with democratic tenets we profess?[52]

Shortly after World War II, the Southern states spent almost twice as much money to educate White children as Black children. White teachers' salaries were 30 percent or higher than Black teachers' and the Southern states spent $86 million on higher education for Whites but only $5 million on higher education for Blacks.[53] To understand the impact of this distribution of resources on Black colleges, in the early twentieth century, it was noted there was only one accredited Black medical school in the South whereas twenty-nine medical schools existed for Whites. A similar ratio held true for engineering schools, law schools, as well as pharmacy schools.[54] Publication of Gunnar Myrdal's *An American Dilemma* in 1944, a documentation of the serious educational disadvantage of Blacks, finally sparked a National Association for Advancement of Colored People (NAACP) legal action campaign against this form of school discrimination.[55]

Clearly, segregation was inconsistent with democratic ideals in the United States, and Blacks understood this irreconcilable position. Many challenged *de jure* segregation but were met with swift sanctions including lynching. After World War II, Blacks' long hostility to segregation, plus the development of an empowered NAACP and a growing awareness among White Americans that segregation was morally wrong made possible the challenge to segregated public schools.[56]

TESTING THE SYSTEM

Schools have been the most prominent arena in which the struggle for racial desegregation has transpired.[57] By the late 1940s, principally under the aggressive leadership of the NAACP and its chief attorney, Thurgood Marshall, the American public schools were identified as the primary place to attack Jim Crow segregation.

With the possible exception of the *Dred Scott* decision in 1857, few judgments of the United States Supreme Court have generated more controversy and conflict over an extended period of time than did its decision in *Brown v. Board of Education of Topeka, Kansas.*[58] In fact, no other decision of the United States Supreme Court likely has precipitated as much fundamental social change or has touched as many families and institutions across the nation as has the *Brown* decision.[59] As Williams and Ryan noted,

> Important social changes generally do not occur without some resistance and friction. School desegregation is not an exception. The change involves established interests, operating customs, cherished beliefs, and deep sentiments.[60]

Even so, few could conceive of the emotion that sparked the resistance to desegregated schools by the majority of Southern Whites. In fact, the *Brown* decision, demanding the total desegregation of American public schools, challenged the long-held values, beliefs, customs, and interests of many Southern Whites. Resistance to school desegregation took many forms. Some communities, typically those with few Blacks, quietly desegregated their schools. Other communities implemented some form of school desegregation plan that eliminated separate schools within several years. Creating international media headlines, communities such as Birmingham and Selma, Alabama, openly and defiantly opposed school desegregation. But the majority of communities, like Austin, covertly resisted desegregating their schools. Therefore, like many communities throughout the South, Austin's Black and White children continued to attend segregated schools even though the justices had ruled segregation illegal[61]

Although Jim Crow laws were unconstitutional, many White Southerners salved their conscience by insisting they belonged to a unique, cultural area within the United States.[62] They proudly believed they were different than Northerners or others within the nation. These White Southerners asserted that racial segregation was part of that uniqueness and was healthy and honored by both races. Guy B. Johnson, for example, an avowed segregationist, declared,

> Segregation is a benevolent and philanthropic institution which "protects" the
> interests of the Negro, which mediates to him the wisdom and virtues of White
> society, which gives him a chance to develop "in his own way" under his own
> leaders in his own institutions . . . he is stirred up by "outsiders," Communists,
> the NAACP or other subversives.[63]

Of course, Johnson was no different than most White Southern segregationists. He, like them, considered segregation a noble cause and asserted it was his duty to protect and defend it. White Southern segregationists liked to depict the South as, after all, a state of mind that elevated Whites over Blacks in every aspect of Southern culture. The state of mind espoused by segregationists included antipathy toward change, deep respect for the status quo, determination to keep the South as a separate and identifiable region, fierce commitment to govern and be governed locally, fidelity to states' rights, paranoid hatred of Communism, Jews, and Catholics, and intense fear of racial amalgamation.[64] To illustrate the intensity of the Southern state of mind, a national poll conducted in the summer of 1954 by the American Institute of Public Opinion confirmed that only 24 percent of Southerners approved of the *Brown* decision, whereas 71 percent disapproved and only 5 percent were undecided.[65]

Within two years of the *Brown* decision, newly formed White Citizen's Councils emerged in many local communities across the South to fight integration legally. Their techniques included mass mailings of pamphlets, newsletters, and flyers, each with the major theme:

> The Citizen's Council is the South's answer to the mongrelizers. We shall not be
> integrated! We are proud of our White blood and our White heritage of sixty
> centuries[*sic*].[66]

The White Citizen's Councils fed on the fears of White Southerners, in particular those fears born and nurtured during slavery; the fear that Blacks and Whites would marry and Whites could no longer claim superiority over Blacks.[67]

Support for the states' overt resistance to the Supreme Court decision increased when, led by Senators J. Strom Thurmond and Sam Ervin Jr., eighty-two Members of the House of Representatives and nineteen United States Senators signed "The Declaration of Constitutional Principles." Popularly known as "The Southern Manifesto," it declared,

> The unwarranted decision of the Supreme Court in the public school cases is now bearing the fruit always produced when men substitute power for established law. . . . We regard the decision of the Supreme Court in the school cases as a clear abuse of judicial power. . . . This unwarranted exercise of power by the Court, contrary to the Constitution, is creating chaos and confusion in the States principally affected . . . . We commend the motives of those States which have declared the intentions to resist forced integration by any lawful means.[68]

While the majority of Southern senators and Congressmen signed "The Southern Manifesto," three senators did not lend their weight to the document. The most important of the three was Lyndon Baines Johnson from Texas. His refusal to sign the document was a harbinger of the 1964 and 1965 Civil Rights Acts, which he championed during his presidency.

From a perspective of forty years, Americans may find it difficult to fully comprehend the ferocious intensity of the South's state of mind that supported resistance to school desegregation. A now little-known book, authored in 1961 by Marvin Norfleet, affords us a glimpse into the mind of an avowed White segregationist. As was common practice then, Norfleet supported his claims of White supremacy through numerous biblical references. His tirades focused on the evils of racial intermarriage and communism.

> The South is now the great bulwark against intermarriage. A very few years of thoroughly integrated schools would produce large numbers of indoctrinated young Southerners free from all "prejudice" against mixed matings. . . . School integration is a "pet" of Communism![69]

Texas was not immune to the ravings of Norfleet and others, nor were Southerners elsewhere. White Texans enacted discriminatory laws and engaged in segregated social practices aimed to keep Black Texans outside mainstream society. Like other Black Southerners, Black Texans lived in a rigidly structured caste system based entirely on the color of one's skin.

A FLAWED AND FAILED
SCHOOL DESEGREGATION PLAN

Historians of school desegregation, to a remarkable extent, have focused on the political struggle for civil equality. In particular, this history is described through major political events and the lives of prominent civil rights leaders. For example,

Garrow's *Bearing the Cross: Martin Luther King, Jr., and the Southern Christian Leadership Conference,* Branch's *Parting the Waters; America in the King years 1954–63,* and Kluger's *Simple Justice* constitute seminal works that portray efforts to desegregate American society.[70] Silent within this public history are the voices of cross-over teachers, Black and White, who were the pioneers in school desegregation. While the courts, parents, school board members, and school administrators determined the education of students during this period, it was the teachers who ultimately made desegregation a reality.[71]

Despite dramatic confrontations, such as Little Rock, Birmingham, and Mansfield, which captured national newspaper headlines, the initial battles for school desegregation were fought between state legislators and federal judges. For example, in Texas, as in several other Southern states, state legislators focused on token compliance with federal school desegregation orders rather than exhibit overt defiance.[72] Token compliance was accomplished through pupil assignments based on a little-known Alabama law.[73] Token school desegregation was seen by Texas legislators and school officials as necessary to provide a legal basis for the assignment of pupils, thus protecting full school desegregation. In other words, token desegregation forced Blacks to remain in their place of inferiority to Whites. [74]

The resistance by most school districts in Texas was magnified by the resistance to school desegregation in Austin. As the state capital and home of The University of Texas, Austin wore a thin coat of liberalism.[75] Its reputation hid a deeply conservative city in desperate need to thwart desegregation of its public schools. In its desperation, Austin's token of cross-over teaching was one of many flawed plans designed to meet the silent criteria of desegregating public schools "with all deliberate slowness." Similar to later school desegregation efforts that first bused Black students to White schools, Austin's cross-over teaching plan initially assigned Black teachers to non-Black schools. Interestingly, these schools did not serve White students as much as the Mexican American community.[76] In fact, Austin's cross-over teaching plan was intended to delay as long as possible Black student entrance into all White schools such as Travis and Austin. Not until three years into the cross-over teaching plan was a Black teacher assigned to a White high school.

The importance of the district's cross-over teachers plan can be seen by the failure of the board's "freedom of choice" plan. Beginning in the fall of 1955 Austin's school board implemented a "freedom of choice" plan for the city's high schools. The plan implied that high school students could transfer to the school of their choice.[77] A few Black students in fact transferred to White high schools. But no White students transferred to Anderson High School, the Black high school. In 1958 the school board extended the freedom of choice plan to the junior high schools. In 1960, and continuing to 1964, the elementary schools were included in the stairstep desegregation plan. Despite media reports of Austin's schools being fully desegregated, the vast majority of Black students remained at all-Black schools. Even though no White student attended a Black school, and the teachers remained segregated, Austin school administrators quietly continued the policy of tokenism.[78] In fact, desegregation of Austin's public schools received minimal attention from school administrators, teachers, or students. Minimal compliance through token school desegregation seemed to work in Austin.

The passage of the 1964 Civil Rights Act changed all that. Shortly thereafter, the Department of Health, Education, and Welfare (the present United States Department of Education) received word from a federal advisory group that Austin's school desegregation plan did not meet federal guidelines. Beginning in 1964, Austin's school leaders, hard pressed to meet federal school desegregation requirements, decided to reassign Black teachers to all White schools. Significantly, they intended to leave Black students in their old schools and not transport them to non-Black schools.

Several years later as the plan developed, White teachers were assigned to Black schools. At this juncture, the lives of Akins, Taylor, Smith, Stoll, Dorsett, Brown, and Allen, as well as others, came together as each teacher, Black or White, participated in the desegregation of formerly segregated school faculties. Their individual backgrounds and stories provide a multivocal perspective of teachers' lives before and during school desegregation in Austin, Texas.

CHAPTER FOUR

Moving from the Shadows into the Sunlight

JIM CROW LAWS separated Whites and Blacks in all aspects of their lives. In 1944, Myrdal observed that "segregation [was] becoming so complete that the White Southerner practically never [saw] a Negro except as his servant and in other standardized and formalized caste situations."[1] In Austin, an invisible line isolated Blacks from Whites. This invisible line hovered above Waller Creek which disconnected East Austin from the rest of Austin. White Austinites seldom came in contact with Black Austinites except in a menial capacity. For example, Alvin Patterson recalled,

> I worked in a lady's yard one day . . . gosh I had no idea what it was going to be like. But she was supposed to pay me a dollar for the whole day! And lunch. When lunch time came—I was [sitting] on the back step and she put my lunch here and the dog's lunch next to mine on the same step! So I never cut another yard and I never did that kind of work, ever again![2]

Treating Blacks the same as their pets was typical behavior for many Whites. This treatment degraded Blacks and they sought change through many avenues, one of which was education. Certainly, for young Blacks born in the South between the 1920s and the 1940s, Jim Crow was alive and well. In fact, Jim Crow governed every aspect of their lives, as they so clearly remembered.

During the period of segregation, understanding the unity of the Black community involved "understanding its basis for solidarity, its implied sense of control, its values and its collective aspirations for its young."[3] In other words, the Black community acted as a collective whole, with a collective will during a collective struggle.[4] Through the Black community's collective behavior, young Black children were protected as much as possible from the racism their parents experienced in their encounters with most Whites.

Part of the collective behavior of Black communities fell upon the school. While Black students learned in segregated schools, its teachers performed an important social role in protecting them. In East Austin, for example, young Black children attended the same segregated schools. That meant that they all went to the same elementary schools, junior high school, and senior high school. In common, their educational journey began at one of the several segregated elementary schools such as Blackshear and culminated with graduation from L. C. Anderson High School. It was not uncommon for Black adults to describe their childhood world to exist within a ten block area in East Austin. For example, Akins recalled he

> was in walking distance to Blackshear [Elementary School] and Kealing [Junior High School] was right across the street . . . Anderson High School was close . . . Huston-Tillotson [College] wasn't that far. I was within walking distance of our church.[5]

For the majority of young Blacks living in Austin during segregation, Akins' description reflected accurately their experiences. In East Austin, young boys would meet at Rosewood Park, especially on Friday nights when the Anderson High School band would play at the park after the softball games. For example, several teachers recalled,

> When we finished playing, there was fellowship. We could play with our friends and do the usual things you do on Friday night. So we enjoyed that. The school [Anderson] was a real part of the community.[6]

But all was not fun and games for Austin's young Blacks. Chambers described a segregated Austin.

> When it's the only society you know, you don't necessarily view it [differently]. I [remember] the "colored" water fountains downtown . . . when we would go to the railroad station, [we'd] be in the back of the station in a dingy room . . . I remember.[7]

Chambers's memories speak of a time and place when Blacks and Whites, by law, were separated. Little wonder Blacks were so determined to achieve equality with Whites.

One method Blacks used to achieve equality was through owning and operating their own businesses. In fact, many Black parents would not allow their daughters to work as maids or domestics for White people. All children, both boys and girls, were expected to attend and graduate from college. For example, Taylor recalled,

> It wasn't a matter of deciding when to go to college. It was a given. There were eight of us and we all went to college. I have a brother who got his Ph.D. when he was twenty-four. We were blessed that we had ability . . . my parents emphasized the importance of using it and giving something back.[8]

Her family emphasized education as the foundation for survival. Similar to other Blacks during segregation, Taylor learned to prevail in a very hostile environment. She eloquently named the hostility as *un-selfing*.

> *Un-selfing* was the psychological kind of interaction that occurs between people that can breed mistrust in any kind of relationship. It means that you either overtly or covertly take a person's dignity. It can be done very, very subtly, but it can be done.[9]

Education was one way Blacks kept their dignity even as they attended segregated schools. For example, Taylor described her experience in a segregated school system.

> We never received new books—never. There was always somebody else's name in them. Which meant that they were books from the White school. They could be ragged and also sometimes they wouldn't have covers. You know they made these books with hardback covers, and sometimes they wouldn't have covers.[10]

Taylor knew many of her teachers bought supplies out of their own money. She laughingly commented that "if you were a good teacher, you would spend something out of your own pocket for your students."[11] Black teachers underscored the importance of an education to their students.

Based on the importance of education, Thurgood Marshall argued before the Texas Supreme Court that segregation was scientifically unjustifiable and socially destructive. A Black father who was a clerk and messenger for the Texas Supreme Court described this event to his young son. His son later reminisced about that time.

> He was there during the time that Thurgood Marshall came to Austin to argue the Herman Sweatt case. He'd come home at night and . . . talk about this handsome man who was before the [Texas] Supreme Court arguing the [Sweatt] case.[12]

Austin's Black parents appreciated the arguments Marshall cited on behalf of Heman Sweatt and all Blacks. The limited professional opportunities available for young Black men required a college degree, and they wanted the best for their children. For example, Akins recalled,

> [My father] wanted his lot to be better . . . the circumstances just didn't allow it. There was a quest on his part that I [go] to school. That was his quest and my mother's, too. They wanted me to do good . . . They were always interested in education to a great degree. They were always advocating to do the very best you could and to be a good citizen.[13]

Doing the best one could and being a good citizen meant, for many young Blacks, graduation from college with teaching credentials. Parents believed in the power of education, a belief some young Black people later fulfilled as Austin's cross-over teachers. But some hurdles still needed to be challenged; the major hurdle being segregated education.

SETTING THE STAGE FOR *BROWN*

The teachers were oblivious to their future roles as cross-over teachers during the period when Thurgood Marshall was arguing vehemently against the "separate but equal" doctrine. The willingness of Blacks continually to challenge the system, while at the same time to work within the system, was exemplified by Marshall and by the cross-over teachers. Understanding desegregation in Texas and in Austin requires an awareness of the impact of three major legal cases, *Sipuel, Sweatt,* and *McLaurin,* upon which the *Brown* decisions were based.

Sipuel v. Oklahoma State Board of Regents

Ada Lois Sipuel was a young, pretty twenty-one-year-old daughter of a clergyman. An honors graduate from the State College for Negroes in Langston, Oklahoma, she applied for admission to the University of Oklahoma Law School in 1946 but was rejected because the state asserted its intention to establish a separate law school for Negroes.[14] The district court further ruled that the university did not have to open a Negro law school until such time as it had sufficient applicants to make one practicable. In April 1947, the Oklahoma Supreme Court upheld the trial court's finding and Thurgood Marshall took this case to the United States Supreme Court. Marshall's major thesis was that, as practiced by the South, the "separate but equal" principle was a "false coin."[15]

The U. S. Supreme Court sent the case back to the Oklahoma Supreme Court, which ordered the university either to admit Sipuel to the White law school or open a separate school for Blacks.[16] The Oklahoma Board of Regents quickly created a separate law school for Blacks by closing off a small section of the state capitol and assigning three law professors to provide instruction to Sipuel and any other Blacks who wanted to attend the law school. Ms. Sipuel refused to attend this pseudo-law school and more than a thousand students and faculty held a rally on the University of Oklahoma campus protesting the regents' decision.[17] Marshall then argued to the U. S. Supreme Court that equality extended beyond facilities to the "free exchange of ideas and attitudes of all groups."[18] The Supreme Court rejected Marshall's argument on the basis that the *Sipuel* case did not meet the standard of the equal protection clause. Although the *Sipuel v. Oklahoma State Board of Regents* case judicially ratified tokenism, the decision laid the groundwork necessary to finally overturn *Plessy v. Ferguson.*

Sweatt v. Painter

Heman Marion Sweatt, a Black letter carrier, applied to The University of Texas law school in February 1946. His application was rejected on racial grounds, and he filed a complaint against the university in Austin, Texas. The district court ordered the state to establish a law school at Prairie View University, a Black college located between Austin and Houston, or to admit Sweatt to The University of Texas at Austin Law School. In response, the state of Texas rented a few rooms in Houston, hired two Black lawyers to serve as its faculty and called the arrangement the Prairie View Law School. The district court, in Austin, found that these makeshift arrangements provided

> substantial equality to the Negro applicant despite its deficiencies in a few areas, such as the absence of a student body, a trained faculty, and a library.[19]

The following March, 1947, the Texas Court of Civil Appeals reviewed the Sweatt case. By that time, the Texas legislature had appropriated $3 million to create a new Texas State University for Blacks in Austin, of which $100,000 was to establish a new law school. The new law school consisted of three small rooms in the building's basement, three part-time faculty instructors who were also first-year instructors at The University of Texas Law School, a library of ten thousand books and access to the state law library. Heman Sweatt could begin classes on March 10, 1947. He chose to return to court. Marshall argued before the Texas Supreme Court that the proposed "law school" was not true equality.[20] A month later, the Texas Supreme Court ruled against Sweatt, and Marshall appealed this case to the United States Supreme Court.

McLaurin v. Oklahoma State Board of Regents for Higher Education

Shortly after appealing the Sweatt case to the federal courts, Marshall agreed to take what would prove to be the final link in the chain of cases building against segregation in higher education. George W. McLaurin had earned his Master's degree in education and applied to the University of Oklahoma to earn a doctorate in education. Like Sipuel and Sweatt, he was rejected on racial grounds. The

NAACP took the case directly to a special three-judge federal district court in August 1948.[21] The Court ruled just thirty days later that

> the state is under the constitutional duty to provide the plaintiff with the education he seeks as soon as it does for applicants of any other group.[22]

In response, the university established a segregated classroom for McLaurin. In addition, the university segregated his use of the library and the cafeteria. Marshall appealed directly to the United States Supreme Court.

Both the Sweatt case and the McLaurin case came before the U. S. Supreme Court in 1950. Each case approached the "separate but equal" doctrine in different ways. The United States Supreme Court ordered Heman Sweatt to be admitted to the University of Texas Law School. This ruling was the first order that a Black student be admitted to a White school on the basis that the Black school established by the state failed to offer equal educational opportunity. However, the *Plessy* doctrine remained alive. The *McLaurin* case, heard after the *Sweatt* ruling, changed the Court's view of "separate but equal" doctrine. The Court found that the restrictions on George McLaurin were inequities and must cease.[23]

The Court's ruling in *Sweatt* found that equality had to be real or the separation was constitutionally intolerable. The Court elaborated on the *Sweatt* ruling in *McLaurin* by finding that if separate facilities were not provided, no individual or group might suffer restrictions or harassments within the biracial school. Each of these cases laid the foundation for the ultimate assault on segregation in education. The NAACP then chose to attack the "separate but equal"doctrine in the public school systems. The case was officially filed with the United States District Court for Kansas on February 28, 1951. Its title was *Brown v. Board of Education of Topeka.*

THE END OF JIM CROW:
BROWN V. BOARD OF EDUCATION OF TOPEKA

The early 1950s found the NAACP Legal Defense Fund overwhelmed with cases. Marshall and his staff decided their fight against school segregation would best be fought by presenting the U. S. Supreme Court with a constellation of lawsuits. Each lawsuit presented before the Court was to be from a different setting so as to place the Justices in a position where engagement with the primary issue of school segregation was unavoidable. Four cases, each with a common legal question of the constitutionality of segregated public schools, came before the United States Supreme Court in late 1952. The cases, from the states of Kansas, South Carolina, Virginia, and Delaware, were consolidated under the first case, *Brown v. Board of Education* in late 1953. In each case, Black children had been denied admission to White schools based on state laws requiring or permitting segregation according to race. The NAACP Legal Defense Fund's strategy of consolidating similar cases with diverse points and localities bore fruit. Prior to the Supreme Court hearing, lower courts had upheld the "separate but equal" doctrine of *Plessy v. Ferguson* in each case. On May 17, 1954, the United States Supreme Court held that the "separate but equal" doctrine of *Plessy v. Ferguson* was unconstitutional and ruled that

> Segregation of white and colored children in public schools has a detrimental effect upon the colored children. The impact is greater when it has the sanction of the law; for the policy of separating the races is usually interpreted as denoting the inferiority of the Negro group. A sense of inferiority affects the motivation of a child to learn. Segregation with the sanction of law, therefore, has a tendency to retard the educational and mental development of Negro children and to deprive them of some of the benefits they would receive in a racially integrated school system.[24]

The United States Supreme Court reversed, in one opinion, fifty-eight years of enforced separation of Blacks and Whites. The NAACP had not identified a single target but a group of targets within a system that it wanted to eliminate—school segregation, lynching laws, Jim Crow laws. In other words, the NAACP efforts attacked the legal basis of racial segregation.

One year later, on May 31, 1955, the Supreme Court: 1) reaffirmed and extended desegregation in education, 2) charged local school boards with responsibility for integration under the scrutiny of federal courts, and 3) instructed the courts to require school authorities to make "a prompt and reasonable start" and proceed "with all deliberate speed" toward integration, but allow reasonable delays to solve administrative problems.[25] The system of racial segregation began an extremely slow process of disintegration. Jim Crow no longer had the legal support of the U. S. Supreme Court.

SCHOOL DESEGREGATION BEGINS IN TEXAS

By the early 1950s, although Blacks constituted 13 percent of the state's population, 90 percent of them lived in Texas' northeast and east central counties. The eighty-eight counties in this part of Texas were politically, socially, and economically closer to the Southern states than they were to the western counties in Texas. Not surprisingly, Whites in east Texas reflected the Southern "state of mind" and participated fully in the concept of "segregation at any price." Allan Shivers, governor of Texas during the 1950s, grew up in east Texas. Having early on set high goals for himself, Shivers quickly gained a reputation for "winning at all costs." The election of Shivers's supporter, John Ben Sheppard, in 1952 as attorney general for the state of Texas helped seal the powerful political machine Shivers developed.[26] At the time of the *Brown* decision, Shivers held immense political power in the state of Texas, and he was not afraid to advocate his cause at the national level. When he heard that the

United States Attorney General had been invited to address the United States Supreme Court specific to *Brown,* Shivers contacted President Eisenhower and offered his opinion as a representative of a Southern state.

> I see in this unusual Supreme Court invitation an attempt to embarrass you and your Attorney General. There is nothing more local than the public school system. . . . I trust he will . . . advise the Court that this local problem should be decided on the local and state level.[27]

Clearly, Shivers was unable effectively to intercede in the Supreme Court's decision to desegregate the nation's public schools, including Texas. Shortly after the Court handed down its decision, Shivers was interviewed by the local newspaper, the *Austin American.* His comments forewarned Black Texans that desegregation would be slow in coming.

> It will take years to comply with the order for integration of schools. . . . Sometimes those who seek reforms go so far that the evils of the reform movement are more onerous than the evils they're trying to remedy. . . . Just saying we abolish segregation doesn't cure it. It doesn't accomplish anything. What is done about enforcing it is the important thing.[28]

The concept of "all deliberate slowness" began to take shape in Texas. Shortly thereafter, June 21, 1954, Shivers clarified his position about segregation during a campaign speech.

> It is an unwarranted invasion of the constitutional rights of the states. . . . . My administration has already told the local school districts that, as far as the state of Texas is concerned, there are no changes to be made.[29]

In the fall of 1954, the Texas Democratic Convention, with Shivers at its head, decreed the *Brown* decision to be "[an] unwarranted invasion of states rights [necessitating the resurrection of] the separate but equal doctrine."[30]

Texas Attorney General Shepperd carried Shivers's and other White Texans' arguments against desegregation to the U. S. Supreme Court in the spring of 1955. On April 13, 1955, Texas Attorney General Shepperd proclaimed,

> This touches the deepest roots of human emotions. . . . It comes dangerously close to interference in . . . the rights of parents to bring up their children in their own customs and beliefs.
>
> Texas does not come here today to argue the cause of other states. . . . It argues only that in Texas, a man-made cataclysm must be made slowly and with wisdom. Our argument may be summed up in eight words. . . . It is our problem—let us solve it.[31]

Like other Southern states, Texas wanted to solve the desegregation order in its own good time. "With all deliberate speed" suddenly took on new meaning.

Given the political climate, school systems in Texas reacted to the *Brown v. Board of Education* decision in various ways. A number of school districts in western counties of Texas quickly began the process of desegregation. Perhaps because the number of Black students in those districts were few, desegregation seemed to be accepted fairly easily. For example, the small Friona school district in west Texas quietly desegregated in Fall 1954, and was the first school district in Texas to achieve desegregation peacefully.[32] The beginning of the 1955–1956 school year found sixty-three additional school districts in the state that had begun the process of desegregation.[33] However, anti-desegregation groups in east and south Texas quickly organized Citizens' Councils and vowed to resist the Court's desegregation orders. The Citizens' Councils only goal was to prevent desegregation of the school systems.[34] Three school districts, Big Springs, Mansfield, and Goose Creek, provide a glimpse of the diverse struggles to eliminate school desegregation in Texas communities. These three examples underscore the reality that the implementation of the *Brown* decision was particular to each community and state across the South.

The first test of the U. S. Supreme Court's decision in Texas occurred in the west Texas ranching town of Big Springs.[35] The local school board discussed the principles of a desegregation policy during the summer of 1955 and developed a written course of action to guide the formation of an official desegregation policy which it would then adopt. The official policy recommended that the elementary schools be desegregated on a voluntary basis during the forthcoming 1955–1956 school year. The Board did not recommend desegregation of the White junior high and high schools, because they were overcrowded and a new Colored secondary school building was scheduled for completion that fall. Thus, junior high and senior high school students were not affected by the Board's desegregation policy.[36] On August 9, 1955, the Big Springs School District Board of Trustees ordered,

> Without changing any of the boundary lines of the areas assigned to these Ward schools . . . grade school students living in these areas be permitted to attend grade school in the district where they reside, regardless of race . . . . Individual students could apply to the superintendent of schools to attend the school of their choice. The applications would be considered on an individual basis and were subject to the long established authority of the superintendent to require the transfer of pupils between grade schools when classes were full in one school and space was available in another.[37]

Reaction to this announcement was swift. The Texas Citizens' Council immediately filed a lawsuit requesting an injunction against the Big Springs School Board's implementation of its desegregation policy.[38] Texas Governor Allen Shivers, as well as Attorney General John Ben Sheppard, supported the lawsuit. These officials argued that local school districts should proceed with caution because rushing into desegregation could cause great harm. They maintained that if Texas laws on segregation were eliminated, the state school laws would disintegrate.[39]

The Texas High Court heard arguments in this lawsuit in September 1955, and rendered its decision October 12, 1955.

> [The Court ruled that] state funds could be spent for schools where Negro and White students were mingled. . . . [T]he U. S. Supreme Court's desegregation ruling did apply to sections of the Texas Constitution and laws requiring segregation of White and Negro students in the public schools [and that] these offending portions were unconstitutional and void. . . . [The Court found] that the school laws prohibiting the expenditure of public funds in integrated schools [were] not supported. [The Court declared] we find in the act no language which would deny the use of such funds to integrated schools . . . [while upholding the legality of voluntary integration, the Texas Court also said] the Supreme Court did not direct immediate and complete integration in all schools.[40]

The attorney general of Texas issued a statement "the ruling settles the law in Texas on a statewide basis, but the time of integration will still be a district by district matter."[41] Segregation had been the law in Texas, as in all other Southern states, since Reconstruction. This ruling changed the law but it did not solve the desegregation problems faced by the two thousand school districts across Texas. Attorney General Sheppard then urged Texas to begin immediately to map plans for a substitute to the state's present system of laws on segregation.

> If we do not have a substitute ready when it is needed, we may be forced by the courts to accept immediate integration. If we wait too long, our school legislation is going to be made by federal courts instead of our own legislature. Texas must take the initiative in solving the problem of desegregation or those nine men are going to solve it for us in a manner we may not like.[42]

Despite the Texas Supreme Court decision upholding desegregation, many communities overtly resisted implementing desegregation. Mansfield, Texas, was one such community. In fact, it was the only community in Texas where law enforcement was used to "keep the peace."

In 1955, Mansfield, Texas, was a small sleepy community on the outskirts of Fort Worth. Like most communities in central and east Texas, a rigid system of segregation kept Blacks and Whites apart. Blacks were relegated to low paying menial jobs, so many of them commuted from Mansfield to the Fort Worth/Dallas area to work. The only Black school in Mansfield was a four room building that served as the elementary school. High school students were required to ride a Trailways bus into Fort Worth and then walk twenty blocks to the Black high school. The only concession Mansfield's White school administrators made to numerous requests by the Black community for educational improvements was to finally issue bus passes to cover the high school students' transportation costs.[43]

Mansfield's Black community was frustrated because of the White school board's continuing resistance to equalizing educational opportunities for Black students. Given this, several members of the Mansfield branch of the NAACP hired L. Clifford Davis of Fort Worth to represent their interest to the school board. Although Davis sent numerous letters to the school board, no progress was made. That spring, in May 1955, the second component of the *Brown* decision was handed down by the United States Supreme Court.[44] Davis, working the Mansfield branch of the NAACP, presented a petition to the Mansfield school board requesting the board "to take immediate steps to end segregation in the Mansfield public schools."[45] Mansfield's Black community was well aware of the inherent risks involved when they submitted the petition, but believed they had no other recourse but to follow the compliance plan sent to all branches of the NAACP.[46] Certainly the Mansfield school board had refused all requests for improvements to Black elementary schools and a bus for Black high school students. The course for a lawsuit was set in place.

In late August 1955, Davis met with Mansfield Superintendent Huffman to attempt the enrollment of three Black high school students in Mansfield's White high school. Huffman stated the students could not be enrolled at the high school because a desegregation plan had not been worked out by the board. On October 7, 1955, Davis filed a class action lawsuit, *Jackson v. Rawdon,* on behalf of Mansfield's Black students at the federal district court in Fort Worth.[47]

Reactions by the White community were swift and not unexpected. Mansfield had a strong Citizens' Council chapter that immediately blamed the NAACP and Communism. The chapter president, Howard H. Beard, emphatically stated,

> If the decision is allowed to stand, our children will be guinea pigs and our days as a national race are numbered. . . . Once mixed they can never be unmixed, and this [is] the surest and most certain way to destroy us. If we don't organize, it will be our children who will pay the price in the next two generations for our cowardice.[48]

The *Mansfield News* cited Beard as labeling the NAACP as "Communist conceived and dominated and really stands for 'The National Association for the Agitation of Colored People.' "[49] Mansfield Whites were adamantly opposed to desegregation and responded as such to the lawsuit. At the court hearing, the school board requested time to develop a desegregation plan beyond the school year of 1955–1956. In November 1955, Judge Estes, who heard the case, ruled for the school board. He believed that (1) the board was making a good faith effort toward desegregation, and (2) desegregation could not take place in the middle of the school year.

Davis and the Black community were not surprised. Their only decision was whether or not to appeal Judge Estes's ruling. In early Spring 1956, Davis filed an appeal of Judge Estes's decision with the United States Fifth Circuit Court of Appeals. On June 28, 1956, Chief Judge Hutcheson issued the opinion of the Court.

The plaintiffs [Black students] have the right to admission to, and to attend, the Mansfield High School on the same basis as members of the white race; that the refusal of the defendants [the school board] to admit plaintiffs thereto on account of their race or color is unlawful; that it [the District Court] order the defendants forever restrained from refusing admission thereto to any of the plaintiffs shown to be qualified in all respects for admission; and that it [the District Court] retain jurisdiction of the cause for further orders . . . to promptly, fully, and effectively carry out this mandate.[50]

Understandably, on August 25, 1956, Judge Estes adhered to the Fifth Circuit's decree and ordered the school board to admit Mansfield's Black students to the White high school. Shortly after Judge Estes's ruling, emotions ran high in Mansfield. The school board tried to find ways around the desegregation order, to no avail. Vehement segregationists held impromptu meetings on street corners around the town. Crosses were burned on the lawns of several Black residents. An effigy painted black with splotches of red paint was hung at the center of town. Painted signs were hung from the effigy, reading, "This would be a terrible way to die" and "This Negro tried to enter a white school." Racial tensions were explosive.[51]

August 30, 1956, was registration day for Mansfield students. Another effigy, similar to the one on Main Street was hung from the high school's flagpole. A White crowd milled in front of the high school with the sole purpose of blocking Black students from entering the high school to register. When Davis learned of the volatile situation, he had the Black students remain at their homes, and immediately sent a telegram to Governor Shivers and to Colonel Homer Garrison of the Texas Department of Public Safety, requesting assistance from the law enforcement agencies.[52] Shivers refused to send additional law enforcement personnel to Mansfield unless requested by the sheriff. Furthermore, he blamed Davis and Mansfield's Black residents for causing the problems.[53] However, several Texas Rangers (nine in total) were sent to Mansfield to "keep the peace." Given direct orders by Governor Shivers, they were not to offer aid or escort Black students into the high school to register. The Black students did not enroll in Mansfield's White high school, and over the next several months an uneasy peace returned to Mansfield. Despite the federal court order to desegregate its schools, Mansfield remained segregated until 1965, when the threat of withdrawal of federal funds was sufficient to accomplish what the Supreme Court could not—desegregation of Mansfield's public schools.

McNair, adjacent to Houston, Texas, was a part of the Goose Creek Independent School District. Shortly after the 1954 *Brown* decision, the Goose Creek school system closed its Black schools and assigned Black students to formerly White facilities with the exception of the Harlem Elementary School in the community of McNair. The history of Harlem Elementary School graphically illustrates the struggle between district officials and communities through the assignment of cross-over teachers.

Harlem Elementary, built as part of the Goose Creek school district in 1928, received its name as a deliberate designation of a Black school. McNair, the community that developed around the school, was Black. Harlem Elementary School had three rooms with dirt floors and outside bathrooms.[54] In 1948, some twenty years later, these conditions were unchanged. The toilets remained outside, children served themselves in the cafeteria, and available classroom space remained limited.[55] The Goose Creek school board apparently gave little thought to the building plans of the school or to the education of the children who attended Harlem Elementary.[56] Like those in other Black schools, Harlem's students were given secondhand books and supplies. However, the Black faculty worked diligently to provide the best education possible under the circumstances to the students at Harlem Elementary.[57]

In 1963, the Goose Creek Independent School District decided to build a Black junior high school near Harlem Elementary School despite the McNair community's strong opposition. McNair's adults believed that only total integration would solve its educational problems. Furthermore, when the school board subsequently decided to renovate Harlem Elementary School, McNair residents voiced strong opposition to this plan as well. The McNair parents were willing to have their children bused to other White schools within the district. The Goose Creek school board refused to even consider their request. Instead, the district renovated Harlem Elementary, built an auditorium, library, five classrooms, and an administration building at a cost of $67,000. In addition, the school district paid $23,000 for air conditioning and a stove on which to prepare the students' lunches.[58] Although the conditions at Harlem Elementary improved, however moderately, it remained an all-Black school.

In 1965, to comply with the Federal Civil Rights Act of 1964, the Goose Creek superintendent of schools said that the district could no longer maintain segregated schools or faculties or the district would lose federal funds.[59] Shortly thereafter, a White teacher, Art Coltharp, volunteered to move to Harlem Elementary School as principal, thereby becoming the first White teacher at Harlem Elementary. Coltharp immediately began to recruit White faculty to cross-over from a White school to Harlem Elementary School.[60] Coltharp promised the White cross-over teachers that they could leave Harlem Elementary at the end of the school year if they were displeased with their assignment. McNair parents, although somewhat suspicious of the cross-over teachers, supported the plan.[61]

In addition to cross-over teachers, the Goose Creek school board initiated a freedom of choice plan, designed to recruit White students to attend Harlem Elementary School. The freedom of choice program allowed parents to choose any school within the district for their children to attend as long as overcrowding did not exist within the school or within the grade that the parents requested. If the school or grades were overcrowded, students living closest to the school would have priority over those living farther away. The school district did not provide transportation to schools away from the neighborhood school. Not surprisingly, the freedom of choice program did not yield a desegregated Harlem Elementary School. The Harlem School was in the midst of a Black community and White parents refused to transport their children across the district to an all-Black school for fear of an inferior education. For the next three years, only the faculty at Harlem Elementary School was desegregated.[62]

The desegregation plan that focused on cross-over teachers and freedom of choice failed to meet the Department of Heath, Education, and Welfare's criteria for legal desegregation, because Harlem Elementary School remained a Black school in a Black neighborhood. Despite the White teachers at the school, HEW declared Goose Creek school board to be in noncompliance and informed the district it would lose federal funds. Students and teachers had to be desegregated. In 1969, the school district designated Harlem Elementary as a magnet school, a move that resulted in an enrollment of fifty-nine White students and 289 Black students. Under this plan, the Goose Creek school board met legal desegregation standards the following year.[63]

Austin school board's desegregation plan closely paralleled Goose Creek school board's plan. Unlike Goose Creek school board, which met the legal desegregation requirements in 1970, Austin's school board for years continued its covert resistance to desegregation through the continued reliance on cross-over teachers.

DESEGREGATION IS IMMINENT FOR THE CAPITAL CITY

Prior to the *Brown* decision, regardless of their residence, Black students in Austin attended one of seven elementary schools restricted to Blacks (i.e., Blackshear Elementary, Campbell Elementary, Clarksville Elementary, Oak Springs Elementary, Rosewood Elementary, St. Johns Elementary, or Sims Elementary School), Kealing Junior High School, and L. C. Anderson High School.[64] Anderson High School and Kealing Junior High School were open residential schools, that is, no matter where Black students lived within the Austin School District boundaries, they attended these secondary schools.[65] During that period, Austin ISD maintained two residential zones: one zone for White students, including Mexican American students, and another residential zone for Black students.[66] Although Blacks lived in some small residential areas outside of East Austin, the majority lived on the city's east side.[67] Austin school board provided funds to transport Black students to the Black schools. Legislation prohibited Negro and White students from attending the same school.[68] During this period, Akins believed that desegregation was not viewed as a viable option by the majority of Austin residents.

Austin High[69] was in existence but the thought of integrating [it] had not surfaced then. It seemed to me that we were pretty receptive of the conditions, the state we were in. The NAACP had some action here. Several people worked hard at it but it didn't take fire because people were afraid they'd lose their jobs [if they joined the NAACP].[70]

Austin's Black community continued its conciliatory attitudes first evidenced during the summer of 1919, when it was one of the few major cities in Texas to escape the summer riots.[71] Certainly, few were willing to risk challenging the status quo.

Shortly after the second *Brown* decision, in July 1955, the Austin school board requested Superintendent Irby Carruth to conduct a feasibility study on the desegregation of senior high school students. One month later, superintendent Carruth proposed the creation of two east side residential zones from the former residential zone of Austin High School. One of the east residential zones already was in place, Anderson High School—the Black high school. The second residential zone would include Johnston High School, a planned but unnamed facility until it opened in 1960. The residential zones for McCallum and Travis High Schools remained unchanged.[72] In addition, the Austin School Board approved a freedom of choice plan based on

> the wisdom of letting students continue their high school careers where they
> have allegiance to the teachers, the program of their school, fellow students and
> student activities.[73]

The freedom of choice plan allowed any high school student (grades 10–12) to attend school in his/her residential zone. As a direct result of the *Brown* decision, the Austin Independent School District Board of Trustees resolved on August 8, 1955, to implement a freedom of choice plan for the city's high schools. The board's decision was understood to be "the first step toward the implementation of a Supreme Court edict declaring color distinction in the nation's public schools illegal and in violation of the Constitution."[74] In other words, all students, regardless of race/ethnicity, were permitted to transfer to the school of their choice.[75] On September 6, 1955, thirteen Black students transferred from Anderson High School to three formerly White high schools, Austin High School, Travis High School, and McCallum High School. Eleven of the thirteen students actually lived within the residential zone of the high school they petitioned to attend.[76] In the 1958–1959 academic year, the school board gave ninth grade Black students the same option it offered in 1955 to the city's high school students. They could attend either Kealing Junior High School or the formerly White junior high school in their residential zone. Nonetheless, in 1958, 95 percent of the Black students attended all-Black schools, and no Black teachers taught outside of a Black school.[77]

Beginning in the fall of 1958, the stair step desegregation plan was extended one grade each year in the junior high schools (grades 7–9). At the end of this process, 3.76 percent (50/1328) of the Black junior high students had transferred to formerly all White schools. Concurrently, 7.2 percent (61/848) of all Black high school students were attending White high schools.[78]

In 1960, the Austin League of Women Voters reported that "all the senior and junior high schools [were] now completely integrated."[79] It also reported that, between 1960 and 1964, beginning with the eighth grade and moving backward, one elementary grade per year would be integrated until the last four grades would be integrated in 1964. In other words, the school board officially permitted Black students to attend one of the Black elementary schools or to transfer to a White elementary school within their residential zone. Some information exists as to the number of Black students who actually transferred from Black elementary schools to White elementary schools. The League of Women Voters report of "integrated" schools seemed more wishful thinking than actual reality. Akins remembered this period in Austin quite differently than that reported by the League of Women Voters.

> We didn't mix a lot. There may be a situation where we'd go on a field trip and some others [Whites] would be there. But there wasn't any planned opportunities for mixing.[80]

Taylor joined the Anderson faculty, as a social studies teacher, in the fall of 1960. She remembered she was surprised to learn about Austin's overt resistance to desegregation. She expected her home town of Hearne to fight desegregation, but not Austin.

> What was most surprising to me was the kind of resistance that occurred, especially here in Austin. I was shocked, that an intellectual community [like Austin] would be so resistant to obeying the law. It was fascinating to me![81]

On September 5, 1963, nine years after the *Brown* decision, Austin's public schools dropped their last racial barrier; freedom of choice was extended to grades one through four.[82] At the same time, about 10 percent of Austin's Black students were enrolled in formerly White schools. Some previously White elementary and junior high schools enrolled between two and seven Black students, but most of Austin's elementary schools remained identifiably segregated.[83] During that same period, Akins and Taylor recalled Austin's district social studies supervisor's desire that all the district's high school social studies teachers meet to develop a common curriculum. They described the process:

> Our social studies supervisor wanted us to meet with other social studies teachers and plan together and then take some field trips together. A cohort of social studies teachers from the high school level, Anderson, Austin, Travis, and McCallum would meet together periodically. For me [Akins], this experience led up to becoming a cross-over teacher.[84]

By the spring of 1964, 14 percent of all Black students in Austin were enrolled in White schools.[85] However, most of Austin's White schools remained untouched by these feeble unidirectional desegregation efforts. Although some Black students transferred to formerly all-White schools, only eight White students attended formerly all-Black schools. The transfer policy proposed by Carruth and accepted by the school board guaranteed the continued segregation of the schools. Despite the plan's apparent neutrality, the transfer numbers were negligible. While some Blacks transferred out of their original residential zone so did the Whites who lived in the zones. At the same time, no White students transferred into Anderson's residential zone. The system's teachers were as segregated as ever. Austin's next step toward desegregation was to reassign a few Black teachers to White schools.

CHAPTER FIVE

With All Deliberate Slowness

THE FALL OF 1964 brought headlines in the *Austin American,* "Austin Faculty is Integrated!"[1] In reality, Superintendent Irby Carruth had assigned three Black teachers to White schools. He transferred William Charles Akins from Anderson High School to Johnston High School and Booker T. Snell and Narveline Dreenan from Kealing Junior High School to Allan Junior High. Both Johnston High School and Allan Junior High enrolled predominantly Mexican American students. Ernest Cabe, Austin Director of Personnel, publicly noted:

> All three teachers have master's degrees and have been active in system-wide curriculum development. They are really tops, master teachers, each one![2]

As cross-over teachers, they were the only Black teachers assigned to White schools for several years. Even then, few Black teachers were transferred to White high schools. Not until the beginning of the 1969–1970 school year, some six years hence, were cross-over teachers transferred in large numbers.

THE ENORMOUS RESPONSIBILITY

William E. Pigford, Anderson High School's principal, notified Charles Akins during the summer of 1964 of his transfer to Johnston High School. Principal Pigford told Akins that superintendent Carruth and personnel director Cabe planned to talk with him about moving to Johnston. Within a few days, Cabe informed Akins of his transfer to Johnston High School and that he should arrange to meet with his new principal, Gordon Bailey. Still, Akins remembers that he realized he had no real choice about the acceptance of the assignment.

> I think Mister Cabe had already made the decision, he and Mister Carruth. My principal said, "They are going to call and talk with you about moving out of here and I hope you go." I said, "Yes, sir, I'll go." I had a lot of anxiety—a lot of anxiety—to be a guinea pig, so to speak. I knew they [White teachers, Black teachers, the entire city] were going to be watching me, scrutinize me. I said, "I don't know why they want me to do it." My principal at Anderson said, "They wanted some youth—wanted a younger person [to be the first cross-over teacher]. Mister Cabe thinks you could probably do the job."[3]

In his recollections of his initial feelings about becoming the first cross-over teacher in Austin, Akins recognized his reassignment as both an opportunity and a challenge. He remembers his concern about his diction and about how he would "fit in" at Johnston High School.

> What I was trying to do was become homogenized and to work with my coworkers so they would not see me as an impediment to being in a good school or teaching but as a colleague. I was less aware of my diction prior to cross-over teaching because we were all in one setting and I could hear no difference. But when I got in a different situation, I could hear the difference and I said to myself, "I need to work on this." I wanted to study so I could be ahead. I had some very adept students and I didn't want them to think "Hey, this guy doesn't know what he's talking about."[4]

Akins knew that his problems were more than diction. He would be the first Black teacher Johnston students, faculty, and parents would meet.

> You wanted to show you were a good citizen. You wanted to get to work early and you wanted to stay late. You wanted to be the epitome of the all-American teacher. You worked hard and put a lot of pressure on your family and yourself to do that. That was important. You take that upon yourself because you think the weight of the success of this endeavor rests upon your success. If I didn't deport myself properly then it [the desegregation plan] would have failed and I would have failed.[5]

As the first cross-over teacher in Austin, Akins knew that he represented all other Black teachers in the district. He remembers feeling enormous responsibility for the success of this part of the desegregation plan.

> If you were going to be there, you wanted to be good and you wanted to be accepted by new friends and new colleagues. Also, you didn't want to fail because you felt if you failed, the whole program would fail. If I don't make it—I don't think it was like that—but it felt like that and it could have been like that for all I know. You start off with one [Black teacher] and then you bring in some

more. If that one had not panned out what would have happened? Such skepticism on the part of the parents and on the part of your fellow teachers and your students. A lot of people are going to take a bad view from how you act. And when they talk with somebody else, you wanted it to be an accolade rather than something unacceptable. So you worked hard, you wouldn't let your guard down.[6]

Akins remembered vividly the multiplicity of feelings he experienced as he began teaching in the White school. He wondered how the students and the teachers would accept him. He knew he had to win over the students. At the same time, he wondered if they (anyone) would try to "run him off." He then recounted his first day as a cross-over teacher at Johnston High School.

We had a faculty meeting. Mister Bailey, the principal, introduced me . . . [he] set the stage pretty well. I had some anxiety and some fear that first day. I don't know if I went to lunch or not; I probably did because I wanted to feel well . . . when the kids came in, they were kind of skeptical of me, too. I don't believe anybody in there, if they had been in Austin, had had an African American teacher before. I was the first one. Especially in high school. If they had one, it was outside of Austin. Thirty kids on the first day. Yes, I was scared. But, I wanted them to know I would help them. I was ready for my first assignment. I had my ditto sheets ready to pass out. I wanted them to know that we had come to try to learn, and I wanted to help them . . . that I wasn't going to intimidate them, and I wasn't going to use sarcasm. That wasn't my style.[7]

Akins was a zealous teacher who wanted his students to do well. He incorporated many of the same methods he had been exposed to as a student at Anderson. He knew these methods worked with his Anderson students, and he expected them to work with his Johnston students as well.

I wanted to be a good teacher, I wanted them [my class] to read the newspaper and be able to keep up with the issues. In fact we read the newspaper every day in class. Had spelling drills every day because I wanted them to be able to spell and to write. Had small quizzes that I could grade quickly. But I also had them do essays. I wanted them to write.[8]

At the same time, Akins never let his guard down. Always careful with his speech, he did not want to slip into his former way of talking because he worried that his students and fellow colleagues at Johnston might judge him negatively. He truly wanted to make desegregation work. Most importantly, he believed in his students.

I didn't sit down much, I walked. I think teachers still do that. And those that don't probably need to. I guess that's taxing—but when you're young you don't think about that being taxing, you just do it. Finally I had some success after a little quiz at the end of the week. I'd try to do a quiz at the end of every week.

Then kids would have a better opportunity [to learn] the more tests that they would take [rather than just] one or two. I said, "Look, if he or she falls down on this one, next week they can do better." So I did a lot of paper grading on weekends to make sure that I could give the kids immediate feedback on how they were doing.[9]

A social studies teacher, Akins began his Johnston career by teaching World History and American History courses. After a few years, Bailey assigned him to teach Economics and Civics as well as the history classes.

I had ninth graders in World History, eleventh graders in American History and a few twelfth graders in Civics or Economics. I think the evolutionary process of my starting with the ninth grade was good. They knew me by the time they were ready to graduate. After a bit kids talk and I got over the hard part, I guess.[10]

Because a few Black students attended Johnston, Akins soon learned he was expected to support them and intervene when other teachers needed help. He was concerned about the Black students but knew he couldn't work with them exclusively or he would be seen as a Black teacher for Black students.

I didn't want that [to be seen as just a Black teacher for Black students] and I don't think the district wanted that. They just wanted me to be a teacher but I wanted those kids to do well. They were being sent home with discipline problems. I didn't seem to be able to do a lot about it. But after I had been there awhile, I began to meet some parents, talked to them about it [the problems]. . . . If you had a Black youngster who was having difficulty in an Anglo classroom, the students would want me to come and be supportive of them. The thought was that they would listen to you faster than they would listen to others. Some of that may have been true. . . . But sometimes you'd catch them in their fit of hostility, they won't listen to anybody when they get to that stage.[11]

Akins cared about all his students, Blacks, Mexican Americans,and Whites. Johnston High School was predominantly Mexican American, so Akins made a point to learn about his Mexican American students' heritage.

I tried to get them [Mexican Americans] feeling good about themselves with personalities. The Hispanic movement wasn't as strong then. But I wanted it to be acknowledged. The movement wasn't as strong, because the focus was on civil rights and African Americans. The Hispanic youngsters were considered part of the majority.[12]

Within the first semester, Akins found all his students began to accept him, especially those who were the underachievers. Gordon Bailey, the principal at Johnston, had established a tracking system, grouping students by color. Akins wasn't sure if the kids knew about the colors, but he thought they probably did.

Mister Bailey had a grouping system there by color—yellow, white, and green. Everybody would have a white class, which would mean that you had some underachievers in there. And then you had these accelerated kids. Well, I always had a class that we considered white, which were underachievers, and then the next level was supposed to be the more average youngsters. But that was his system. Trying to get to the kids to save them.[13]

He remembered that he had students of all three levels in his courses. However, most of his students were the underachievers and some at the middle level. He remembered working as hard with the underachievers as he did with the average and above average students. For the next two years, Charles Akins was the only Black teacher at a predominantly White school in Austin.

The Austin School Board continued its freedom of choice plan for students. Only a few Black students moved into White schools and no White students transferred to Black schools. Moreover, the administrative leaders made no further attempts to continue the desegregation of Austin faculty until the summer of 1966.

At that time, Austin personnel director Cabe informed Iola Taylor of her transfer from Anderson High School to Johnston High School. There, she joined Akins in the social studies department. She described the process as *un-selfing*, a term that meant that the school administration did not recognize her as a professional. Taylor recalled how she felt when she received the reassignment letter.

The way I was transferred was—I received a letter. Telling me of my assignment. They never called you in to talk to you—implying you would make it [desegregation] better. I called and asked about the letter. All they did was remind me what my contract said—which was that you were subject to assignment by the administration. They could assign you wherever they wanted to send you. If you wanted the job, you went. I think they never ever took the vantage point of at least talking to you, encouraging you, making some type of support commitment to you. You never got that; you just got a letter . . . I don't know if they did the same with Anglo teachers. That's all we got, a letter assigning us. You would get the letter and they would have contacted the principal at the campus where you were going and the principal would contact you.[14]

Taylor remembered her immediate concerns when she went to Johnston. She recognized that she needed to be sensitive to three cultural groups of students rather than just one. Johnston had a predominantly Mexican American student population with some Blacks and a very few White students.

I had to be sensitive to the kids, the involvement of the young people. Sometimes there was a little bit of jealousy. You had to be sure that you were being equitable in terms of involvement of the students . . . that there was no indication that you were favoring one group over another. Johnston was predominantly a Mexican American high school. That's the way Austin integrated.

That's just the way they integrated. They integrated by making the first steps by Blacks with Mexican Americans and then the next step—they had no choice because they were fighting a court battle all along—was to move Black teachers into Anglo-American schools.[15]

Taylor characterized Johnston principal Bailey as a gentleman who wanted his school to succeed. She thought that he was more adaptable than other Austin principals to new and different situations. She described his approach to students.

He knew those young people, and he would follow them home in a whistling minute and when they would play hooky, he knew where they would go, and he would get in his truck and go get them and bring them to school. So, he was a man who was part of AISD, but his domain was Johnston High School, and he wanted Johnston to succeed. He had sense enough to know that the Black teachers he had were the best and the brightest. And so he supported us to a point.[16]

Perhaps because she was female, Taylor's initial experiences at Johnston differ somewhat from those of Akins. She remembers that her students had a "wait and see attitude," but they were not hostile. She keenly recalled a particular incident early in her assignment at Johnston. Teachers at the school were required to stand outside their classroom and welcome students to the class.

I didn't speak Spanish at all, but I picked up certain parts. One time, I was standing outside my door and a young lady who was a student teacher right across from me was standing outside the door of her supervising teacher's room. These students came up the stairs. They knew who spoke Spanish; they were saying something in Spanish. I looked at him, and he was smiling and going on. Then, they went on in my room and sat down. I knew they were up to something but I didn't know what. The student teacher came over to me. She spoke fluent Spanish. She asked me, "Do you know what he said?" I said, "No, because I don't speak Spanish at all." So, then, she told me, "He said something very nasty." Well, I thanked her and I remembered the words. I called him out and chatted with him. Then I took him down to Mister Garza's office, [the] Dean of Young Men, and he had a talk with him. I chose a Mexican American young lady from one of my classes to be my student aide. I made a deal with her to teach me Spanish, especially the key words, so [that] every day we had an hour, so she could teach me basic Spanish. She was a very good student and a very nice young lady.[17]

Taylor learned Spanish so that she could not only talk with her students in their language, but also so that she could communicate with their parents. If she didn't know something, she would learn about it. Her philosophy was that "you teach but the students learn." Taylor believed that both components were necessary—teacher and student—for learning to take place. She described herself as "being creatively responsible for her students."[18]

Johnston High School was important to the Mexican American community in much the same way as Anderson was to the Black community. Taylor recalled her experiences at Johnston as she learned about a new culture.

> I had never had any interaction with the Mexican American culture before I went to Johnston. I had never been to a Roman Catholic church but the kids invited me and so I went. I don't remember having had too many parents—Mexican American parents—that were hostile. They were pretty open to receiving you as a teacher . . . Johnston was very significant to the Mexican American community. There was a Catholic priest who worked very closely with Mister Bailey and the young people at Johnston. So there was liaison there and with Jackie McGee who was the Dean of Young Girls. She worked closely with the Mexican American community. There was the Mexican American holidays—like Cinco de Mayo—as a matter of fact we learned how to celebrate many kinds of holidays.[19]

Neither Akins nor Taylor were seriously ostracized by students, administrators, teachers, or parents at Johnston High School. Nothing changed in the overall desegregation plan of the school district. In fact, the school administration issued reports and memoranda alluding to the completion of the desegregation plan first begun in 1955. A letter dated May 10, 1966, was sent to each parent of a school age child informing them of the U. S. Department of Health, Education, and Welfare's requirement that "each student or parent choose the school the student would attend in the upcoming school year." Superintendent Carruth specified the requirement that a choice of schools must be completed before the end of the current school term.

> A choice of school is required for each student. A student cannot be enrolled at any school next school year unless a choice is made . . . once a choice is made, it cannot be changed except for serious hardship.[20]

Carruth's letter implied that desegregation had been accomplished, and the school district was being required to "jump through some hoops" by the U. S. Government. The district would do so reluctantly. Few students chose to participate in the freedom of choice plan. The Black schools remained Black schools. The four White high schools had only two Black teachers, both at Johnston. Anderson High School had one White teacher. The Austin school board began to feel the pressure to move more rapidly with their desegregation plan, so they attempted to relieve the pressure by moving more teachers.

THE FALL OF 1966

In the Fall of 1966, Austin's desegregation plan was not working. The school board, as well as the school administrators, appeared uninterested in moving to full desegregation of the public schools. The freedom of choice plan, most recently updated in the spring of 1966, implicitly encouraged White students' transfer out of Anderson's attendance zone. A few Black students transferred to White schools. The desegregation of school faculty proceeded even more slowly than the student desegregation. Twelve years after *Brown II* and three years after the Civil Rights Act of 1964, Austin's schools remained segregated by student and by faculty.

Yet, desegregation was occurring in other areas affecting teachers and students at the state level. Each would have an indirect influence on the Austin school board. After strong debate, the Texas State Teachers Association (TSTA) accepted the ideals of total desegregation. It modified its membership policy, which read, "any White teacher or White friend of education" to read:

> Membership in the Texas State Teachers Association shall be open to school related personnel holding certificates or qualifications appropriate to their respective duties.[21]

One year later, the Black Teachers State Association of Texas voted to join the TSTA, thereby presenting a single classroom teachers association to the state. Prior to the final vote for dissolution by the delegates, TSAT President Robert L. Curry eloquently reminded all those present:

> [TSAT] has meant the opportunity to engage in spreading the "success story" of practices in school administration, supervision, and methodology, the promulgation and interpretation of educational policies and procedures. TSAT has been the pointed accusing fingers and the suspended sword of Damocles continuously nudging and constraining in the fight for equal educational opportunities and equal professional opportunities in Texas. . . . Deep in the "shadows" of events leading to the progressive era into which we have emerged as a professional organization, let us not be led to believe that there has always been "smooth sailing" and the lucky ones found the proverbial pot of gold at the end of the rainbow. . . . We owe a debt of gratitude to the "unsung heroes" of the Teachers State Association of Texas—a debt we should never forget. . . . The decision is yours alone to vote. With constructive thinking, *we can effect the challenge of "uniting the teaching professions in Texas."* . . . Not only are the eyes of Texas upon you, *"the eyes of America"* are upon you![22]

As the teachers' associations desegregated, so did the University Interscholastic League. This statewide organization was the governing body that fostered and regulated athletic and literary competition among White Texas public schools. Mirroring the Interscholastic League was a separate organization reserved for Black schools, the Prairie View Interscholastic League. However, after 1966, negotiations between the two statewide organizations resulted in the invitation of Prairie View to join the University Interscholastic League. For the first time in Texas history public school students participated equally in academic and athletic events.[23] To further bring the races together, the state legislature introduced legislation permitting school attendance figures for both White and Black students be reported as a single unit.

Back in Austin, another Black teacher, Mrs. Vernice Smith, was transferred from Anderson High School to all-White Austin High School. Smith was unique among cross-over teachers. She became the first Black teacher to cross-over directly from a Black to a White school. That meant she now was teaching in Austin's White west side.

During her seven year tenure at Anderson Smith developed an excellent teaching reputation. Her professional abilities were finally noted by her principal when she was appointed Chairperson of the English Department. In 1965, she was awarded a three year grant entitled "Teacher of the Culturally Deprived and Academically Challenged" from the Southern Education Association. Through the grant she intended to introduce her tenth grade students to significant out of school activities which would increase their cultural awareness. She firmly believed that when her students graduated from Anderson in 1968, they would be much better prepared to succeed in college. During the first two years her students were able to attend such events as the Long Horn Jazz Festival, and the Russian Ballet Company. They saw traveling Broadway plays such as *The Sound of Music,* and toured the president's Texas White House at the LBJ Ranch. At the beginning of the program's third year she received notice of her reassignment.

> Mister Pigford called me, I think. I went to the personnel office to talk with Mister Cabe and when I came back, I asked Mister Pigford if there wasn't something he could do because I didn't want to go to Austin High School. I had these special kids. I had had these kids two school years and I had one more year to go—the twelfth. When I came back from Mister Cabe's office, I was disappointed because I had this program that I was committed to and he [Mister Cabe] said, "The other schools need your expertise." When I spoke with Mister Pigford, he said, "You know, Missus Smith, you [should be] flattered that they want you."[24]

Despite Smith's pleas to remain at Anderson one more year so her students could complete the program, she was transferred to Austin High School. Her worst fears about her program were realized; the program ceased after she left.

After her reassignment notification in midsummer of 1967, Smith organized her resources to begin the fall semester at Austin High. During the school's initial faculty meeting, Principal Robbins introduced her to the faculty. She remembered vividly her introduction to the faculty as the first Black teacher.

> It was really kind of embarrassing. Everybody else in there was White. Mister Robbins had me stand up in front of all these Anglo men who were whistling at me. It was . . . embarrassing.[25]

In the late 1960s, Austin High School was considered the city's flagship school. Being near the University, many professors' children attended it, and teachers expected students to attend college. Smith recalled some acutely painful times at Austin High School with fellow teachers. On several occasions, other teachers chastised her. They accused her of having lower teaching standards than other Austin High teachers. She knew that she was accepted at Austin only because the "law said she had to be accepted." In fact, some of her English colleagues ignored her completely.

> I would be talking to the chairperson of the English department and this woman would walk up and start talking as if I were not there. I would ask [her], "How are you today?" She would say, "Oh, why, uh, how are you?"[26]

In fact, early in her tenure at Austin High School, an unsuccessful attempt was made by her colleagues to dismiss her. She sadly described what occurred.

> Now that I look back, it was a . . . difficult time. There were some other things. Negative things are easily accepted. That's so unfortunate. They even tried to say I came to school drunk every morning because I gave F's to some of the students whose people run this town. But if the students didn't do the work, they didn't get the grade with me.[27]

Smith's teaching standards extended to her former Anderson students, several of whom transferred that same year. As she was completing her lesson plans late one afternoon, a young boy rushed in, excited to show her his paper. She recalled how beautiful his handwriting was:

> He said [to me], "Just looky here, look at this paper that I made an A on." I tried to read the paper. It made about as much sense as my five year old granddaughter's papers. I said, "Ira, whoever gave you an A on this paper should be fired." Because all she had done was glance at it. [Although] he had beautiful handwriting, she couldn't have read it. It was unreadable![28]

Shortly after she began teaching at Austin High School, her students reminded her that an upcoming Friday was "color day." The colors at Austin High were maroon and white, so Smith wore her maroon dress with white pearls. One teacher commented that she had never worn the school colors during her twenty-two years at Austin High. Smith replied, "Somehow, kids expect more of me than they do other teachers!" Within two weeks, almost every teacher and W. R. Robbins, the principal, wore the school colors on Fridays. Smith recalled laughingly how she served "Maroon Punch and Good Fortune Cookies" to her class whenever Austin played Reagan High School.

> I sent a bowl of Maroon punch with Good Fortune Cookies to the principal's office. He [Mr. Robbins] just couldn't believe it. . . . Others said, "Did he know that you were serving punch in your room?" I said, "Yes." He wrote me a note

one Thursday, "Ms. Smith, please fix us some of that Maroon Punch with Good Fortune Cookies." People were coming in the office, and he just wanted some nice gesture such as punch and cookies to serve them. Mister Robbins was a "good ole boy." If you said, "Mister Robbins, I'm going to the restroom." He'd say, "Yea, Missus Smith, I 'preciate that." He appreciated everything![29]

One wonders if Principal Robbins asked any of his White teachers to bring punch and cookies for his visitors. Probably not.

ACROSS TOWN AT JOHNSTON

Because Principal Bailey wanted Johnston High School to succeed, he readily included Charles Akins and Iola Taylor in all the school's activities. Both Akins and Taylor described how Bailey knew all the students' names, where they lived, and where they played hooky. He knew where they would go, and he would "get in his car, go get them, and bring them to school."[30] Bailey learned early on that Taylor had sponsored the Future Teachers of America at Anderson, so he made her the sponsor of the FTA club at Johnston. Taylor recollected,

> He had sense enough to know that the Black teachers that he had were the best and the brightest. He knew that, so he supported us up to a point. But to me he was kind of paternalistic too. I don't take to paternalism at all. But . . . I'm a professional, I do my job so I never got close to him and let him be paternalistic to me. [She described him as] A good ol' Texas boy . . . every Fall he would have a big barbecue. He would barbecue half a cow on the grounds at the school. This was his welcoming of all the teachers back to school. This was the kind of person he was.[31]

The general attitude of the teachers and the principal at Johnston supported desegregation. Perhaps the school administrators knew of Bailey's approach and that knowledge guided their first cross-over teaching assignments. Certainly, Akins remembered the inclusivity of the atmosphere at Johnston. He attributed the sense of inclusion to Principal Bailey's "down home" approach with both faculty and students. Akins obviously enjoyed teaching at Johnston as he recounted,

> I made friends [with fellow faculty]. We went to football games and I sat with them. I didn't miss any football games. I was the only African American on the faculty [and] I wasn't going to miss anything. I liked to be with people. I didn't make a sacrifice. I hear people complaining about being in the portable buildings. Well, when I first went there [to Johnston], I taught in a portable. If I had been overly sensitive, I would have said something about the portables. It didn't bother me. It was my classroom.[32]

Through his increasing reputation as a teacher, Akins came to be regarded as a valued and trusted professional by principal Bailey and other school administrators.

Not surprisingly, in the summer of 1966 Akins became the first cross-over summer teacher at Reagan High School.

> They sent me to teach summer school at Reagan High School. I think they told me they wanted me to be the cross-over teacher when they opened Reagan High School in nineteen sixty-six. When the school opened, in the summer, they sent me there to teach—mostly Anglo kids.[33]

Initially, the administrators planned to transfer Akins to Reagan the fall of 1966. However, Bailey had other plans. He wanted Akins back at Johnston. Akins reminisced about the summer of 1966 at Reagan.

> Reagan High School was the most beautiful high school I had ever witnessed. And I still think it is. I had never been in a situation where there was an office for a teacher. So I had a classroom, a desk, and when I would leave my classroom, I could go to my office. There were cubicles [in a separate room] for each of the teachers in the department—outstanding![34]

Regardless of Akins's fascination with the beauty of Reagan High School, he was aware of the potential discipline problems. He thought about that summer teaching experience at a new school.

> [The separate offices] could cause a discipline problem because you had a tendency to run to the office to get something. In the old days, at Anderson or Johnston, my office was my desk in my classroom. I was always there. There's a sense of importance, like the college prof who says, "Just a minute, let me go to my office to get something." You have to get accustomed to that. You have to train your kids [not to be disruptive], because when you are out of the room things happen. You need to be around![35]

After Akins's return to Johnston High School, Bailey talked with him about becoming Dean of Boys at Johnston. Akins, poised to begin his climb up the Austin administrative ladder, became Dean of Boys at Johnston the following year, 1967.

His colleague Iola Taylor was also developing a successful teaching career at Johnston. She experimented with different types of social studies curricula and teaching methodologies. Looking back, by incorporating Black history into her classes, Taylor was developing an educational philosophy, which years later would be referred to multiculturalism. For example, during that period, Ralph J. Bunche became the United States' first Black United Nations ambassador. Taylor inserted his position into a simulation program that was a popular teaching method during that period.

> We had simulation programs about war and peace. It set up a particular scenario for students and divided the students into groups. The students had to negotiate with each other in relationship to certain kinds of interests on the parts of the groups. The groups represented imaginary countries. One group

might have been a group that didn't necessarily like Z country but had some dependence on Z country because Z country had oil. And then on the other hand, Y country that had nothing to do with Z at all, but at the same time, this country may have needed Y country for some other reason, such as water or other resources. The young people had to familiarize themselves with the scenario, where their country sat in the particular scene, and then make decisions regarding relationships with their country. So then the United Nations had to deal with what these [imaginary] countries' relationships as they ironed them out between one another. In that way, young people learned about diplomatic relationships.[36]

Taylor, as the first Black supervising teacher for White university teacher candidates, developed a mock congress with one of her student teachers. They prepared the program carefully and were pleased with their results.

> She and I worked out the mock congress all the way from the constituents at the grass roots level, to the representatives and assemblies, and then the committees. We went through the entire committee system. Students got an idea of how committees worked, and to subsequently making decisions on the floor. We were able to pick up some contemporary issues. Issues that the kids were interested in, but also issues that were related to a particular culture, such as the Mexican American culture, the Black culture, and the Anglo culture. We brought issues in like that. We could incorporate information and yet, at the same time, not be dogmatic about any aspect of it. Let the young people handle it and work with it.[37]

Shortly after Taylor was transferred to Johnston, she joined the National Council for Social Studies. She found their materials and information very helpful, even though they provided little about integrating cultural diversity into her social studies programs.

> NCSS gave you information on technique for teachers. . . . I had to determine what would be useful to me and then I had to adapt it to my particular situation, to my students, and to the milieu in which I was operating. . . . I'll tell you something that was extremely useful to me . . . the references in the handbooks. Those were extremely useful. You could go look up materials and find them. That's the way I came into contact with the first book written by Jonathan Kozol.[38]

Taylor challenged her students academically. However, she expressed her frustration at Bailey's emphasis on vocational courses. He encouraged students to learn a trade, to learn a skill in a particular vocational area. Taylor called his approach "the old Booker T. Washington" philosophy.

> For all the students, we had printing, cosmetology, woodworking, agricultural kinds of things. At Johnston, there was a wide spectrum of vocational

courses as part of the curriculum. The young people were encouraged to enroll in those courses. Now this is not to say they were not encouraged to go to college. [However] the assumption was that most would not be going to college and would need some type of vocational training for the future. . . . Booker T. Washington was more appealing to the concept that people of color should be hewers of wood and drawers of water. People of color were a step below [Anglos] in terms of their ability to think and to reason, to learn and to understand. His was a justification philosophy.[39]

Nonetheless, Taylor believed Booker T. Washington originally meant vocational training as a means of facilitating African Americans' movement into professional occupations. But his philosophical approach to education became a way of tracking minority students into either remedial classes or special education classes. She maintained:

> Tracking is a mechanism that starts so low in grades that once you get a kid into a particular track, it's hard to move him because he doesn't have what he needs to remove himself from that track. Then there is the overwhelming number of young people who are relegated to special education classes. I guess it is relatively easy to do that, rather than rise up to the challenge that a young person may be able to think effectively if you would devote the material means to alleviate some of the problems that retard his [her] growth.[40]

Despite Taylor's disagreement with Bailey's emphasis on vocational courses, she applauded his ability not only to listen to the students, but also his willingness to find innovative solutions to potentially explosive situations. For example, she recalled a divisive incident that occurred near the conclusion of her second year at Johnston.

> One of the big problems that the students had was what kind of music they were going to have for the prom. The Mexican American young people wanted Spanish music and the Black young people wanted soul music. Both groups said they couldn't dance to the music of the other. It became a big problem. Mister Bailey solved the problem after meeting with the student council who were the ones trying to decide. He said, "We will have half with Spanish music and half soul music." That night when they danced, they danced in groups according to their music. The prom came off okay without it becoming a big hostile kind of thing![41]

Unfortunately, events did not proceed as smoothly for Smith at Austin High School as they did for Akins and Taylor at Johnston High School.

Tensions often ran high between White teachers and Smith. As well, there were conflicts between her and some White students. Yet, the differences proved to be positive because her presence there gave her students opportunities they never would have had to learn about others. During her first two years at Austin High School, Smith recalled a particularly difficult, but eventually validating event.

> A person had her child taken out of my class because I definitely wasn't giving grades to students who didn't earn them. The next semester, the younger brother was in my class. I called him into class and said, "You may not want to stay in here because your parents had your brother taken out of my class." He said, "I don't care." He did very poor work and he confessed to me later that he was an alcoholic . . . he made an F. You can't imagine how I felt when that second semester rolled around—this boy that I had given a F was sitting on the second row from the front. I said to him, "Do you realize you got an F under me? That I gave you an F?" He said, "No, Missus Smith, I made an F, and I'm going to show you I can do better." And he made a B.[42]

On the last day of school the following May, Smith's students gave her a potted plant, an ivy, because they enjoyed her class so much. Smith remembered that a little later in that same afternoon, the young man who previously failed her class, came to see her.

> He was kind of shy, and he had this box, a long flat box, and he said, "Missus Smith, I just wanted to give you a gift." I replied, "But you have already given me a gift." He said, "No, I went in with them, but I wanted to give you my own personal gift." I thought it was a handkerchief, but it was the most beautiful billfold![43]

Smith treated everyone the same: no untied shoes, no bandannas dangling from pockets, no rude behavior, and no caps in class. She took time to teach her students to get along with one another. Smith, as did Akins and Taylor, provided opportunities for students to see and think more honestly and realistically about all people. Each teacher tried to provide an enriching and empowering experience for every student. Sharing their knowledge about their Black history was one way of enriching all the students.

TEACHING BLACK HISTORY

Black teachers, particularly those who taught history and government, were in a special and difficult position. Information contained in textbooks misrepresented this nation's history. In fact, most textbooks completely ignored the contributions of Black Americans and other minorities. The distortion of the Black American's past has always had a purpose. The assertion that Blacks have no history worth mentioning was basic to the theory that they had no humanity worth defending. Deliberate misinformation was used to justify slavery and discrimination. Until recently, most historians ignored Black American contributions to most phases of American life, particularly the exploration of the new land and the post–Civil War industrial growth.

In particular, for Black students a correct portrayal of the Black American's part in history served justice as well as truth. *Amsterdam News* columnist James L. Hicks recalled his days at Central High School, in Akron, Ohio,

> I was the only Negro in my history class, and the way my Beard and Beard history book presented the Negro and the way my history teachers taught what little they did teach about the Negro was more than enough to make me cut history classes and almost enough to make me cut out from school altogether.[44]

Such Black students could have learned that their forefathers also had important historical roots deep within the soil of their new homeland.

While Akins, Taylor, and Smith, as well as other Black teachers, continually experienced ideological contradictions each day of their lives, they had a deep and abiding faith in the power of education. However, Black teachers knew they were solely responsible for bringing their history into the curriculum.

Early in her teaching at Austin High, Smith recalled that neither students nor faculty knew of Black History. She decided to include Black History into her English curriculum. She wrote out her lesson plans and sent them to the principal's office with a note that she planned to teach Black History as part of her English classes.

> I explained to my students what Black History was all about, and I let them choose different Black people to write about. And one group were to report on Malcolm X. Our librarian went crazy because—I think the Unitarian church— had given them that book *[Malcolm X]*. And this girl knew they had given Austin High this book. She went to the library to check out *Malcolm X,* and they did not have it on the shelf. And what ever this church was—had given a number of books—they took back all the books when they found out that the librarian had not shelved *Malcolm X.* And of course I went to the librarian and raised a little Cain—the librarian was too late—the kids went to the city library and got the books that they wanted! During this time, I was ill for several days and when I returned to school, my students were just angry. A young substitute teacher had decided to improve on my lesson plan and she told them "that Blacks ate salt pork and molasses for breakfast," and Blacks fought with guns, Mexicans fought with knives, and Whites fought with bare hands. When I came back—my kids were so upset—apparently it had made her [the substitute] mad that my kids had done so well on their papers. She had even made notes on my lesson plans about Blacks—she was way back in slavery times![45]

Laughing, Smith remembered how many of her students at Austin High were amazed at her color, which was a very light brown. During her discussion of Black history, they wanted to know:

> How did you get to be that color? [Because] for these kids, Black should have been dark brown or black.[46]

Her students then learned about the different degrees of color among Blacks. More importantly, they learned how "a drop of Negro blood" defined a person as inferior under Jim Crow laws. Smith taught her students that the color of a person's skin meant no more than the color of a person's eyes.

At Johnston, Taylor's classes learned of the unheralded role Black Americans played in the history of the last Western frontier. She involved Black history with traditional White history, such as the following.

> The Ninth and Tenth Calvary, composing a fifth of all the cavalry assigned to pacify the West, were all–African American regiments. Despite discrimination they earned their share of Medals of Honor and could boast the lowest desertion rate in the Army. Among their proud commanders was John J. Pershing, who won his nickname of "Black Jack" leading a company of the Tenth against Indians and bandits in Montana, against Spaniards in the charge at San Juan Hill and against Pancho Villa in Mexico.[47]

Taylor, Smith, and Akins sought to instill a sense of pride and understanding of Black American heritage. Although each approached this in a different way, their goals were

> to demonstrate the contributions of Black Americans despite slavery and the legalized repressions of the Jim Crow system; to show the Black American contributions to the many aspects of American life since their arrival with the Spanish explorers; to help students understand the Black American's role and difficulties in American history and how they have contributed to this nation's culture and institutions; to show the Black American's part in history must be seen in the context of the greater picture of American growth and problems; to demonstrate that Black Americans never willingly accepted slavery or second-class citizenship but battled in valiant and practical ways to achieve the promise of America; and to help students understand that the fight for equal rights was a reform movement aimed at the democratization of American life and the completion of America's promise of freedom for all.[48]

EDUCATION FOR DEMOCRATIC CITIZENSHIP

As the mainstay of desegregation, Austin's freedom of choice plan had failed by the fall of 1968. Of Austin's eight high schools, one remained a Black high school, five remained White, and the remaining two White high schools shared three Black teachers. Not surprisingly, the Department of Health, Education, and Welfare demanded that Austin's school board submit a new desegregation plan by early 1969, or face the loss of federal funds.[49]

Nevertheless, attention to the problems of desegregation in the classroom came on several fronts during the 1968–1969 school year. The Austin Classroom Teachers' Association (ACTA) elected its first Black officer, Iola Taylor, as Recording Secretary.

Her article, "The Forward Look of a Minority Teacher," demonstrated the necessity of viewing desegregation as positive social change.

> It is evident that social change is reshaping the position of the teacher who is a member of a minority group in our society. Facing this teacher are challenges and adjustments that must be met by the teacher, education, and educators, in a manner that will secure active participation, worthwhile contributions, and security.
>
> This is significant, for positive accomplishments in this area on the part of all involved in the education of our children, can only serve to enhance the fulfillment of the goal—education for democratic citizenship. Awareness of these facts have led to techniques and proposals designed to facilitate adjustment. However, it is generally agreed, there is no single answer.
>
> One avenue open to the minority classroom teachers is the opportunity to become a vocal part of a classroom teacher organization that reflects awareness of the social milieu and the changing role of teachers without exception.
>
> The Austin Classroom Teachers Association offers an unrestricted chance to participate and activate the forces of change.[50]

Taylor remembered this period in Austin's history as a time of pushing people to do it (integrate) and to do it well. In fact, the University of Texas Extension office had a program called the Texas Educational Desegregation Technical Assistance Center, or as it was commonly known TEDTAC.[51]

> It was a program designed to take teachers who had effectively made transition into integrated situations and to use those teachers as resources to teach teachers from small towns and rural communities.[52]

TEDTAC was part of the old University extension office, and Taylor was one of the group leaders in that program.

> [As part of TEDTAC] we shared with teachers in small, rural communities that were beginning to integrate, techniques and methods that had worked for us. We had workshops and role playing. The teachers came from small communities like that in an effort to foster desegregation in the classroom.[53]

Taylor recalled that TEDTAC looked at desegregation from both the teacher's perspective and the student's perspective. Both Black teachers and White teachers participated in the sessions. They came from the little surrounding communities near Austin, including a teacher from Taylor's home town of Hearne, Texas. Taylor was invited to be part of TEDTAC as a result of her role, as a cross-over teacher, in the Austin Independent School District. As a group leader, she had a key role in the teaching laboratory, sensitivity training, and oral communication activities in the TEDTAC program. Using small group processes, group leaders gained valuable insight and proficiency in leading small groups. Taylor recalled her experiences with TEDTAC.

We broke down into groups with facilitators. It was a very interesting experience. The teachers were invited from all over. TEDTAC arranged everything. The teachers lived on campus, probably in a dormitory. The director, Maurice Dutton, coordinated this program with the Department of Education. The consultants would present a premise, then they would raise questions and issues. Then, if I remember correctly, teachers reacted to the consultants in open sessions. Then we broke into groups. As facilitators, it was our responsibility to make the sessions comfortable enough for the persons to open up, to really express what was on their minds, to express their feelings and their concerns, to express their reservations, and to interact with each other in terms of their own experiences. We [our small group] would go to lunch together. After lunch, the small groups returned to the large group and each group would report their activities. Then the large group had opportunities to react to the small group reports. It was a good experience.[54]

Taylor believed the purpose of TEDTAC was to pave the way for teachers, both Black and White, returning to their home town to integrate the schools. Her role, as a facilitator, was to stimulate the discussion, and ensure a comfort level where people would really say what was on their mind. She found her role to be easy because people's jobs were "on the line." The facilitators would meet with the consultants and with the director once or twice during each six-week session. Taylor remembered their sessions covered many areas.

Behavior of young children—some cultural things—cultural differences, techniques, different teaching methods, things that had worked, that we felt would work—sensitivities, things to be sensitive about, I guess we even got into teaching methods. Because whenever you get a group of teachers together [lots of laughter]. They share and share and share. We had a lot of materials and reacted to those stereotypes. There were stereotypes about Blacks in terms of their ability to handle children, in terms of discipline. Another one was the perception of noisiness. There seemed to be a perception that Black children were inherently noisy.[55]

Taylor enjoyed working with TEDTAC for many reasons, one of which was her belief that her contribution helped ease the transition for teachers and students during the desegregation process.

However, the Austin school board continued to delay total desegregation of the schools' classrooms. Although the University of Texas assisted surrounding communities to desegregate through the TEDTAC program, Austin continued to drag its feet.

WHATEVER STEPS NECESSARY

[Given the *Brown* timetable, school boards with a history of *de jure* segregation were] clearly charged with the affirmative duty to take whatever steps might be necessary to convert to a unitary system in which racial discrimination would be eliminated root and branch. . . . [School boards were expected to give] meaningful assurance of prompt and effective disestablishment of a dual system. . . . The burden on a school . . . is to come forward with a plan that promises realistically to work, and promises realistically to work *now.*"[56]

By 1969, Austin's school board had not developed a plan that would effectively desegregate its public schools. Freedom of choice and cross-over teachers were not meeting federal guidelines as set forth in the 1964 Civil Rights Act. At the beginning of the 1968–1969 school year the district was visited by representatives of the Dallas branch of the Office of Civil Rights. The specific purpose of the visit was to gather information to judge if the district was in compliance with Title VI of the Civil Rights Act. The resulting findings clearly stated "the district's plan has not been effective in eliminating the dual school structure and providing an equal educational opportunity to minority students." Specifically, J. D. Ward's [Dallas Educational Branch chief of the Office of Civil Rights] letter charged the following in language the School Board could understand:

1. Eight schools [including Anderson High] constitute visible vestiges of the dual structure in that they were established as traditional Negro schools, and . . . still have enrollments that are totally Negro.
2. The zone for Anderson high, which has not changed since it was established in 1955 . . . follows the residential patterns of Negroes in east Austin.
3. The transfer provision which permits any student, regardless of his residence, to attend Anderson . . . does not conform to the requirements for voluntary desegregation plans based on Geographic Attendance zones . . .
4. The free choice offered to students residing in the Anderson zone . . . has not been effective in removing the racial identity of Anderson.
5. Students that reside in the Johnston zone are given a choice between Johnston (94% minority) and Anderson (100% Negro) . . .
6. Prior to 1954, the district established one set of attendance zones for White children and another for Negro children. . . . The zones for the Negro schools continue to be superimposed over the zones for the traditionally White schools. . . .[57]
7. The present school zones and student assignment policies have not worked effectively to eliminate minority group schools . . .
8. The educational program at Anderson high is not equal to that offered at the predominantly Anglo high schools, partly because the enrollment is not large enough to support a comparable educational program . . .
9. Student teachers from Huston-Tillotson, a Negro college, are assigned exclusively to all-Negro schools.
10. Negro teachers assigned to predominantly-Anglo schools have more teaching experience than Anglo teachers assigned to Negro and minority-group schools.
11. During the 1967–68 school year, only 31 Negroes were assigned as classroom teachers to 28 schools where the enrollment was predominantly Anglo.[58]

Ward emphasized that Austin's school administrators had the responsibility for adopting and implementing a desegregation plan that promised meaningful and immediate progress toward disestablishing the dual school system they described. Cutting to the heart of the matter, Ward and his associates suggested Austin school board members consider policies that would establish a single system of attendance zones that would eliminate the racial identity of the city's Black schools. Further, they encouraged the board to consider rezoning and utilizing L.C. Anderson High School as a desegregated school. Or, and most worrisome to the board members, L. C. Anderson be closed and both students and teachers assigned to other schools.

Unwisely, Austin school board members rejected these suggestions but refused to put forth alternative suggestions. In response to the board's position, a federal advisory group on school desegregation immediately reviewed the existing desegregation plan and, at the beginning of the 1969 school year, recommended that Anderson High School be converted to junior high school status and change Kealing Junior High School to a "middle school." That is, Kealing would house only grades five and six. The third recommendation was the board must "move beyond" token faculty desegregation.[59]

Reflecting the board's inability to come to terms with school desegregation, the members were split in their response to the federal advisory plan. One member, former elementary school principal Hage, maintained that the plan was not realistic. Hage said,

> You can't rejuggle a whole city. We've got to deal with the reality of people, not geographic mobility. . . . Don't expect us to deal in a dialogue of the impossible.[60]

Another school board member, Mrs. Bob Wilkes, expressed deep disappointment. She had expected, "[the advisory committee] to bring us a magic panacea. This is no solution at all."[61] Of the three recommendations, the board focused on the last, the movement of teachers. Not only would Black teachers be reassigned but now White teachers would be recruited to teach at Anderson. In fact, despite two separate federal proposals the school board adopted an entirely different plan. The board members' inability to objectively evaluate their desegregation plan left federal agencies with few options except through civil litigation.

The consequences of the school board's resistance to the *Brown* decision resulted in the voluntary reassignment of White teachers to Anderson High and the continued involuntary reassignment of Black teachers to White high schools. In other words, Austin school board placed the responsibility for desegregation squarely on the shoulders of teachers, Black and White. How the teachers coped with this responsibility unfolds in the next chapter.

CHAPTER SIX

No White Missionaries
Need Apply

IN AUSTIN, TENSIONS ESCALATED rapidly during the fall of 1969. Earlier that year, Austin's ISD school board rejected firmly the federal government's two desegregation proposals.[1] Instead, the board retained the original desegregation plan, which focused on freedom of choice and cross-over teachers, with the stated goal of

> [r]etaining Anderson, with an all-Negro enrollment of 627, with its present boundary lines; moving ninth grade from Kealing junior high to Anderson high, increasing the enrollment about 300 students; and "further integration" of the Anderson faculty as well as efforts "to strengthen and broaden the curriculum significantly."[2]

Not surprisingly, HEW dismissed the proposal, noting little change in the current plan from the school board's original desegregation recommendation.[3] Gillespie C. Wilson, President of the Texas chapter of the National Association for the Advancement of Colored People, strongly denounced the school board with a bitter statement employing sarcasm and disgust:

> So you believe in law and order. Then what about Anderson high school (an all-Negro school) which evidently you, as citizens of this city, fully intend to maintain until someone outside the state solves your integration problems for you? [he then accused Austin of being] a magnificent example of the breaking the law of the land.[4]

Rumors ebbed and flowed among the citizens of Austin, and in particular, among the teachers and students at Anderson High School. Patterson, who was teaching at Anderson, characterized this time as chaotic.

> Oh, this was a tumultuous time. We had been told, "You are going to be assigned and your students are going to be assigned," and then, at the end of the summer, they [the school administrators] decided they weren't going to do that.[5]

In the meantime, the school administrators scrambled to comply overtly with the federal desegregation guidelines as they covertly resisted full desegregation.[6] They transferred Black teachers from Anderson High School to Austin's White high schools and, at the same time, they assigned White teachers to Anderson High School. As part of the recent desegregation plan, the district school board administrators designated Anderson High School as the district's new vocational education center. Chambers, an Anderson High School teacher recalled,

> Vocation [al education] had a high priority back then [1969–1971]. Before Anderson closed, we had [vocational classes] such as building construction, auto mechanics, agricultural class, office education, data processing, and distributive education.[7]

In fact, in the summer, just prior to the opening of the 1969–1970 school year, local automobile dealer Roy Butler, Austin's school board president, sent a letter to parents of the district's high school students explaining its most recent approach to meet federal desegregation guidelines. His letter was intended to be a recruitment device encouraging White students and teachers to cross-over to Anderson High School. The administration's goal was to have an Anderson teaching faculty that was equally Black and White and a student body that comprised both races, although, in the case of the student population, the school board was more interested in increasing the number of White students attending Anderson than equality of numbers. Board President Butler's recruitment letter described Anderson as a "comprehensive high school with an excellent academic, vocational and technical program."[8] In addition, he listed the vocational and technical courses to be offered at Anderson.

> Vocational Agriculture, Distributive Education, Trade Auto Mechanics, Vocational Home Economics, Cosmetology, Refrigeration and Air Condition, Vocational Office Education, Building Trades, Data Processing and Mechanical Technology.[9]

Few responded positively to Butler's recruitment letter. Although no White student transferred to Anderson, some White teachers volunteered. At the same time, to immediately increase White teacher percentages at Anderson, the board developed a policy in which the district's newly hired White teachers would be assigned to Anderson.

WHITE IS THE COLOR OF MY SKIN

The White teachers who volunteered to teach at Anderson, like the school's Black teachers, were different than the older generation of teachers. Because these teachers had grown to maturity after the *Brown* decision, they viewed race relations differently than school administrators and members of the school board. But their similarity ended there, not because they were younger, which they were, but because they were White. Growing up White in the South during segregation automatically ensured more opportunities, better schools, higher paying jobs, and easier access to college. Being White also meant minimal, if any, interaction with Blacks.

Common to the White teachers who crossed over to Anderson was the belief in equality of education for all students regardless of color. One of these teachers, Elizabeth Ann Stoll, was a young, newly married teacher who had just moved with her husband to Austin from Arkansas. Her first teaching assignment in Austin was at Lanier Junior High School. Her father, a minister, and her mother opposed racial segregation and she remembers many discussions over dinner about the evils of segregation.[10]

Similar to Stoll's experience, Tom Allen's family also opposed segregation. Growing up in east Texas, Allen vividly remembered the rigid separation of Blacks and Whites.

> This was the era [1950s] of side by side drinking fountains, White and Colored, and side by side restrooms, White and Colored, if they even offered restrooms for the Colored. If the Blacks were allowed in the theater at all, they sat in the balcony, so there was almost no chance for contact in public.[11]

Allen's parents also did not tolerate racist attitudes to be expressed by their children. Allen's views toward Blacks mirrored his parents' approach. Allen returned to teaching in 1969 and was assigned to Anderson.

James Dorsett, like Allen, grew up in east Texas. After earning his bachelor's degree in physical education and his master's degree in education, he taught at several Texas schools. Dorsett and his wife moved to Austin in 1964 and began teaching at University Junior High School.

Another White teacher, Herbert Brown, spent his early years in California, moving to east Texas during the eighth grade. Brown remembered segregation as a new and unpleasant experience. He recalled working in his father's east Texas cafe.

> I did have a really unique experience because the cafe that we bought [had] a front half for the Whites and a back half for the Blacks. I worked there so I had a better opportunity than most of my classmates in the White school to be around Black people in an informal way. I formed a lot of positive feelings.

I really preferred to wait on the folks in the back than the folks in the front because they were a lot more fun to be around. That probably was a big influence on me.[12]

After earning his bachelor's and master's degrees in education in 1966, Brown applied to Austin School Board and was assigned to Fulmore Junior High School. He stayed there three years before his reassignment to Anderson High School.

As district school administrators sought White teachers to volunteer for teaching duty at Anderson, they were also involved in critical negotiations with federal officials. They wanted Department of Health, Education, and Welfare officials to give them more time to meet the deadline for full desegregation.[13] Unknowing to them or federal officials, newly elected President Nixon was about to aid their cause. In September 1970, the Nixon administration scrapped the mandatory deadlines for full desegregation that the Johnson administration established in March 1968.[14] Assuming the Austin School Board would take the administration's new school policy literally, a Justice official cautioned,

There's got to be some movement, They've got to get some school desegregation, some faculty desegregation, some [extra-curricular] activities desegregation. School Districts must make some movement toward desegregation this fall [1969].[15]

Austin's school board expressed relief. Most members felt that more time would give the board's desegregation plan a "chance to work." Board president Butler said, "With a little more time, we [Austin School Board] may get to where HEW is wanting us to go."[16] In the meantime, plans were moving ahead at Anderson to accommodate the multitude of changes expected over the next two years.

ANDERSON WELCOMES NEW TEACHERS

Cross-over teachers would have been enough of a concern for Anderson High School in 1969, but much more was happening. Principal W. Pigford was reassigned to Reagan High School as assistant principal. Hobart Gaines was appointed principal of Anderson High School, and he recruited Charles Akins from Johnston High to return to Anderson as assistant principal. Akins recalled his being asked to return to Anderson.

[Mr.] Gaines became the principal. He had been a friend of mine and my mentor. He came to my house and asked me to come back as assistant [principal]. Said I had been dean [of boys], and he wanted me to come back as assistant principal. This was an opportunity so I went to Anderson as an assistant principal. He said, "We're probably on shaky ground because they may close us, but if we do a good job they'll have a place for you."[17]

Akins appreciated returning to Anderson as assistant principal, but he also was sad to leave Johnston High School. He knew what he was doing at Johnston and he had enjoyed his roles as teacher and Dean of Boys.

> When Mister Gaines asked me to come back to the old Anderson and be an assistant principal, I hated to leave Johnston because they had been so nice to me. I knew what I was doing at Johnston. I didn't know what I was getting into [at Anderson] because they were getting ready to close Anderson. Tensions were high . . . with students because of the anticipation that "they were going to close us." I went back to Anderson and that was the kind of atmosphere that was there at that time.[18]

Akins was the only Black teacher to return to Anderson High School in 1969. District administrators transferred most of Anderson's Black teachers to White high schools and replaced them with White teachers.[19]

A notable difference about perceived empowerment between Black and White teachers became obvious between 1969 and 1971. Black teachers were subject to assignment. In other words, personnel director Cabe arbitrarily reassigned Black teachers to White high schools. In contrast, White teachers were recruited, asked to volunteer to cross-over, or were new hires assigned to Anderson.[20]

Dorsett, Brown, Allen, and Stoll met and became colleagues when they began teaching at Anderson. Of the four colleagues, only Allen was hired to teach at Anderson. Two, Brown and Stoll, volunteered and Dorsett was asked to transfer. Each teacher's experience was slightly different.

Dorsett was teaching Industrial Arts and coaching at Martin Junior High School when he received a telephone call from district athletic director Tony Burger one Sunday afternoon in 1969.

> Mister Burger, [Austin School Board's] athletic director at that time, called me. It was a Sunday and [he] asked me if I would take a coaching job at the old Anderson High School. Well, I said, "Can't you get anybody else to go?" And he said, "No." I said, "okay." Well, we'd known each other a long time, ever since I'd been in high school. Anyway, I went over there.[21]

Burger explained to Dorsett that the district needed to desegregate its schools and asked him to help by crossing over to teach at Anderson.

> He said, "We needed to integrate and cross-over, student wise and teacher wise." And I guess through [me], he gained a coach plus a teacher. I was just kidding him when I asked [him] if they couldn't get anybody else to go! I laughed, but I went down and talked to Mister Timmons [Anderson HS head coach] that day. In fact, I called him and told him I wanted to come and talk to him as [he was Anderson's] head coach. We talked all evening, nearly three hours. I liked Mister Timmons, a very good coach, and a fine fellow. Very gentlemanly. We got along real good.[22]

Dorsett remembered that he could choose not to go to Anderson and his teaching position would not be in jeopardy.

> There wasn't any pressure to go. Burger said he sure would appreciate it if I would go after he talked to me. I said, no, not until after I talked to Mister Timmons.[23]

Brown and Stoll responded affirmatively to the district's letter requesting volunteers to transfer to Black schools. Brown recalled the process.

> In the spring of nineteen and sixty-nine, the school administrators sent a letter [to all the teachers] that they were going to staff some other schools, as far as integration was concerned, and asked if anybody would be willing to sign up. I thought it was a good idea and I put my name on the list. They assigned me to Anderson. Yes, I think Mister Burger called me in, the district athletic director, and told me . . . if I wanted to . . . they'd move me to Anderson in a coaching position so they did. It was not a pressure kind of thing at all. If I didn't want to go I didn't have to, [I] wouldn't lose my job or anything like that.[24]

He was very clear that he could refuse to transfer, and knew he would not lose his teaching position if he later changed his mind about the transfer.

Stoll's experience of transferring to Anderson was very similar to that of Brown. She also recalled that the school district asked for volunteers to teach at the Black high school.

> They asked for volunteers and, actually, I was teaching summer school at McCallum. They [district personnel] came to summer school and told us what was going to happen and I thought, well, I could do that. Really believed in school integration and integration in society, I really kind of felt that I should do that. So I called up the personnel department and said I was willing to go. And I received a letter pretty soon saying I was being reassigned. Something along the lines that they wanted to desegregate the faculties of the schools of the high schools and needed volunteers to go.[25]

Like Brown and Dorsett, she, too, felt no pressure to transfer and did not believe her job was on the line if she later refused to go.

Allen, on the other hand, was assigned to Anderson after his initial interview with the district's personnel department. His previous teaching experience included one year at the junior high level in Houston, Texas.

> So I didn't leave a teaching position to become a cross-over teacher—I entered the Austin school system teaching at Anderson high school in East Austin. I think . . . took the assignment. I was employed by the district and that was the attitude I had.[26]

Having no choice about going to Anderson did not concern Allen. He understood his assignment, and he went. In fact, most newly hired White secondary school teachers were assigned directly to Anderson High School during the 1969–1971 school years.[27] The remaining teachers were either recruited, or they volunteered.[28]

Anderson High School faculty and students were determined to make the White teachers feel welcome. McPherson, a Spanish teacher who was not reassigned, remembers the time of cross-over teachers.

> It was great. The ones [the teachers] who volunteered to come, they came because they wanted to be there [at Anderson]. We accepted them. I thought it was great of them to come over to the Black school. They didn't have to be there. They definitely didn't have to be there and I thought it was great of them to come.[29]

Patterson, who also remained at Anderson, described the faculty's approach.

> We put up a big Welcome sign. We wanted them to feel welcome, to feel comfortable.[30]

Stoll, Brown, Allen, and Dorsett also remembered how Anderson's faculty welcomed them at the beginning of the school year. Allen recalled his initial experience at Anderson.

> I already knew the term—cross-over teacher—and I knew why I was there. I knew they wanted White teachers from the other side of the Interstate [I-35] to come into the Black school and to mix. Well, we had some exercises in the week before school where the teachers interacted. Black teachers and White teachers. That experience was totally natural. Then we had the experience of talking with some of the student leaders and they were expressing some of their expectations or fears. I was impressed with the fact that their expectations were just like mine and just like the kids that I would have been teaching on the other side of the Interstate too. It was all just a great unknown. So there wasn't anything uncomfortable about those two weeks.[31]

Allen also noted how nice the school appeared and concluded that the administration had made a real effort to get it into shape for the new teachers. Brown's experience was similar to that of Allen. Although he was apprehensive because he did not know anyone, he quickly was put at ease.

> I was a bit apprehensive. I didn't know anybody going over there. I had never really talked to anybody over there [at Anderson] until it was time to report for athletics, which was in August. I was a bit apprehensive but when I arrived . . . I immediately was put at ease and I felt really comfortable with the professionals and the administrators, even before school started. I feel like I just slipped right in. I really had no problems, initially, with any of that. I felt really comfortable.[32]

Brown believed the transition went so well because the Anderson faculty wanted it to go well. He thought they were committed to the desegregation process.

In contrast to Brown, Stoll recalled minimal staff development prior to the beginning of the school year.

> I believed we just showed up for school—the teachers always have the staff development and that sort of thing, for about a week. I met Mister Gaines [the principal]. I may have gone over to the school and met him so I would know where to go. But as far as any formal thing, you just showed up for staff development. I didn't feel any different than usual, starting school. I was probably naive at that point. I met some new people and liked them. I don't remember any special preparation for that we were White and going to work with all Black students. Mister Akins was the assistant principal at that time. He was the most gracious man in the whole world. The Black teachers, what ever they felt about our coming, made us feel very welcome. The staff development [focused on] starting school and learning [the] procedures of a new school.[33]

Because Stoll had only junior high school teaching experience, she was more concerned about that aspect than about differences between Blacks and Whites. She was worried about learning Anderson's policies and procedures as well as learning about the differences between junior high and high school curricula and philosophies.

A ROLLER COASTER TIME

In 1969, for the first time in Anderson High School's history, the majority of its faculty members were White. For many Black students, it was their first time interacting for any length of time with Whites, on a personal level. The reverse was also true for the White teachers. For most of them, this would be their first opportunity to interact with Blacks. As might be imagined, their involvement was distorted by the many myths and stereotypes present during that period. As the White teachers soon learned, Black students no more knew what to expect from their White teachers than they knew what to expect from their Black students. Each would learn from the other, as Stoll, Brown, Allen, and Dorsett quickly discovered.

Stoll reflected on her experiences during her first year at Anderson. She described them as difficult because, for the first time in her life, the color of her skin became important.

> I can remember the first weeks—they [my students] reacted differently [than I expected]. I guess it was the first time I had ever been judged, or I was conscious of being judged, by the color of my skin. Some of the kids were very curious because I was the first White person they had ever really talked to up front. . . . Some of them wanted to touch my hair and talked to me about how I felt about Black people. Some of them just openly didn't like me because of the color of my skin.[34]

Stoll recalled for the first time having significant student discipline problems. That caused her to doubt her abilities as a teacher.

> I did have discipline problems. I think it was because of that transition. I was White and I was young. I was about twenty-four, but I never had real discipline problems before, even when I first started to teach. I just [began to] doubt my ability to teach. I would go into Mister Akins and say "My husband Bill and I have figured out my finances, and we can get along without my salary. I just can't take this any more!" He would say, "Now, Missus Stoll." He saved my teaching career because I really was just about ready to go. I was called names I had never heard . . . [such as] "Motherfucker" . . . I was twenty-five years old and I had never heard that . . . I said, "What?" One of them called me "a raggedy ass bitch!". . . it was a real awakening.[35]

During one faculty meeting at Anderson, Stoll was forced into evaluating her motives for volunteering to teach at Anderson. She then realized how offensive a "missionary" approach was to her colleagues.

> I don't remember if it was Mr. Gaines or some teachers who said they really didn't want White missionaries over there [at Anderson]. And I thought . . . that's probably what we're acting like . . . we're coming over here and [implying] aren't we wonderful because we're coming to an all-Black school and we're going to change [it] . . . make everything good . . . we're willing to do this . . . it was kind of a crusade. I had never thought about that before but I thought . . . that would be very offensive. So I think that was something that I learned that Black people did not want nor did they see all this [cross-over teaching] as wonderful and good.[36]

Stoll then described her first year at Anderson as one during which she was being repeatedly tested by her students. She attributed part of her problems to her youth as well as her inexperience with teaching.

> During the second year, things were infinitely better. I had a reputation for the [new] kids that I was tough but I was fair. When they came in, we started to work. I'm not saying I never had minor discipline problem[s]. I was a young teacher and I had learned some things about preventing misbehavior. By that second year, things were okay. So as far as discipline, I didn't have the same kind of situation where the kids were testing me. [But] I think that whole first year was a test.[37]

Things were much better for Stoll and her colleagues in their second year at Anderson. Laughingly, she described a dance that she and another teacher sponsored the spring of 1970.

> Another teacher and I sponsored the ninth grade and they [the ninth grade class] wanted to have a Blue Afro Ball. So we said, "Why not?" They dressed up in dashikis and African clothes, and they had blue

bread and blue punch. I don't remember all the stuff we did at that little park by Hancock Center. I didn't know much about high school, and I didn't know all these community people would come. The dance turned out [to be] successful, but I am sure the assistant principal and the principal wondered why these women had agreed to do this. Because you had to keep the older kids in the community out. So I learned a lot about high school dances that night![38]

As the sponsor of the ninth grade, Ann Stoll attended most of the school's football games. At times, she drove students to a game with her.

I really liked the kids and I went to football games. I know I left for a game in a little Volkswagen with three boys. Mister Akins came out and asked, "Missus Stoll, where are you going?" I said, "I'm going over to McCallum to the ninth grade football game." "Okay [he replied], but you be careful." When I came back, being the responsible adult that I was, I insisted on taking each one home.[39]

She remembered the students were reluctant for her to take them home. Stoll wasn't sure if her students just wanted some free time away from adult supervision or if they were ashamed for her to see where they lived.

Stoll described the faculty at Anderson as very close and committed to making the situation work. She also felt supported by the Anderson parents.

The parents were very supportive of the school. If you called home and said the student was misbehaving, the parents got right in there. If you needed a parent conference they came.[40]

Parental support was a common theme iterated by individuals who taught at Anderson High School. Teachers contacted parents when their students had problems with their studies. They also contacted parents when students misbehaved in class, and parents were quick to solve the identified problems. In fact, Herbert Brown described Anderson High School as a "family." Because of this concept, he found parents very helpful to the resolution of problems with his students.

The one thing about was when we had problems, the parents and the families had a much higher regard for teachers [at Anderson] than in an ordinary school. If I ever had a problem with a student . . . I vocalized it to the parent. I don't think there was ever a time, I didn't get an immediate response from the parent. That's another thing I really felt positive about—the kids that had parents—they were strong.[41]

He concurred with Stoll and others that Anderson parents supported the teachers. Brown further defined the role some teachers assumed as parents for some students. He remembered,

The teachers also took the role of parent for those kids who didn't have parents. The teachers had students they had to give an extra measure of care to. . . . We worked hard to be a family.[42]

Brown then recalled a time when his wife was ill and he took his children with him to a track meet. As he recalled, his daughter remembered that time as "really great!"

I know my kids, even now my oldest one talks about the time my wife was sick . . . we had a track meet on a Saturday [in San Antonio] and so I took the kids with me to the track meet. The track guys and the cheerleaders took care of my kids. My oldest daughter remembers that in a very good way to this day![43]

As will be discussed later, however, this concept of family by L. C. Anderson's teachers, parents, and students exacerbated their loss when Anderson was closed in the summer of 1971.

Brown believed the Anderson High School faculty was committed to desegregation. Because of that commitment, he thought Anderson's use of cross-over teachers went smoothly. He recalled,

I'm sure they worked a little harder than just meeting folks on the street. I never felt tension or anything bad. . . . There was some limited amount of transition problem there. Basically the students really accepted me very easily. It was a rare student that I had any problem with and I didn't take it to be any more than I would have had at a White high school. I never really felt uncomfortable.[44]

After Brown's first month at Anderson, he felt very comfortable, not just with the teachers, but also with the students. Rather than believing he was being judged on the color of his skin, he saw his difference as positive.

When it came to the student body as a whole, after the first month or so, I felt really totally at home. And I felt really that I had an advantage over the average teacher going to the average high school, because I stuck out like a sore thumb. When I walked down the hall, after two or three days, everybody knew who I was because I was so different.[45]

Brown developed a strong relationship with his students, which he attributed, at least partially, to his identifiable difference.

It was really easy for folks to identify with me as far as [my] name was concerned . . . if I was doing obvious things it was easy for them to pick up on. . . . I feel like I had a better relationship with students in that school than I have ever had with students at other schools. . . . I think a big part of it was the advantage I had of being different. People looked for me, I did positive things . . . [so it was] easy for them to relate to me.[46]

Despite the obvious difference of skin color, these White teachers wanted their students to know them as people. Stoll, Brown, Dorsett, and Allen were committed to teaching at Anderson. They, like Anderson teachers before them, expected their students to do their best.

Nonetheless, Brown as well as other teachers confirmed that problems existed at Anderson. He attributed some of the problems to Anderson's location directly opposite the housing projects.

> Occasionally we would have folks come on to campus who were not supposed to be there. We were right across the streets from [the] real bad housing projects. There wasn't a fence, so sometimes folks, who weren't the best people in the world, would come over and manage to get in the halls. . . . I caught one guy in the hall with a chain and that was pretty hairy for awhile but we calmed it down, and it worked out all right. It was [people] who weren't supposed to be in school, who weren't supposed to be there, [who] were the problems.[47]

Brown also found many of his students needed extra assistance with even basic skills. But he worked with them on extra assignments and developed creative methods of teaching his health classes.

> There were more of those students who had problems with the basic skills. Most of them ended up doing okay. I don't have any glaring memories of academic problems as far as them trying. But there were definitely some [academic] limitations.[48]

James Dorsett, a coach and history teacher, described his experience at Anderson as difficult. In particular, he identified problems with his students, such as their reading abilities.

> It was a challenge. The students couldn't read. You couldn't give them assignments to read in their book. They just couldn't read and retain what they read. You just see it in their eyes. Not all of them, but about seventy-five percent couldn't read very well.[49]

Dorsett believed his students read at a junior high school level rather than at the assumed high school level. Because few reading teachers had been assigned to Black schools during that time, reading was difficult for many students. To help them, he developed new and different methods of teaching history.

> I had guidelines [for my history and civics classes]. . . but there was just no way you could follow them, not in this situation . . . the kids were pretty well behaved, most of them. [But] we had a few discipline problems.[50]

Some of Anderson's problems related to the overall racial tensions at the national level. In many states, civil rights marches were taking place. Speeches to raise the consciousness of Black students were on television and, sometimes, the local street corner. Anderson students were caught up in the overall rebellion. Some of those students were at Anderson High School. For example, Dorsett recalled,

> If I remember right . . . you'd be teaching and all of a sudden all of the kids would get up and leave because they'd be having demonstrations. They'd march up and down the halls for a couple or three hours.[51]

Dorsett was not the only teacher who had students leave his classroom to march in the halls. Stoll also recalled how she would stand at her classroom door and tell her students to "get back to work on their class assignment." She was always surprised when her students quietly went back to their class assignment rather than argue with her.

Like Stoll and Brown, Dorsett recalled being treated quite nicely by the Anderson teachers. He also believed that his fellow teachers believed he was a difficult grader.

> They [the Black teachers] were very cooperative, very congenial. I didn't see any outward animosity at all. We seemed to get along just fine. About the only bad problems I had were because of bad grades. . . . I guess I graded a little hard, not because of the race, but like I had always done. Guess I should have backed off a little bit because of their [the students] inability to understand.[52]

Allen, a chemistry teacher, agreed with Dorsett. He also believed that his students lacked academic preparation. Allen clearly believed the students' academic problems were not based on race but rather on their home environment.

> I concluded it was a matter of what happened before they got to that level [high school]. I was told by some [Anderson] counselors that one of the problems was the students didn't have real good modeling at home. For example, they didn't see father sitting in an easy chair reading a book. There was very little reading in the families and consequently the reading levels were really quite low.[53]

Adding to the problem, Anderson High School was situated in the landing and take off pattern for Robert Mueller Airport. Allen recalled that during classes, he would have to interrupt his lecture because of the noise level. He then described an example of academic limitations that occurred in his class.

> One day a plane on a landing pattern made such noise I had to stop. I thought I would just take a break and lighten the moment and we talked about where it [the airplane] might be going. That discussion led to a long debate about practical geography. I found that the kids, in general, had no concept of jurisdiction of city, state, country. For example, Paris, France, and Fredericksburg, Texas, were just out there instead of geographically located.[54]

Although these White Anderson teachers admitted that many of their students had difficulties, they attributed their students' academic deficiencies to the district's freedom of choice plan. Simply, they argued that Anderson's best students likely enrolled in the city's White schools. In fact, Patterson recalled many of the White high schools had actively recruited Anderson's best and brightest students. The remaining students were those with easily identifiable academic deficiencies. Problems were also exacerbated by the rumored closure of Anderson, rumors that continually surfaced during the 1969–1970 and 1970–1971 school years.[55]

ON THE OPPOSITE SIDE OF TOWN

Problems were not confined to Anderson High School, however. Obviously, the uncertainty of the times contributed to the potential for problems. Personnel director Cabe reassigned several Black teachers from Anderson to formerly all-White high schools. Furthermore, he transferred Iola Taylor from Johnston High to McCallum High School. Identical to her earlier notification of reassignment, Taylor received a letter informing her of her new position. No central office administrator asked if she wanted to volunteer. Rather, she was told that she would teach at McCallum High School beginning in the fall of the 1969–1970 academic year. In contrast to Johnston, with a large Mexican American population, McCallum was predominantly Anglo with a few Mexican Americans and a very few Black students. Her experiences at McCallum High School were much different than those at Johnston. Taylor reflected on her experiences with fellow teachers.

> There were teachers who were open and accepting and there were those who would prefer that you not be there. Then, there were others who were independently aloof. One of the places where you could discern the attitudes of the teachers with whom you worked was the teachers' lounge. Sometimes, if you went in, those who were not accepting would leave. Then, there were others who would converse, would interact with you, would sit down and talk to you. There were others who might see you in the teachers' lounge and not come in. There were people who would rather I not be there. Some felt it [desegregation] would never work, it was just something that would never work. It was an onerous burden that was being heaped on them that they should not have had to bear. And there were those for whom it was just part of the teaching profession. They felt it was about time![56]

Patterson concurred with Taylor. He recalled,

> [When you'd walk down the hall [at McCallum], you were nothing. You didn't exist. The other teachers would turn their backs.[57]

Even though not all White teachers were so prejudiced, still many would ignore their Black colleagues when they met off campus. The veneer of pseudo-liberalism coated the interactions between Blacks and Whites at many of the White high schools.

But all was not negative for Taylor at McCallum High. She laughingly recalled how some of her McCallum students played tricks on her.

> I assigned seats to my students but they played little tricks on me. I do have a sense
> of humor. Little tricks that I had never had students play. These were Anglo stu-
> dents. They would come in [into class]. So I would have the movie set up and
> everything in the back of the room and the plug was in the back of the room. And
> they would pull it out! [Laughing] I'd turn on the machine, and it wouldn't work.
> They played games. I would say what in the devil is wrong with this thing? And
> they'd say—hmmm—wonder what's wrong? And then one of them would jump
> up—and then I'd look back and see the plug [had been pulled out the socket]![58]

Obviously, Taylor's sense of humor carried her through some very funny but potentially difficult times. As she remembered her teaching experiences at McCallum, Taylor shared her "best team teaching experience" with John Shelton, a
White fellow English teacher.

> John and I wrote up our curriculum, and all we wanted our students to do.
> Mister Sloan had agreed that we didn't have to do "the usual contained class-
> room kind of thing." The American History unit and the English unit were
> combined to make the readings in English and the writings in English coalesce
> with the writings and readings in American History. It was great and we had
> some great students. We had it well planned. We turned them loose and they
> did some great work, they really did. We would give them their units and then
> they could freely go to the library and do their research. They had to report
> back to us, make reports in class, and share information. But it was a beautiful
> experience for us. We did it for a whole year. It was a wonderful experience.[59]

Perhaps an integral part of this class, especially for the students, was watching a
Black female teacher and a White male teacher cooperate as equals.

As Taylor was reassigned by Austin's district personnel department, so were
the majority of Anderson's Black teachers. Melvin Chambers recalled the transfer
process.

> It didn't come as a shock. They notified us that they would like for us to come
> down at such and such a day and such and such a time and talk with Mister
> Ernest Cabe, who was the personnel director at that time about reassignment.
> The time that I moved, they had us in line. We would just sit out in the hall
> and they would go from one [to another]. We had thirty minute appointment
> times. One would come in and one would go out.[60]

Chambers laughed as he continued his story about his reassignment. He chose
Crockett High School although he had just told his wife he didn't want to go there.

> I had told my wife that Sunday, we went for a ride after church and rode out
> to Crockett. And I told her, "This is one place I don't want to come." Crockett

was three years old but the distance was so great [from our house]. When I got there in that interview, Cabe says, "The options are Reagan, Austin High (Austin High was over on Rio Grande then), and Travis and Crockett. I said Crockett. I had been in a science institute at the University of Texas so I knew some of the science teachers over there. And I thought, well, at least I'll be going into a situation where I know the people. I knew people in the other places but the lineup at Crockett just seemed to be the better lineup. That's why I chose it.[61]

As Chambers reflected about his reassignment, he described Cabe as not supporting the Black community.

He had already lined us all up, and he just basically said, "I want you all to come on such and such a day at such and such a time and talk about reassignment." Mister Cabe was not a staunch supporter of the African American community. [For example] when I graduated from college and went for an interview with him, he told me that the line of Black teachers started at the college door and that basically, if I'd been White, he'd have given me a job right off. And that was in nineteen fifty-eight. He didn't make it easy for any of us.[62]

Chambers knew the Black teachers who remained at Anderson were ready to transfer by then. Anderson's administrators and faculty believed the school would be closed soon. They were "tired of the decision as to whether or not it would close." As Chambers reflected, "We just wanted to get it [the reassignment] over with." However, he acknowledged the difficulty of closing Anderson because it was a community school. Parents, students, teachers, and administrators were fiercely loyal to Anderson High School.

Austin School Board decided, during the summer of 1971, to close Anderson High School as a way of complying with the federal desegregation guidelines. Its closure stopped the cross-over teaching process at the high school level as a major component of Austin's school desegregation plan. Still, the story did not end. More was to come.

Photographs of L. C. Anderson High School

1. Laurine C. Anderson (far left) and faculty members standing in front of the Anderson High School building located on Olive and Curve Streets, c. 1907.

2. Anderson High School Band members and director Benjamin L. Joyce (black uniform) stand on the west side of the Huppertz house in Rosewood Park, Dec. 6, 1937.

3. Industrial Arts class with instructors Mr. G. E. Emery (left rear) and Mr. James E. Mosby (right rear), c. 1954.

4. 1943 Anderson High School Band.

5. Anderson High School Beauty Pageant, c. 1950s

6. Class of 1960.

7. Members of the 1971 Anderson High School Band: (kneeling l–r) Gayle Manning, Louie Nelson, and Carla Gregg; (standing l–r) Leroy McDonald, band director Alvin Patterson, and Jerolyn Black.

8. 1971 Yellow Jacket Band clarinet section in their new uniforms: (sitting l–r) Toni Larry, Barbara Fennen, Donna Carter, Charlotte Gauntt, Cheryl Thomas, Shirley Harrell, Joyce Russell, Louie Nelson, Janice Prosser, Laura Gooden, Melba, Cassandra Mials, Jerolyn Black; (standing l–r) Eddie Lewis, Clara Baker, Trina Knox, Helen Mays, Jackie Lee, Clarise Thomas, Patricia Miller, Patsy White, Rita Mannie, Herman Grier, Vickie Taylor, Mae Patton.

9. The Jackette Twirlers (l–r): Joan Arnold, Nancy Houston, Addie Powell, Nelda (Wells) Spears, Brenda Pleasant, Gloria Arnold, and Brenda Douglas, 1964.

10. First VICA Club at the 1953 Anderson High School campus at Thompson and Hargrove Streets, 1969.

11. The 1913 Anderson High School building on Pennsylvania Avenue in east Austin.

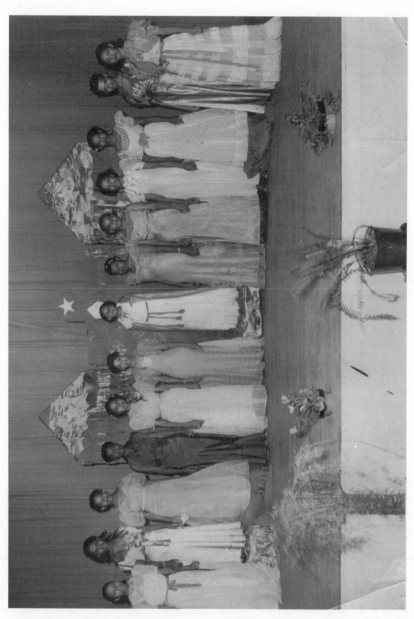

(7)

Death of a School

School Board Wins Integration Fight Against HEW with New Superintendent [was prominently displayed on the first page of Austin High School's Yearbook in 1971] Fruitbasket turnover was the name of the game as the Austin School Board fought it out with the Federal government over the question of desegregation of the Austin Public Schools. . . . One of the headaches that followed the School Board for more than nine months was the order to desegregate.[1]

UNDERLYING THE *BROWN V. BOARD OF EDUCATION*[2] decision in 1954–1955 was an assumption that the desegregation of public schools would result in better life opportunities for Black children. The *Brown* decisions set in motion a slow and tortured quest for equality of educational opportunities through the desegregation of the nation's public schools. By the early 1960s, the Civil Rights movement initiated the dismantling of the Jim Crow system of *de jure* segregation in Southern states. Initial challenges focused on public symbols of segregation that separated Blacks and Whites in public schools, transportation, hotels and restaurants, residential areas, and other parts of the nation's social infrastructure. Nevertheless, the progress of desegregating public schools in communities across the South, including Austin, was painfully slow.

Fourteen years after the Supreme Court's ruling that school segregation was unconstitutional, Austin's school board faced a January 1, 1969, deadline to submit a plan that would meet federal guidelines. The school board received notice the previous August that its freedom of choice plan, begun shortly after the *Brown* decision, resulted in fewer than 20 percent of all Black students enrolling in White schools. Freedom of choice had not met the federal requirements for desegregation. Desegregation of school faculty moved at an even slower pace. In fact, the Department of Health, Education, and Welfare's Office of Civil Rights forcefully argued that

> [t]he Austin school district should move beyond token faculty desegregation and assign several cross-over teachers to every school within the district. . . . Of the 212 Negro teachers presently assigned in the predominantly or Negro schools, no fewer than 106 of them [should] be assigned to schools where their race is in the minority; also a reciprocal number of Anglo teachers should be assigned to replace them . . . further, it is recommended that no fewer than three cross-over teachers be assigned to any school.[3]

In fact, only three Black high school teachers (Akins, Taylor, and Smith) had been transferred to White high schools and three White teachers (Stoll, Brown, and Dorsett) had been transferred to the one Black high school. Obviously, most of Austin's White schools remained untouched by this meager desegregation effort.

Despite the federal agency's rejection of Austin's desegregation plan, the school board focused on volunteer integration as the solution to the federal mandate. In June, 1969, Austin district board president, Roy Butler announced, "We are going to enlist the aid of any interested citizens hoping to effect this voluntary integration." The only Black school board member, Mrs. Exalton Delco Jr., concurred, "HEW told us to integrate or close Anderson High School. The success of our plan depends upon the degree to which Whites will volunteer to integrate."[4] At the same time, district personnel director Ernest Cabe explained, "You can't move a teacher where he or she doesn't want to go. If you do, they won't do the job."[5]

As a note, his comments applied only to White teachers. The request for White volunteer teachers began immediately and over the next two years, Austin's school administrators scrambled to transfer teachers, Black and White, as part of their modified desegregation plan.

The summer of 1971 found the Austin school district and the Texas Educational Agency in Federal District Court as defendants in a lawsuit. Federal agencies had charged that Austin had a dual school system and that segregation of Black students still existed.[6] Finally, the covert resistance to full desegregation by the Austin school board was publicly exposed in District Court. The lawsuit forced the board and school administrators to take steps they had resisted for years, the closure of Anderson High School. School board president Will Davis argued that closure of Anderson High School was necessary because "it was the vestige of a dual system that was ordered removed by the Court."[7] The Austin school board approved a plan to transfer the city's Black students and teachers to White schools. Students would be bused.

Few scholars have focused on the impact Black school closures have had on Black communities.[8] Early in the desegregation process, Charles Johnson of Fisk University predicted that, as a result of the *Brown* decision, not only would racially separate schools cease to exist but the Black community's institutional structures would undergo dramatic changes.[9] Certainly, the teachers' (such as Aikens's and others') remembered experiences inform the reader of a fuller and more complete understanding of some of the unintended consequences the desegregation of L. C. Anderson High School had on East Austin.

The public history of segregated schools has focused almost entirely on the observation that Black students suffered an inferior education. This national memory assumed, "Black children suffered immeasurably and received little of educational value until they were desegregated into superior White systems."[10] In other words, while the memory of inequality was correct, the historical picture was incomplete. Thus,

> [The] historical recollections that recall descriptions of differences in facilities and resources of White and Black schools without also providing descriptions of the Black schools' and communities' dogged determination to educate African American children have failed to tell the complete story of segregated schools.[11]

Nonetheless, few if any people realize the extent to which both historically Black schools and communities changed. Supporting the teachers' remembered experiences about the historical picture of Black schools, Billingsley asserted that prior to desegregation,

> [i]n every aspect of the [Black] child's life a trusted elder, neighbor, Sunday School teacher, or other community member might instruct, discipline, assist, or otherwise guide the young of a given family . . . as role models, community members show an example to and interest in the young people . . . as advocates, they actively intercede with major segments of society (a responsibility assumed by professional educators) to help young members of particular families find opportunities which might otherwise be closed to them . . . as supportive figures, they simply inquire about the progress of the young, take a special interest in them . . . in the formal roles of teacher, leader, elder, they serve youth generally as part of the general role or occupation.[12]

The lives of millions of Black Americans were changed profoundly by the United States Supreme Court decision that struck down racially segregated schools. Specifically, in Austin, a city that did not want to desegregate its schools, the lives of teachers, administrators, students, and members of the Black community were forever altered through their pursuit of public school desegregation.

HISTORICAL BACKGROUND

At the turn of the century, *de jure* segregation existed in seventeen states and the District of Columbia.[13] During Reconstruction, Texas, as did other Southern states, passed legal statutes that mandated separate schooling facilities for White and Black children. In 1876, the Texas Constitution mandated that "Separate schools shall be provided for the White and colored children, and impartial provisions shall be made for both."[14]

The Early Years of Anderson High School

In the late 1870s, one of the first public schools for Black children in Austin was built on Robertson Hill. The Robertson Hill School consisted of two rooms whose teachers taught grades one through eight. The Travis County Superintendent's Report noted that

> [t]he colored common school district public funds in 1877 were used to build Robertson Hill, Evans and Wheatsville schools . . . the colored population owned a public building in the 1870s and had been using it for a number of years.[15]

In 1905, twenty-nine years later, Texas mandated separation of public funds for the schooling of White and Black children:

> All available public school funds of this State shall be appropriated in each county for the education alike of White and colored children, and impartial provisions shall be made for both races. No White children shall attend schools supported for colored children, nor shall colored children attend schools supported for White children. The terms "colored race" and "colored children," as used in this title, include all persons of mixed blood descended from Negro ancestry.[16]

Even so, for Blacks, literacy was a fundamental bulwark against oppression. In other words, literacy and formal education were Blacks' means to liberation and freedom.[17] Clearly, the Black community viewed education as a safeguard against fraud and manipulation. However, White schools received three times greater funding than did Black schools. Separation of public school funds empowered White school administrators to purposely and legally allocate less monies to Black schools.[18] These government policies of minimal funding guaranteed that the Black community would be forced to either remain satisfied with their present circumstances or find other methods of funding their schools.[19]

Illustration of the intentional evil of this form of segregation can be seen in Austin. In 1889, Austin's Black community wanted a high school to help their children continue their education. The school board denied public funding for the expansion of the Robertson Hill school, so the Black community "taxed" and completed the expansion themselves. In Austin and throughout Texas, Black communities pursued public education for their children with a tenacity and determination that put to shame the majority of White Texans. For this tenacity, they paid a heavy price. They were "double taxed." Anderson noted,

> It was terribly unjust. Black Southerners paid their taxes as citizens, and while White taxpayers got a system of free public education, [B]lack taxpayers got virtually nothing except when they taxed themselves again.[20]

The Black community supported Anderson High School both socially and financially. In 1926, the high school's first annual was published. At that time, Anderson High School encompassed grades seven through eleven. Anderson was no different than Austin, the White high school, in that both high schools only went to the eleventh grade. Anderson High School's Year Book, *The Geyser,* presents an interesting picture of the teachers, students, and East Austin. Anderson's faculty numbered sixteen teachers including the principal, L. C. Anderson. Of the teachers, six were men and ten were women. The curriculum included Latin, English, Mathematics, History, Science, Manual Training, Domestic Science, and Music and Art. Similar to other high schools, Anderson had a spring and winter graduation. The spring graduates were listed as 11B and the winter graduates were listed as 11A. A and B designations were used from grades one through eleven. Alvin Patterson, who graduated from Anderson High School in 1940, remembered that the Austin school district changed its grade levels in the late 1930s along with other Texas districts:

> The school district changed from eleven grades for graduation to twelve. They just moved everybody up a grade so that those coming into the first grade at twelve years while those others of us had graduated at eleven years. But they called it twelfth grade at the time. So that made many of us graduate[d] at around sixteen years old from high school.[21]

The 1926 graduating class denoted as 11B entered Anderson in the seventh grade with a total of seventy-seven students, thirty-two boys and forty-five girls. Reviewing the class history gives a glimpse into the life of Black students during this period. Several students dropped out during the eighth grade and one student died, noted by the *Geyser* as, "Suddenly, the Death Angel came and called one of the classmates, Miss Novella Haws, to rest." During the junior year, the pupils who lacked a B+ average were not allowed to continue studying both Latin and science and had to drop one of them. By the class's senior year, another student had died, and others dropped out, leaving a graduating class of thirty-nine.[22]

Yellow Jackets: To Be The Very Best

Six years later, in 1929, L. C. Anderson resigned his position as principal due to ill health. He died January 8, 1938. On January 10, 1938, the school board unanimously renamed the Anderson High School, as the L. C. Anderson High School.[23]

A. N. McCallum, superintendent of schools at that time, remembered L. C. Anderson at his funeral.

> In every town, all over the country, in various colleges and universities some of his teachings are being carried on today. He was one of the most respected educators of his time. . . . He taught young men and women the right way. He was true, loyal, steadfast and outstanding in his dealings with men. . . . He was honest, dependable, trustworthy, competent, and a Christian gentleman. His work will live and be carried on this earth.[24]

Despite McCallum's tribute to L. C. Anderson, Austin's Black teachers and students continually experienced social and ideological contradictions every day of their lives as a direct result of segregation. Regardless, a basic tenet of American Black culture was a deep and abiding faith in the power of education. W. Charles Akins remembered fondly his school days at Anderson High School.

> There was a quest in Austin for us to have a good school system because the principal, Mister Campbell at Anderson, used to indicate that we wanted Anderson High School to be the very best school in the state—plus we were ranked very high with the other African American schools around the state. You know we all took pride in the fact that we wanted to be able to qualify to get into school—no sense of qualifying for the university [The University of Texas at Austin] because we couldn't get in at that time. We were talking about getting into Huston-Tillotson [College] and into Prairie View [A & M] which was a big state school.[25]

Shortly after World War II, the Southern states spent approximately twice as much to educate White children as Black children. During the late 1940s in Texas, salary differentials were quite marked. White high school teachers earned between $1,035 and $1,485 per school year while Black high school teachers earned between $900 and $1,125 per school year. Not until the early 1950s, with the passage of the Gilmer-Akin laws, did all high school teachers, regardless of race, receive the same pay based on a salary schedule.

In 1951, during Texas Education Week, Anderson High School sent information packets to students' parents entitled, "Know Your Anderson High School." The information was intended to give the parents basic knowledge about Anderson so that when they visited or talked with teachers, they would have a better idea about their children's education. Parents learned for example that Anderson was an accredited member of the Southern Association of Colleges and Secondary Schools with a faculty of thirty teachers. Fifteen teachers held advanced degrees. All faculty members were members of professional organizations such as the National Educational Association, the Texas State Teachers' Association, and the local Teachers' Association. Of these three organizations, only the NEA was integrated. The other two organizations remained segregated until the early 1970s. There were 774 students at Anderson, of which 393 were boys and 382 were girls. The length of the school year was 175 days. Seventy-five percent of the 1950 class were enrolled in college. Akins recalled fondly his school days at Anderson High.

> We wanted to be good. So that was what was coming out of Anderson at that time. Many of the teachers had master's degrees at that time. The teachers and parents believed there weren't any students any better than those coming out of Anderson. That was the prevailing spirit and the pride that we built and taught. . . . We had a sense and feeling that you needed to be professional . . . you needed to quest for a degree, move as high in education as you could. . . . When the superintendent would come to Anderson, the parents would want the building to be clean. You know you took pride in being a Yellow Jacket.[26]

ANDERSON HIGH SCHOOL: A MEETING PLACE

Austin's Black community was primarily located within a twenty block radius just east of the downtown business district. Like many Black communities in American, East Austin was a thriving, self-sufficient community with schools, businesses, restaurants, hotels, and homes. Anderson High School was a social cornerstone, acting as a meeting place for community events. Akins described growing up in Austin. Akins's father was both clerk and custodian for the Texas Supreme Court justices. His mother worked as an aide at Brackenridge Hospital in Austin. His parents were committed to his education. He related a particularly significant event,

> My father . . . would take the Supreme Court justices' money to the . . . Austin National Bank. He'd take the [legal] briefs to many of the top attorneys in Austin at the time [1930s and 1940s]. He always wore a tie to work. I don't remember seeing him without a tie . . . then he would clean up – custodian, clerk, messenger.[27]

Despite a college education, few occupations were available to Blacks prior to the late 1960s. Akins related that "most students wanted to be teachers." Of course, Black teachers lived on Austin's east side. East Austin then was a small, tightly knit neighborhood in which everybody knew each other. The Black teachers who moved into Austin also lived on the east side. They, too, quickly became members of the Black community.

Teaching at Anderson High School

Many teachers at Anderson High School had attended it as students. They did their student teaching there while studying for their undergraduate education degrees and then returned to Anderson to teach. However, others were recruited by the principal when local teachers were unavailable. Therefore, until the late 1960s, in the midst of desegregation, Anderson's faculty was stable, numbering approximately between thirty-four and thirty-six per year with an average student population of about six hundred students.

Taylor, who came to Anderson from Hearne, Texas, in 1960, described her teaching experiences at Anderson.

> I taught social studies and at Anderson I sponsored the Future Teachers Club—that was another kind of responsibility. Again, you did all kinds of things. The club I sponsored was the Future Teachers. I was pretty proud of them. They did a good job. They were large—I remember that and usually I would have—oh I have had as high as thirty students in a classroom. I guess they would range from twenty, twenty-five, thirty, like that.[28]

She recalled her approach to discipline in the classroom. Taylor was clear that her methods worked better at Anderson High School because the parents welcomed her into their homes, whereas, when she later taught in White high schools, the parents were less willing to discuss problems with her about their children.

> And I was this way about the parents—and I could do this in a segregated school—I would tell my students, "I'm going to have supper at your house." Which meant I was going to be at their home and visit with their parents, their mother and their father. When you are teaching in a segregated system, as it was at Anderson, I think you can do that.[30]

Vernice Smith's daughter also attended Anderson High School and shared with her mother how she viewed her teachers.

> The teachers did the best they could. My daughter wrote that when she thought of her kindergarten through her graduation, she never had a bad teacher. And I feel that way . . . I just felt that every teacher did the best she could and the best he could. I would really stack them up against anybody.[31]

Akins, an Anderson graduate, also completed his student teaching there. Recalling his interview for a high school social studies position, he first mentioned Mr. Cabe, who would become prominent in Austin's desegregation history.

> Mister Ernest Cabe. In fact, I recall when I was interviewed by Mister Cabe, he wanted to know what news magazines I read. I always had the Time Magazine and all. Still do—that was during the time they wanted to know about your church affiliation too. They wanted to know about your family and where did you go to church. It gave him a picture of your character, of citizenship. This is a guy who goes to church and this may be the kind of person we need to teach our young people.[32]

Clifford McPherson's experiences as a teacher at Anderson were slightly different from Akins's and Patterson's experiences. McPherson was born and raised in

Panama. He received a basketball scholarship from Huston-Tillotson College. McPherson always believed he was treated differently by Whites because he was foreign born. Regardless, he experienced segregation for the first time when he moved to Austin. He spoke very highly of Anderson and described its central role in the community.

> We had great students. We had great teachers back then. Great football teams [laughs]. The school is like the community, I mean, when they had football games on Friday or Saturday nights, the community was there. That was a happening and they probably told you that, you know, that was a happening back then and track time and stuff—that was a happening because like I said, we were over here and all the activity was over here and that's what everybody took part in. So that sense of community and so forth was there, you know. And they all looked forward to taking part in that type of stuff. So, you have your different clubs and all that stuff and it was great.[33]

FORESHADOWING THE CLOSURE

A major component of Austin's district school board's desegregation plan was cross-over teaching. Thus, only three Black teachers were transferred from Anderson High to Johnston and Austin High Schools between 1964 and 1969. Two White teachers were transferred into Anderson High School during the same period. Beginning in 1969, district school administrators actively recruited White teachers for Anderson High, increasing the number of faculty to fifty-seven teachers by the opening of school in 1970. Forty-eight teachers were White and nine were Black. At the same time, the district engaged in a massive remodeling program at Anderson High. Like Goose Creek's remodeling of Harlem Elementary, the purpose of these efforts were the same. They wanted to maintain the dual system of education in Austin.

Patterson, band director during that time, recalled the terrible climate at Anderson High School.

> It was a terrible two years. They started a building program at Anderson. They were doing a lot of renovations, so the building was open a lot of the time, dust all around. . . . I had over seven thousand dollars worth of instruments stolen so we couldn't even play at the first football game.[34]

During this time, Akins was reassigned to Anderson as Assistant Principal. He was aware of the rumors that Anderson was supposed to be closed so the school district could meet the legal definition of desegregation. He believed he could make a difference with Anderson's students and faculty even if it was slated for closure.

DEATH OF A SCHOOL

[The closure of L. C. Anderson High School] was devastating to the Black community. Because Anderson High represented, for the Black community, something more than just a high school . . . it was a social center . . . a symbol of history, a symbol of achievement and a symbol of accomplishment for the community. I think that was part of the devastation.[35]

Clearly, Taylor believed the Black community paid a great price for the desegregation of Austin schools. Austin lost a community center with the closure of Anderson High School. Several of the teachers believed that

[w]hen the school was closed, there was a feeling on the part of Austin's Black community that one of the major institutions of the community—the center of the community—had been closed. Anderson's teachers, administrators, and staff were leaders in the community—did a whole lot of things in the community. It was a center and focus of the Black community.[36]

In particular, McPherson recalled that when the school district closed Anderson High, a sense of community was eliminated.

At Anderson High, you had the PTA, and the Black parents ran everything and made decisions and stuff like that. Once you [Black students and parents] go across town, you're in the minority now. You don't run anything and you don't help run anything. So, the sense of community wasn't there.[37]

In other words, students caught the school bus, attended their assigned school, and then caught their bus back home.

By closing Anderson, the Austin school board insisted White flight to the suburbs was avoided. They were praised because busing children was minimized (only the Black students would be bused). Now the school district had an opportunity to assist in the development of a new teacher educator program at the College of Education at The University of Texas. Regardless, the community's response to the school board's plan was mixed. Many in the Black community voiced strong opposition to the closure of Anderson High and Kealing Junior High, in part, because their children would be the ones bused to White schools. Marsha Woods, president of Anderson High's student council said, "Anderson had been given to the Blacks as 'a toy.' When they saw we were making something of it, they took it away."[38] She believed Black students would not have the same opportunities of school leadership at White schools that they had experienced at Anderson. Velma Roberts, chairperson of the Welfare Rights Organization, agreed with Woods.

They [Austin school board members] know if they close Anderson and Kealing they won't have to bus White children over there. There's no reason that Anderson and Kealing could not be kept open and integrated in compliance with Federal law.[39]

However, Black parents pointed out that their children would bear the burden of integration. The very arguments that White parents raised against busing their children to Anderson High and Kealing Junior High were given by the Black parents as reasons for not busing their children to White schools. Simply stated, parents knew the added time requirements imposed on students by busing would reduce attendance and increase dropout rates among their children. It also decreased the parents' ability to interact with teachers about the education of their children. This was inappropriate in a society that valued children, schools, and education.

Black parents also knew that busing to achieve racial balance would create problems not yet totally understood by educators. For example, they expressed concern about their children being introduced into hostile environments that would create obstacles to their learning or present problems that would not be understood by children too young to understand dramatic social change. Like their White parents-colleagues, Black parents knew too well that the financial costs of busing were too great for rewards so small.

In reality, segregation severely limited the choices available to Austin's Black residents well into the 1970s. As we have noted, Anderson High played a major role in Austin's Black community. Specifically, it was a focal point for the Black community. Anderson was a source of deep pride for Blacks in Austin. The high school band, which won many of the state competitions authorized by the Prairie View Interscholastic League, played for the Black community on weekends at the high school. In fact, Anderson High School had been the civic center for Austin's Black community until it was closed in the summer of 1971.

LOSS OF COMMUNITY

> Community is the tie that binds students and teachers together in special ways, to something more significant than themselves; shared values and ideals. It lifts both teachers and students to higher levels of self-understanding, commitment, and performance—beyond the reaches of the shortcomings and difficulties they face in their everyday lives. Community can help teachers and students be transformed from a collection of *I*'s to a collective *We*, thus providing them with a unique and enduring sense of identity, belonging and place .[40]

Thus, the collective "We" join in a tightly knit web of members engaged in meaningful relationships. Sergiovanni contends that the defining characteristics of schools as communities include a social structure that bonds people together in special ways through shared values and ideas.

> Communities are defined by their centers of values, sentiments, and beliefs that provide the needed conditions for creating a sense of "We" from "I's."[41]

Thus, community members—teachers, administrators, students, staff, and parents—connect with each other "as a result of felt interdependencies, mutual obligations and other ties."[42] The collective "We" develops and passes on to new members a community of memory.

This metaphor yields benefits for schools that encompass social and academic goals. Schools become communities in several forms, such as caring communities, learning communities, professional communities, collegial communities, inclusive communities, and inquiring communities. To become any one of these communities, the school must become a purposeful community whose members have developed a community of mind that bonds them together through shared values and ideologies. Ideologies are the means by which people make sense of their lives.[43] The culture of a community is potentially as important a causal agent of change as are laws or demographic growth.

Throughout the South, Black communities created a sense of "We" as an effective defense against the depersonalization of segregation. The communities were a caring, learning, professional, collegial, inclusive, and inquiring collective "We." The Black communities' collective "We" developed and passed on to their children a community of memory. It is this community of memory that Walker articulated so fully in her description of a community's determination to educate its children within the context of segregation. Billingsley described Black community members as advocates for their children.

In this book, the teachers' narratives support the metaphor of the school as community. Austin's Black community supported L. C. Anderson High School socially and financially. Akins described the teachers and parents as having pride that Anderson's students were the best. The collective "We" expected, even demanded, that each student be as good as he or she could be. Parents welcomed teachers into their homes. Students knew that if they misbehaved at school, they would be punished at school and at home. This sense of community within Anderson High School assisted the administrators, teachers, students, staff, and parents to reach beyond the shortcomings and difficulties Blacks faced every day of their lives. At Anderson High School everyone engaged in the meaningful relationship between students and learning. Teachers such as Taylor, McPherson, Patterson, Akins, Smith, and others, described Anderson High School as "the major institution of the community, center of the community, a symbol of history, and of accomplishment."

> Austin was hypocritical. . . . On the one hand you [Austin school board] played the game; you [Austin school board] were . . . trying to move the schools into a democratic type of situation and on the other hand, we're [Austin school

board] resisting like hell. Not doing what we [Austin school board] really know we should do to go ahead and get things done . . . the superintendent finally met with the NAACP . . . with people in the community. Now if they had done that from the beginning, from the beginning had gone ahead and said, "This is the law—adhere to the law!" Just think of the money they spent . . . how many kids it could have helped in terms of the school district. [It wasn't] nickel and dimes they spent on the legal cases—it was enormous.[44]

The closure of L. C. Anderson High School destroyed the school as a community. The history of accomplishments through the collective "We" of the Black community was ignored, particularly for the students. Black students were bused across town to White schools. The White schools maintained their collective "We" at the expense of the Black students. Black students were deliberately excluded from the school as community. Their collective "We" became of a collection of "I's." In fact, the closure of Anderson High School devastated the Black community. Parents were no longer welcomed at their child's school. Closing the Black school accomplished two goals: The overt symbol of a dual system of education no longer existed, and, though few realized it, the covert symbol of exclusion was further entrenched in Austin society.

CHAPTER EIGHT

Reflections and Memories

WHEN CHARLES AKINS, Iola Taylor, and Vernice Smith started their journeys into White Austin's schools as cross-over teachers, their feelings ran the gamut from exhilaration to apprehension. As professional teachers, their thoughts reflected the questioning wonderment of the now-expected reality of Black teachers teaching White students in White schools. While that vision had been with them all during the years after the *Brown* decision, the thought of it becoming a fact had been far from them. They knew that their professional preparation had been based on an assumed continuation of school segregation.

This book recounts how, after the *Brown v. Board of Education* ruling, White Austin's school board attempted to thwart desegregation. Even Akins, Taylor, and Smith assumed, like others who wanted to desegregate education, that White Austin's racial attitudes would not change. They recalled the *American Statesman* newspaper reports of Travis and Austin High students' reaction to the *Brown* ruling immediately after the decision. Just as they recognized in the press releases White social disdain of Blacks, they were forced to read the words. They knew student attitudes were reflections of their home environments, and these views were supported by White teachers. In fact, they recognized the board's cross-over teaching policy for what it really was—only an attempt by the White community to develop some sort of window dressing that would satisfy the Supreme Court's ruling without integrating students.[1]

Understanding the dynamics of social change, Blacks recognized that if Austin were to integrate, some outside force would be needed. It was not that

Austin Blacks had lost hope in *Brown*, rather, it was the stark fact that school integration would never be implemented if it was left to the White Austin school board. On one hand, they were aware the 1957 Little Rock riots that forced that city to face its racial problems. Because there was no difference in racial attitudes between the two cities, the question became, Was Austin to suffer the same national humiliation simply to be given the same answer?

On the other hand, the year 1964 was pivotal for school integration and race relations in Texas. As the Austin school board agonized over its new policy of "racial integration" by reassigning Black teachers to White schools, the presidential election was waged. This extraordinary election was conducted during the then longest economic boom in American and Texas history. It also had a "down home Texan"[2] running for president. Faced with major social and political issues (civil rights and Vietnam), Americans were asked to chose between two political philosophies. One philosophy, advanced by the Republican candidate, Senator Barry Goldwater of Arizona, was a call for the nation to return to its conservative roots. The second philosophy, advanced by President Lyndon Johnson, was a call for the nation to continue its successful military presence in Vietnam, and at the same time, create a society in which all Americans could participate.[3] Americans voted overwhelmingly for peace and prosperity.[4] Prosperity touched Austin and its African American community with stunning repercussions.[5]

Describing impoverishment as if it were an enemy to be eradicated, Johnson called upon Americans to fight a "war on poverty"[6] in the same manner as if the nation was fighting a military conflict.[7] During its first year, Congress allotted one billion dollars to improve health care, social services, and education of disadvantaged children.[8] In 1965, Congress, with Johnson's political urging, passed the Elementary and Secondary Education Act (ESEA).[9] This extraordinary piece of legislation was one of the federal government's major cornerstones aimed at implementing the Supreme Court's *Brown* ruling. Its focus was to help disadvantaged children, regardless of race, participate in enrichment programs.[10] Perhaps the best known program that earned the respect of Texans was Project Head Start.[11] It was an immediate success, and Austin teachers, like their colleagues throughout the nation, discovered the extent and brutal power of poverty in the lives of children.[12] In Austin, Head Start programs were organized in schools. But they could also be found in churches and other public facilities. For many Black Austinites, this was the first time they recognized the overwhelming influence of the school in areas beyond that of acting as a community focus within a segregated city. Now children had the opportunity to learn and, at the same time, be treated for sickle-cell anemia, hearing and eyesight deficiencies, and diseases that would otherwise not be discovered until it was too late.[13]

Yet, White Texans had great difficulty accepting the extent of change these programs required. White Austinites, like those who lived in Dallas, San Antonio,

Houston, and El Paso, were first-generation migrants from the country. Because the vast majority of White migrants moved only a short distance to the city, they experienced little or no culture shock.[14] Seldom did they meet others who voiced values that challenged their ideas about life. Therefore, living much as they had in their small rural towns or on their farms, White Texans were able to transfer their living styles to the city. They maintained their own level of social, economic, political, and religious comfort, including the conservative distrust of change that was forced upon them from outside the South.

Perhaps it was the Civil Rights Act (1964) that White Texans distrusted the most.[15] Politicized by fellow Texan, President Lyndon Johnson, the Civil Rights Act, for the first time in the twentieth century, returned to the federal government its power to bar discrimination. Most visibly in Austin, gas stations, restaurants, movie theaters, and other public spots were integrated. For many Whites, this brought those who lived in East Austin closer to their homes, shopping centers, and places of work and entertainment. White business owners construed the Act to mean interference with their daily business practices. Now they had to prove to a non-Texas authority that they were not discriminating in their employment practices. In the same way, schools and universities were required to prove they were not discriminating against minorities if they wished to continue to receive federal monies.[16]

While Austin Blacks found the Civil Rights Act gave them much,[17] it was obvious that the Black community had a long ways to go to catch up. As a consequence, Black militancy became the watchword of the decade. Unlike the riots that were provoked by the Ku Klux Klan during the post–World War I period, these were executed by Blacks. While there were no major riots, such as those in Washington and Watts, demonstrations took place in the larger Texas cities. Austin, true to its history, remained silent.[18]

In the same fashion, Vietnam played a strong role in race relations in both Austin and the United States. Unlike other wars, Vietnam could not be defined as an immediate threat to the nation or even as a conflict that could be won on the battlefield.[19] Within that context, for young men of draftable age, between eighteen and twenty-six, Vietnam was an enigma in which a possibility of death played an important role.[20] Reminiscent of previous wars, race played a strong part in Black attitudes about who should fight in what some called a "White man's war." Although Black Texans had a tradition of joining the military, the Vietnam War was proving difficult for them to understand. Antiwar demonstrations in the early part of the Johnson administration were basically led by White students, many of whom were petitioning their draft boards for military deferments. Whites knew that staying in college effectively meant staying out of Vietnam. However, as Black organizers became aware of the disproportionate number of Black soldiers in Vietnam and their high death rate, Black demonstrations throughout the country merged with the White protest movement.[21] And so the polarization of national attitudes continued. In Austin, as in communities throughout the country, people took sides over issues they did not always understand.

WHITE FLIGHT: LEAVING AUSTIN'S CORE

In the same fashion, White Austinites found it difficult to believe what was happening to their school district during the summer of 1971. As described in preceding chapters, the school board could not prove in district court that its cross-over teachers policy was an effective method to desegregate Austin schools. Austin joined a growing list of Southern communities in which the federal judiciary mandated change.[22] White Austinites reacted to the federal court order by following a pattern developed in other parts of the South.[23] Bluntly, unable to accept the reality that their children could learn as well in integrated classrooms as in White classrooms, Whites began a process of urban emigration. Simply put, White Austinites rejected their school board's contention that busing Black students to White schools was an effective means to avoid White flight. Whites, who referred to themselves as Anglos, wanted their children to learn about the Texas they knew and not that of other races. For example, White parents could tolerate their children learning Hispanic history because the mythology of the Alamo seemed to justify that culture's existence. But Black history, at best, made White Austinites cringe.

In Texas fashion, emigrating from the city was not difficult. Just as it had not been difficult to bring their rural values into the city earlier, it was comforting to know those same values were still accepted in suburbs.[24] Unlike Northern urban emigrants, Texans had little need to develop mass transit systems to leave the city. Austin, like Houston, Dallas, El Paso, and other Texas communities was surrounded by land. Land was available within driving distance, mostly on the periphery of the city.[25] In Austin's case, it was a matter of moving north and northwest from the city center. The new interstate highway system pointed the direction. Running north and south from Dallas to San Antonio, the Interstate acted like an artery, giving White Austinites access to the open land. Requiring new services, multilane roads such as Mopac,[26] Lamar, and Research Boulevards crisscrossed north Austin.

As Austin's northern suburbs grew, services and businesses followed. Small shopping centers, theaters, banks, and entertainment centers quickly dotted the neighborhoods. At the same time, in the city's center, churches faltered, businesses lost customers, and entertainment centers emptied. As in other cities experiencing this demographic shift, Austin churches and those businesses that depended on customers recognized that if they wanted to remain viable they would have to move to where their parishioners and customers were. Eventually, Austin's city center lost much of its seven day a week bustle, leaving it to the lawyers, legislators, office workers, and tourists who came to see the Capitol or walk down Sixth Street.

Whites did not mind leaving Austin. Like most Texans, Austinites considered themselves Texans first before they identified themselves by location or community. As a consequence, Whites found it easy to move to small farming communities that dotted the land around Austin. Most of these communities, such as Georgetown and Pflugerville, had long, lazy histories that had begun in the mid-1800s because of some immediate economic need of the local farming area. Some communities located at a river's edge because that location allowed travelers to be ferried from one shore to the other. Some were established by small business owners. Round Rock was one of these communities, founded in 1848, by Jacob M. Harrell, a blacksmith.[27] Throughout its first century's history, Round Rock remained a small agrarian community watching various agricultural businesses succeed and fail, and a private college attempt success before closing, and briefly experiencing an outlaw. Perhaps its most exciting time was when a railroad company laid tracks close to the settlement. Recognizing the importance of transportation, the community moved en masse to the railroad site, leaving its original settlement to stand empty.[28] Round Rock's population remained stagnant, never increasing above 1,400 citizens and never decreasing below one thousand.[29]

While Round Rock's growth increased marginally in the 1960s, it flourished in the 1970s as White Austinites moved north. Within a short period during that decade, Round Rock became demographically tied to Austin.[30] Graduating to the status of a bedroom community, Round Rock attracted Austinites by giving them quiet residences built on large lawns, quality roads, neighborhood churches, convenient shopping centers, and a small town government that was responsive to citizens, who could talk to the mayor in person. Residents knew each other by their first names. Round Rock also had schools that supported curricula parents could understand. Most importantly for White Austinites, their children would learn in classrooms alongside those of their neighbors.

The 1971 district court order also caused Black Austinites to move, but in fundamentally different ways. Unlike Whites, who were in the process of building new homes in north Austin and the newly developed suburbs, Black Austinites remained in their East Austin neighborhoods and watched their children being bused to White schools on the other side of the interstate highway. As we described in the previous chapter, this was a difficult process for Black parents because of their concern for their children's education. Now their children would be learning with others from different racial and cultural communities.

WHITE SCHOOLS AND THE CULTURE OF INTEGRATION

Like schools throughout the South and, eventually, the North, Austin's previously White schools felt the consequences of integration. The fabric of the school experience became broader and more complex for students and teachers alike. Cultural unknowns, racial stereotypes, personal feelings, family histories, and values clashed in classrooms, schoolyards, parking lots, and hallways. It was common for White students and parents to believe their schools no longer belonged to them. It was the same attitude White families voiced when they expressed their fear that they might become different if they lived in integrated neighborhoods or worked with Blacks. Likewise, White parents feared their children would become different if they attended integrated schools. Yet, as narrated earlier, Black Austenite students and parents had no false assumptions. They knew the White schools didn't belong to them. They pictured themselves as guests of unwilling hosts. While Blacks thought of integration to mean shared power with Whites, White students rejected this idea because they interpreted it to mean Blacks would have power over them. Blacks embraced the idea of equality.[31]

Consequently, schools became biracial battlegrounds in which students and teachers struggled with their personal reflections of individual separation.[32] It was through these struggles that Black students developed different avenues to learn and live with White students. One method was called "fronting."[33] Fronting, while difficult for Whites to understand, is an easy technique for Blacks to master. Black students who wanted or needed to communicate with White teachers and students used it effectively to protect themselves from threatening racial situations. It allowed Black students to keep their culture without the daily fear it would be downgraded by Whites. Yet, the price of fronting is expensive because it causes Black students to publicly depreciate their cultural histories with White teachers and students while privately valuing them.[34] To protect their culture within a White school setting, Black students sought each other out. Through school clubs and organizations, or simply sitting together in the cafeteria or mingling in the hall, Black students rekindled their culture. Like a protective web, the group had a chance, by talking, gossiping, listening to music, dancing, or relaxing to refresh themselves within their heritage.[35]

Another avenue Black students used to cope with Whites in a White student–dominated school was to purposely fail. In many ways, Black students did not find that difficult because many areas of the curriculum were vestiges of White or European cultural traditions. While White students may have had out-of-school experiences supporting the curriculum, Black students usually did not. Therefore, the meaning of the curriculum was usually lost or misunderstood.[36] What is not misunderstood by Black students, however, is that failure in White schools will not erode the loving support of the Black community. In fact, success in White schools may raise questions about whether students want to remain in the Black community.

THE STALEMATE

By the last decade of the twentieth century, it was clear that competition between the traditions of equality and assimilation had ended in a stalemate. White Austinites, like others who have faced this same issue in other communities, had clearly voiced their reaction by moving from the city's central core, taking their tax monies with them. Politically, many White parents became actively interested in state and national politics, seeking out candidates who promised them public monies and tax breaks so that they could afford to send their children to private schools. Some parents even "double taxed" themselves so that charity groups and churches could build schools for the faithful.

Within the Black community, the same issues developed. However, they were discussed from the vantage point of whether their students would receive an equal education in a White school. For the majority of Blacks in this period, the answer seemed to be in the affirmative. For example, in 1970, the year prior to the district court's orders ending Austin school segregation, more than half of all Blacks questioned in national opinion polls supported busing as an effective method of seeking equal education opportunity. In fact, Black acceptance of busing continued to grow during the decades.[37] It was because of this positive feeling that racial equality could only come about through equal education that East Austin was willing to close L. C. Anderson High School. The closing also reflected Black willingness to support outside agencies' solutions to local problems, something White Austinites despised.

Yet, almost a half century *Brown v. Board of Education* and thirty years after district courts throughout the United States forced school boards such as Austin's to integrate, Black communities are continuing to ask whether Black students are receiving an equal education in White schools. Although the question is consequential to Black parents, it is obviously important to everyone. In a major study investigating school attendance by race, Orfield[38] reported what teachers, parents, and students already knew. The flight of White parents from the cores of the cities divested those schools of their tax bases and left them to the poor. In turn, those who remained floundered for lack of avenues of escape. As a consequence, equality in school settings has not opened the doors of opportunity. Black parents recognize indicators of disparity that exist at every level, including the economic status of first-year college graduates.[39]

Walking through the streets of East Austin, passing small businesses and homes with busy front yards, and eventually entering Huston-Tillotson College, it is easy to place yourself back on May 17, 1954. On that day Charles Akins's spirits soared. *Brown* finally gave him and his family, friends, neighbors, and all those who looked like him an opportunity to experience equality. He, like Iola Taylor and Vernice Smith, intuitively knew that *Brown* was the result of generations of labor, both by those whose names they had learned at L. C. Anderson High School and others who would only be recalled by friends and family. They had also learned from their teachers that nothing had been given them except what they gave themselves. It is for these who labored in the classrooms and others like them to tell us whether crossing over to White schools brought their visions of opportunity and equality closer to reality, or whether the struggle is unending.

CHAPTER NINE

Creating Places
of Engaged Listening

And the old shall dream dreams,
And the youth shall see visions,
And our hopes shall rise up to the sky.
We must live for today, we must build for tomorrow.
Give us time, give us strength, give us life.
                            —*And the Youth Shall See Visions*

THE LIVES OF MILLIONS of African Americans were forever altered through their pursuit of educational equality.[1] Yet, few studies have focused on African American schools, the closure of those schools, the impact of those closures on African American communities, and what we might learn from those schools.[2] This chapter is intended to give the reader an opportunity to reflect on the experiences of Austin's cross-over teachers as its school board grudgingly was forced to integrate by the federal government which demanded the laws be obeyed. Highlighting the voices of cross-over teachers in this book within the context of conflicting histories, we encourage readers to raise questions regarding the voices of social, racial, and cultural conflict they hear today in a society still complicated by continuing inequality at all levels.

The educational history of segregation conveys the many difficulties faced by African American students, teachers, administrators, and parents. African American schools were historically underfunded, if funded at all, by the states in which *de jure* segregation was operative. Outdated, used textbooks from White schools were passed on to African American schools. School supplies were minimal and supplemented by teachers. African American teachers and administrators received substantially lower pay than comparable White teachers and administrators.[3] The concept "separate but equal" did not apply to education or other areas of society for African Americans. In fact, we argue in this book that the phrase "separate and unequal" was substantially more descriptive of educational opportunities during segregation. Although the decision of the U. S. Supreme Court in *Brown v. Board of Education*[4] affirmed these findings, segregated schools continued to exist for another fifteen to twenty years in the majority of Southern states. In this book we have grappled with issues of complex relations among what is known and what has yet to be learned about segregated African American schools and the subsequent effect of desegregation on both individuals and the African American community as a whole.

We assert that African American schools during segregation accomplished wondrous achievements not extensively reported in the literature. We contend that parents, teachers, and administrators value education, as did the students and community. What, then, happened to the African American students, teachers, administrators, and communities during the process of desegregation? This paradox permeates our research in the field of desegregation. In other words, we struggled to identify, to frame, what happened in these communities prior to, during, and after the *Brown* decision. Until recently, our research has focused on telling of the story of desegregation through African American teachers' narratives documenting their experiences. However, just telling their stories is insufficient to examine the question continually raised by ourselves and others. Thus, if the African American schools were so substandard—historically underfunded, with outdated, used textbooks, minimal school supplies, and low pay for African American teachers and administrators—how did they do so well with their students? African Americans' commitment to educational equality requires, historians, educators and others to more fully investigate this event in our cultural educational history.

The purpose of this book is to discuss the struggle and to frame theoretically this research. In it, we have engaged in a multilayered, multivocal discourse as we have worked through the paradoxical nature of segregated schools. We first examined the structure and words of segregation that have privileged Whites while marginalizing African Americans. We then argued that African American schools constituted safe places where students, teachers, and administrators re-worked the histories of slavery and segregation, empowering students to understand the marginalization they encountered in the world outside their community. The teachers created a place of active learning engaged listening as they and their students struggled to find meaning in and understanding of the events of their lives in a segregated world. Thus, we contend, communal experiences were created within the curriculum of segregated African American schools. We then examined the unintended consequences of the abrupt closure of African American high schools for students, teachers, administrators, parents, and communities.

Based on these findings, we now examine how some identities within desegregated White schools were privileged and others marginalized. We maintain that privileging by Whites was often invisible in that they themselves did not see it happening. That is we maintain White privilege was couched in terms of normalcy, authenticity, and desirability. By adopting these positions, Whites confirmed their social dominance by maintaining the privilege of defining what was normal and normative. In other words, Whites adopted ways of thinking, acting, living that privileged some—Whites—and excluded others—African Americans—while failing to acknowledge the ways this marginalization occurred. As you read this last chapter, we encourage you to actively engage with the text as we deconstruct the concepts of privilege and marginality using, at times, concepts and quotations from previous chapters.

STRUCTURES AND WORDS OF SEGREGATION

> *Un-selfing* was the psychological kind of interaction that occurs between people that can breed mistrust in any kind of relationship. It means that Whites either overtly or covertly take away an [African American] person's dignity. It can be done very, very subtly, but it can be done.[5]

"Un-selfing," or "Othering" by Whites normalized oppressive behavior and created the context of authenticating marginalization of African Americans.[6] For example, in Southern states, an invisible line, segregation, isolated African Americans from Whites in all aspects of their lives. Whites seldom had contact with African Americans except in a menial capacity. An African American teacher recalled his experience as a young boy:

> I worked in a lady's yard one day . . . gosh I had no idea what it was going to be like. But she was supposed to pay me a dollar for the whole day! And lunch. When lunch time came—I was [sitting] on the back step and she put my lunch here and the dog's lunch next to mine on the same step! So I never cut another yard and I never did that kind of work, ever again![7]

Treating African Americans the same as their pets was typical denigrating behavior for racist Whites. Within the context of segregated social structures, every aspect of African American life was determined by those who wanted to maintain White supremacy. For example, the simple act of buying candy marginalized this African American child.

> It was . . . so segregated in terms of racial treatment that I can remember several of the real negative kinds of experiences. For example, the experience of not being treated in the same fashion [as Whites]. . . . If I went to the store to buy a bar of candy, the storekeeper would hand me the candy, but he would never

hand me the change. He would always put the change on the table. I would
pick up the change from the table. It was a no-no for him to touch me and for
me to touch him. . . . When I would pay him, I would put the money on the
counter and he would pick it up. There was never any touching between Blacks
and Whites. You just didn't do that![8]

These White racist Southerners asserted that racial segregation was part of their
uniqueness, was healthy, and was honored by both races. For example, an avowed
segregationist declared:

Segregation is a benevolent and philanthropic institution which "protects" the
interests of the Negro, which mediates to him the wisdom and virtues of White
society, which gives him a chance to develop "in his own way" under his own
leaders in his own institutions . . . he is stirred up by "outsiders," Communists,
the NAACP or other subversives.[9]

White Southern segregationists considered segregation a noble cause and asserted
that it was their duty to protect and defend it. They liked to depict the South as,
after all, a state of mind that elevated Whites over African Americans in every aspect of Southern culture. The state of mind espoused by segregationists included
antipathy toward change, deep respect for the status quo, determination to keep
the South as a separate and identifiable region, fierce commitment to govern and
be governed locally, fidelity to states' rights, paranoid hatred of communism, Jews,
and Catholics, and intense fear of racial amalgamation.[10]

The White segregationist society created their dominant culture through tex-
tural artifacts that included gestures, words, symbolic objects and practices. They
were woven through conversations, declaring attachment to particular locations,
to particular neighborhoods, and through everyday habits with Whites only. Re-
membering a segregated city, a teacher recalled:

When it's the only society you know, you don't necessarily view it [differently].
I [remember] the "colored" water fountains downtown . . . when we would go
to the railroad station, [we'd] be in the back of the station in a dingy room . . .
I remember.[11]

These memories speak of a time and place when African Americans and Whites,
by law, were separated. The dominant White culture created boundaries, marked
off territory with words and signs. An African American teacher described her feelings as a young child:

Growing up in a segregated society was like being put in a closet with the doors
shut with a little hole where you could peek out to the real world. It was like
looking up in the sky and you could see the sun but only like it was a shadow.[12]

Although such sentiments were the norm for African Americans during segregation
in the South, most Whites disregarded any consequences for African Americans.

As we discussed within two years of the *Brown* decision, newly formed White Citizen's Councils emerged in many local communities across the South. Their goal was to fight integration legally. From a distance of forty years, Americans may find it difficult to fully comprehend the ferocious intensity of the South's state of mind that supported resistance to school desegregation by such organizations as the White Citizens' Councils. However, a now little-known book, authored in 1961 by Marvin Norfleet, affords us a glimpse into the mind of an avowed White segregationist. As was common practice then, Norfleet supported his claims of White supremacy through numerous Biblical references. His tirades focused on the evils of racial intermarriage and communism.

> The South is now the great bulwark against intermarriage. A very few years of thoroughly integrated schools would produce large numbers of indoctrinated young Southerners free from all "prejudice" against mixed matings. . . . School integration is a "pet" of Communism ![17]

White racists enacted discriminatory laws and engaged in segregated social practices aimed at keeping African Americans outside mainstream society. African Americans lived in a rigidly structured caste system based entirely on the color of one's skin. But there were places where African Americans' histories were honored—the African American community and its schools.

CITING DIFFERENT HISTORIES AND CONVEYING DIFFERENT MEANINGS

> How do I change the history of these words and the structures of society so that we can see and hear and read and feel these words as citing different histories, conveying different meanings and producing different effects?[14]

African Americans were incredibly vigilant and were obsessively concerned with racial uplift. They had an ongoing recognition of the need to oppose and denounce stereotypes of African Americans developed by racist Whites. Therefore, it is not surprisingly, the public history of segregated schools has focused almost entirely on an inferior education for African American students. Walker explained that this national memory assumed, "Black children suffered immeasurably and received little of educational value until they were desegregated into superior white systems."[15] She believed that, while the memory of inequality was correct, the historical picture was incomplete. Thus, "[the] historical recollections that recall descriptions of differences in facilities and resources of White and Black schools without also providing descriptions of the black schools' and communities' dogged determination to educate African American children have failed to tell the complete story of segregated schools."[16]

Nonetheless, few, if any, people realized the extent of the changes for both African American schools and communities. Those few who did, expressed great concern. Supporting Walker's argument about the historical picture of White and African American schools, Billingsley asserted that prior to desegregation,

> In every aspect of the [African American] child's life a trusted elder, neighbor, Sunday School teacher, or other community member might instruct, discipline, assist, or otherwise guide the young of a given family . . . as role models, community members show an example to and interest in the young people . . . as advocates, they actively intercede with major segments of society (a responsibility assumed by professional educators) to help young members of particular families find opportunities which might otherwise be closed to them . . . as supportive figures, they simply inquire about the progress of the young, take a special interest in them . . . in the formal roles of teacher, leader, elder, they serve youth generally as part of the general role or occupation.[17]

Teaching against oppression requires teaching about oppression. By explaining the White racist stereotypes, African American teachers created classrooms where students could affirm one another and understand the meanings of the crises they encountered in the public world of segregation. They created and re-created safe spaces in their schools as a bulwark against the White segregationist world.

For example, as we have noted, L. C. Anderson High School in Austin, Texas, was an accredited member of the Southern Association of Colleges and Secondary Schools with a faculty of thirty people. Ninety-nine percent of the faculty held Bachelor's degrees and half held advanced degrees. All the faculty were members of professional organizations including the National Educational Association, the Texas State Teachers' Association, and the local teachers' association. Of these three only the NEA was integrated. The other two organizations were segregated. The student population was 774, with 392 boys and 382 girls. The school year was 175 days in length. *Seventy-five percent* of the 1950 graduates attended college. A student recalled fondly his school days at this high school.

> We wanted to be good. So that was what was coming out of our high school at that time. Many of the teachers had master's degrees at that time. The teachers and parents believed there weren't any students any better than those coming out of our school. That was the prevailing spirit and the pride that we built and taught. . . . We had a sense and feeling that you needed to be professional . . . you needed to quest for a degree, move as high in education as you could. . . . You know you took pride in being a Yellow Jacket.[18]

Nonetheless, with the public school as a symbol of American democracy and equal opportunity, many African American teachers and students asked:

> [I]f democratic behavior [wa]s one goal of our educational program . . . in the public school our youth must be indoctrinated with democratic ideals. . . . C[ould] this be done in a segregated system? Does the segregation of the Black present a situation inconsistent with democratic tenets we profess?[19]

Even though this question remained unresolved, understanding the unity of the African American community involved "understanding its basis for solidarity, its implied sense of control, its values and its collective aspirations for its young."[20] In other words, the African American community acted as a collective whole, with a collective will during a collective struggle.[21] Through the African American community's collective behavior, young African American children were protected as much as possible from the racism their parents experienced in their encounters with most Whites.

In Southern states, African American children attended segregated schools, which meant that they attended the same junior high school and senior high school. The educational journey for young African Americans began at one of the several segregated elementary schools. Many youngsters described their whole world as living

> within walking distance to African American elementary school and the junior high school was right across the street . . . the high school was close . . . and the college wasn't that far. We were within walking distance of our church.[22]

For the majority of young African Americans during segregation, this description reflected accurately their experiences. Young boys would meet at their local park, especially on Friday nights when the high school band would play after the softball games. For example,

> When we finished playing, there was fellowship. We could play with our friends and do the usual things you do on Friday night. So we enjoyed that. The school was a real part of the community.[23]

But all was not fun and games for young African Americans.

At school, the teachers created a context and location to learn about Black culture that was excluded from the dominant culture's histories.

> We learned about Black people who had made contributions such as Black writers, I was extremely interested in Black history, in high school we would study Black history for a week around Lincoln's birthday.[24]

In fact, the teachers created an atmosphere where students felt safe enough to take risks to ask real questions about their lives. Thus, one former student and crossover teacher described her family's commitment to education as the foundation for survival.

> It wasn't a matter of deciding when to go to college. It was a given. There were eight of us and we all went to college. I have a brother who got his Ph.D. when he was twenty-four. We were blessed that we had ability . . . my parents emphasized the importance of using it and giving something back.[25]

African American schools, such as L. C. Anderson high school, provided a bridge between the racist public world and the loving, safe private world. The teachers encouraged acts of thinking and helped students develop an awareness of and appreciation of themselves. In this way, the students re-ordered and re-created themselves. They learned that writing stories and narratives created connections and possibilities despite risks and dangers.

One teacher's daughter, now a psychologist, shared with her mother how she viewed her teachers.

> The teachers did the best they could. My daughter wrote that when she thought of her kindergarten through her graduation, she never had a bad teacher. And I feel that way. . . . I just felt that every teacher did the best she could and the best he could. I would really stack them up against anybody.[26]

Rewriting themselves through stories and narratives provided students with reflective dialogue between who they were in their community and who they became in the segregated world of the White racists. The classroom was a place of engaged listening in which students could find meaning and understanding of events in their lives. For African American students, it was a process of identity making. In other words, teaching/learning became a way of co-living and co-constructing positive identities.

The African American communities supported their schools socially and financially. Teachers and parents were described as having pride that their high school students were the best. The cultural narratives of the communities expected, even demanded, that all students do their best. Parents welcomed teachers into their homes. This sense of community within the African American schools assisted administrators, teachers, students, staff, and parents to reach beyond the shortcomings and difficulties they faced every day of their lives because of segregation. Everyone was engaged in the meaningful relationship of education. African American teachers described their high schools, in particular, as "the major institution of the community, center of the community, a symbol of history, and of accomplishment."

In reality, segregation severely limited the life choices available to African Americans well into the 1970s. Therefore, the African American high school was more than just a high school where students learned. Rather, as we learned, L. C. Anderson High School was a meeting place, a focal point for the African American community. It was a source of deep pride for African Americans. In fact, African American high schools were the civic center for the African American communities until they were closed.

GRASS ONCE MARKING A HIGH SCHOOL

> The grass, once marking a high school no longer there, now a sign of leaving; a tracing of passion caught now in encroaching weeds. How do we mend the broken heart of separation? Or do we?[27]

Desegregation satisfied the policy requirements of the dominant group's assumption while denying the concerns of African Americans. In particular, this White denial of the African American culture was a denial of "community and place" as an effective defense against the depersonalization of segregation.[28] The communities were a caring, learning, professional, collegial, inclusive, and inquiring collective "We," which bonded them together in special ways through shared values and ideas and imparted a sense of place to its members. The African American communities' collective "We" developed and passed on to their children cultural narratives valued by community members. Thus, the collective "We' joined a tightly knit web of members engaged in meaningful relationships. Accordingly, community members—teachers, administrators, students, staff, and parents—connected with each other "as a result of felt interdependencies, mutual obligations and other ties."[29] The African American school became a purposeful community whose members developed a community that bound them together through shared values and ideologies based on learning, inquiry, and inclusivity.

> [O]ur ignorance about desegregation and its impact on African American culture has persisted partly because we have failed to recollect and celebrate the stories . . . lost in the desegregation era. . . . School desegregation . . . ignored the possibility that there could be desirable elements in African American culture worthy of maintenance and celebration . . . did not even consider that school desegregation could have destructive consequences for African Americans . . . could actually destroy important elements of African American culture.[30]

Dempsey and Noblit argue that Whites in general, and educational policy makers in particular, ignored African American efforts to enlighten them about the positive and negative consequences for the African American community. They label this type of behavior cultural ignorance and believe that cultural ignorance "is presumptive in that it devalues aspects of what is known so that we act is if these were not known."[31] In other words, policy makers publicly and privately denied the immense burden placed upon African Americans by desegregation. For example, when African American schools were closed, students were bused to formerly White schools, and many teachers and administrators were fired or demoted when transferred to White schools. The dominant White culture presumed that either mere association with White culture would benefit African Americans, or African American teachers, administrators, and students had low academic standards and/or abilities. Our research through teachers' narratives demonstrates the metaphor of the school as community.

> [The closure of the high school] was devastating to the African American community. Because the high school represented, for the African American community, something more than just a high school . . . it was a social center . . . a

symbol of history, a symbol of achievement and a symbol of accomplishment
for the community . . . that was part of the devastation.[32]

Clearly, these African Americans believed their community paid a considerable
price for desegregation. In fact, African Americans lost a community center with
each closure of a high school.

> When the school was closed, there was a feeling on the part of the African
> American community that one of the major institutions of the community—
> the center of the community—had been closed. The high school teachers, ad-
> ministrators, and staff were leaders in the community—did a whole lot of
> things in the community. It was a center and focus of the Black community.[33]

The closure of African American high schools cut away the roots of the African
American communities. The history of accomplishments through the collective
memories of the African American communities was ignored when students were
bused across town to formerly White schools. The White schools maintained their
culture while deliberately excluding the African American students, teachers, and
administrators. African Americans' culture was denigrated and isolated, when parents were no longer welcomed at their children's schools. Our research found that
closing the African American school accomplished one thing: The overt symbol of
a dual system of education no longer existed. Yet few realized was that the unintended consequence of exclusion was further entrenched in American society.

Closure of the African American schools removed the safe place affirming
African American children. We discovered that, in many ways, African Americans
had little choice about the decision to close their schools, if they wanted to achieve
educational equality. Because psychological, political, and geographical places provide a sense of comfort, African American students suffered hostility and fear when
forced to leave the security and comfort of their ideological home—their school.
Teachers and students had created a sense of attachment to their school. They honored it and the people who inhabited it. Separation from these places necessitated
grieving, by the African American community, the students, teachers, parents, and
administrators. But grieving was not honored as the schools were closed even
though African American communities had long, vibrant histories of schooling that
demonstrated generations of families' love of, and value for, education.[34]

DESEGREGATED SCHOOLS: WHO LOST?

In the early and mid-1970s, school boards such as in Austin were ordered to complete full integration, thereby closing African American high schools. African
American teachers were either reassigned to other schools within the district, or
they lost their positions. Much against their parents' wishes, African American students were bused to White schools.[35] Previously all-White schools throughout the

South, and eventually the North, felt the consequences of integration. The fabric of the school experience became broader and more complex for students and teachers alike. Cultural unknowns like rumors, were amplified. White students and parents no longer believed their schools belonged to them. It was the same attitude White families voiced when they expressed their fear that they might become different if they lived in integrated neighborhoods or worked with African Americans. Likewise, White parents feared their children would become different if they attended integrated schools.

African American students and parents held no false assumptions. As we mentioned earlier in the text, they knew the White schools did not belong to them. They pictured themselves as guests of unwilling hosts. School integration forced African Americans to change beyond the anticipation of equality promised by *Brown v. Board of Education.* Few realized that their children's lives would change in ways they did not totally understand. For some parents, inequality had been equated with "opportunities lost." Now, they were to discover that equality could also mean the loss of neighborhoods, schools, and families. Those who looked saw their communities decline.[36]

In the school culture of desegregation, the traditions of equality and assimilation competed. While Whites thought of integration as assimilation, African Americans thought of equality.[37] Consequently, schools became biracial battlegrounds in which students and teachers struggled with their personal reflections of individual separation.[38]

It is now abundantly clear that competition between the traditions of equality and assimilation has ended in a stalemate. Whites, disliking equality, have clearly voiced their reaction by moving from cities' central cores, taking their tax monies with them. Politically, many White parents have become actively interested in state and national politics, seeking out candidates who promise them public monies and tax breaks so that they can afford to send their children to private schools. Some parents even "double tax" themselves so charity groups and churches can build schools for the faithful.

Within the African American community, the same issues developed. However, they are discussed from the vantage point of equality and community. Regarding equality, the majority of African Americans in mid-twentieth-century America believed that desegregating schools was good. For example, in 1970, more than half of all African Americans questioned in national opinion polls supported busing as an effective method of seeking equal educational opportunity. In fact, African American acceptance of busing continued to grow during the succeeding decades. It was because of this positive feeling that racial equality could only come about through equal education that African Americans were willing to close their high schools and put their neighborhoods at risk. The ruin of African American neighborhoods, at the expense of failed attempts for equality of educational opportunity have forced the African American community to reevaluate the meaning of biracial education. De facto school resegregation is sparking intense discussions within the African American community about the many positive features of schooling in those days when African American parents sent their children to African American schools. There, they were taught by African American teachers who espoused familiar values of community and family.

Dawning on both African Americans and Whites is the realization that the institutions of schools, community, and family are unalterably intertwined. In many ways, African Americans and Whites are also discovering that the transplantation of one of the institutions, for example the school, from one racial community to the other has extraordinary impacts upon that "other." In this case, the unintended consequences of integration for both the African American and White communities was that biracial schools would not give students an interracial education.

For both communities, therefore, it was this ignorance about the unintended consequences of desegregation that caused that generation of educators to ignore the many positive aspects of African American culture. It is this thought that Dempsey and Noblit were discussing when they voiced the concept of cultural ignorance and school desegregation that we mentioned earlier in this study. We can conclude that these now-closed schools do represent for this generation of educators an opportunity to learn about the fragility of school, family and, community. In fact, we now have the opportunity to study the fragility of culture itself.

It is now we are able to understand hooks, who argues that racism constructs images.[39] In the case of school desegregation, African American images were codified by others so they could be understood outside the African American community, yet not from within. It is this competition between the critiques each community represents that can both enrich our minds and challenge our understandings. It enables critical interventions transforming oppressive structures of domination and articulates a freedom to control one's destiny through common ground and counter hegemonic marginal space.[40]

Lastly, this book is a cultural critique, a historical and personal interpretation of the segregation and desegregation of schools. The interpretive discussions in this text are neither meant to resolve the narratives of segregation and desegregation, nor to explain their roles in the present. Although we allow such ideas as cultural fragility, institutional transplantation, and the unintended consequences of desegregation to emerge, it is our intent to raise difficult questions about the relationship between the elitist history of books, documents, Supreme Court decisions, and official statements of public policy with the common history of peoples' memory. What we are saying is that the confluence of these two histories, elite and common, is tightly woven and is distorted by both Whites and African Americans during our recent past. It is this point Sumara and Davis are advancing when they remind us that

> radical change and cataclysmic events are not only the result of large gestures, but collections of small ones—gestures that are often unnoticed, but significant.[41]

For example, how did these African American teachers and administrators do so much with so few resources for so many students? Why were these successes not recognized by the African American communities when they discussed equal educational opportunity for their children? Also, why were Whites slow to understand these same issues when they countered African American arguments of equal educational opportunity with the tenets of assimilation? It is questions such as these that allow us to discuss the implications of the closures of African American high schools. These should allow us to recognize that the space of human understanding is within the lived world of practice and human relations. Without this, as Greene argues, we cannot escape the pervasive influence of culture. That "freedom cannot be conceived apart from a matrix of social, economic, cultural and psychological conditions."[42]

> Today's the day I take my stand, the future's mine to hold.
> Commitments that I make today are dreams from days of old.
> I'll have to make the way for generations come and go.
> I'll have to teach them what I've learned so they will come to know:
> That the old shall dream dreams
> And the youth shall see visions . . .[44]
> —*And the Youth Shall See Visions*

Notes

CHAPTER ONE
INTRODUCTION

1. Because race specific terminology changed dramatically during the period of this study, Black will be used to refer to African Americans and White for Caucasians. Black and White will be capitalized when denoting race. Primary sources when cited will be historically correct. The teachers' narratives will be as spoken.

2. Oral History Interview with Iola Taylor, October to December 1996, at her home in Austin, Texas. Mrs. Taylor, an African American teacher now retired, lives in Austin, Texas. She taught secondary social studies before, during, and after school desegregation. The interview tapes are deposited at the Oral History Collection, Center for the History of Education, The University of Texas at Austin. Hereinafter referenced Taylor Interview, OHC. All interviews in this collection subsequently referenced are designated OHC.

3. The origin of the term *Jim Crow* applied to Blacks is lost in obscurity. Thomas D. Rice wrote a song and dance called "Jim Crow" in 1832, and the term had become an adjective by 1838. The first example of "Jim Crow law" listed by the *Dictionary of American English* is dated 1904. C. Vann Woodward, *The Strange Career of Jim Crow,* 3rd edition (New York: Oxford University Press, 1974), 7.

4. David J. Garrow, *Bearing the Cross: Martin Luther King, Jr., and the Southern Christian Leadership Conference,* New York: Vintage Books, 1988; Taylor Branch, *Parting the Waters: American in the King years 1954–63,* New York: Simon and Schuster, 1988; and Kluger, Richard, *Simple Justice: The History of Brown v. Board of Education and Black America's Struggle for Equality,* New York: Random House, 1975; are seminal works in the public presentation of desegregation. Garrow's and Branch's books focus on the elites in the Civil Rights movement. In particular, each author has as his main players Martin Luther King Jr. and the people immediately surrounding him. Kluger's book, on the other hand, focuses entirely on the events leading up to and including the Supreme Court's decision, *Brown v. Board of Education of Topeka, Kansas* (347 U.S. 483 [1954]), overturning the separate-but-equal doctrine. A more recent book, Robert Mann's *The Walls of Jericho: Lyndon Johnson, Hubert Humphrey, Richard Russell, and the Struggle for Civil Rights* (New York: Harcout Brace & Company, 1996), presents a slightly different view of the civil rights movement. While focusing on elites, Humphrey, Johnson, and Russell, Mann narrates a powerful story about Congress' reluctance to legislate civil rights for all Americans. A plethora of books and

articles about segregation, desegregation, and integration were published in the 1960s and 1970s. Some of these were written as a direct response to the *Brown* decision, others as a response to Kluger's *Simple Justice*. Some focused on individual communities' struggle to desegregate their schools, public places, buses, etc. Although not exhaustive, the majority of these books and articles are listed in the bibliography. Of particular importance to this project are five books recently published. Alwin Barr's *Black Texans: A History of African Americans in Texas 1528–1995* (2nd edition, Norman: University of Oklahoma Press, 1996), covers the history of blacks in Texas from the 1500s to the present time. Robyn Duff Ladino's *Desegregating Texas Schools: Eisenhower, Shivers, and the Crisis at Mansfield High* (Austin: University of Texas Press, 1996) and Glenn M. Linden's *Desegregating Schools in Dalls: Four Decades in the Federal Courts* (Dallas: Three Forks Press, 1995) are recent publications that tell the story of desegregation in Mansfield, Texas, and Dallas, Texas. Gary Orfield, Susan E. Eaton, and the Harvard Project on School Desegregation's *Dismantling Desegregation: The Quiet Reversal of Brown v. Board of Eduation* (New York: The New Press, 1996) reviews the progress of desegregation and concludes that many cities, including Austin, Texas, are in the process of resegregation. Michele Foster's *Black Teachers on Teaching* (New York: The Free Press, 1997) is the first book that shares "the perspectives, values, and pedagogical insights of a group of excellent African American teachers from diverse communities across our nation" (1997: xi). Several of Foster's teachers describe their experiences during segregation and desegregation. Hers is the only book that gives voice to African American teachers' remembered experiences. However, none of her teachers participated in cross-over teaching as part of a desegregation plan. V. S. Walker's *Their Highest Potential: An African American School Community in the Segregated South* (Chapel Hill: University of North Carolina Press, 1966) book chronicles an African American high school during segregation in which she "captures the special circumstances of a particular time and place in history" and seeks to "understand the type of schooling that was created in response" and she "retells a community valued kind of schooling" (p. 11).

5. O. L. Davis Jr., "The American School Curriculum Goes to War, 1941–1945: Oversight, Neglect, and Discovery," *Journal of Curriculum and Supervision*, 8,2: (Winter 1993) 112–127.

6. See, for example, Anna V. Wilson, "Stranger in a Strange Land: One Black Student's Experience of Desegregation of a Birmingham, Alabama High School," *Midwest History of Education Society Journal* 23 (1996):117–123.

7. The cross-over teaching plan began at the high school and junior high school levels. Some elementary teachers were later included as cross-over teachers. This study focuses only on high school teachers. AISD maintained historical archives, some of which date back to the early 1900s. As a primary source of historical information, the archives also contained the School Directories for the years 1964 to 1971 inclusive. A careful search of these directories enabled the identification of high school cross-over teachers in the school district. In addition, the initial cross-over teachers were able to confirm the identity of later cross-over teachers and, in many instances, were able to provide introductions to them. In some cases, the first cross-over teachers were able to verify those teachers who were still living as well as those teachers who were deceased.

8. These audio tapes were then transcribed, summarized, indexed, and placed in the Oral History in Education Collection, Center for the History of Education, The University of Texas at Austin. A log, or master list, was kept for each interview, including who was interviewed, for how many hours, on what dates, using how many tapes, the dates of tran-

scription of the interview, what restrictions may have been placed on the interview. A file for each interview was established and included biographical information, letters arranging the interview, a copy of the legal consent form from the interviewee, an abstract of the interview, and explanations of any restrictions on the interview. The interviews, description, analysis, and interpretation were shared with the participants for accuracy. Seidman advocates a sharing of material with the participants so that the interviewer will know if, in working with the interview data, the interviewer has done anything to make the participant feel vulnerable. Donald A. Ritchie, *Doing Oral History* (New York: Twayne Publishers, 1995);I. E. Seidman, *Interviewing as Qualitative Research: A Guide for Researchers in Education and the Social Sciences* (New York: Teachers College Press, 1991).

9. Richard Marius, *A Short Guide to Writing About History,* 2nd edition. (New York: Harper Collins, 1995)

CHAPTER TWO
SOCIAL CONSTRUCTION OF RACE

1. Mrs. Charlotte Filmore, 100, was invited to the White House by President Clinton for remarks from the Oval Office on Dr. Martin Luther King Jr.'s seventy-first birthday on January 15, 2000. The President commented, "A good while ago she worked at the White House—back then, even here, she had to use a side door. Well, today, Charlotte Filmore came to the White House through the front door and all the way to the Oval Office." "Hate crimes leave deep scars," The Nation, Oklahoma City *Daily Oklahoman,* January 16, 2000, 17.

2. Lucy is a fictional person constructed from many conversations with Whites about attention given to African Americans in the media.

3. Grace Elizabeth Hale, *Making Whiteness: the Culture of Segregation in the South, 1890–1940* (New York: Pantheon Books, 1998), 1–11. Hale's text focuses on Whiteness as a social/political essential of Southerners who saw themselves outside the national environment. A hub of the text is that integration has taken on new meaning of our future. Said she, "If we cannot imagine less racially binary pasts or raceless futures, who will? If we cannot craft a dance of time to do more than deepen and elaborate racial difference—and set the hued fragments in motion until the jig reveals the pattern and the colors blur—who will make this time? Integration, created from within our history now, is our only future" (11).

4. Sanford's name would be incorrectly spelled as "Sandford" in the United States Supreme Court records.

5. The Nat Turner Rebellion in the 1830s sparked White resentment and fear of Blacks. While the rebellion was never discussed in the *Dred Scott v. Sanford* (19 Howard [1857], 393) arguments, it played a part in the deep undercurrents of White public sentiment, especially in the South.

6. Not all slaves ran away. Some chose to remain at home on the plantation while their "masters" went to war to defend the "peculiar institution" called slavery. It was not uncommon for the slave owner to give to a slave the responsibility of running the plantation. The irony of these trustful situations must have been marveled at by both groups through the years.

7. Not all politicians liked Lincoln's philosophy about Reconstruction. They felt his policies were simply too easy and that many Confederate leaders would go unpunished. Johnson was from Tennessee, a Confederate state. The Radical Republican Congress found

him difficult to work with and eventually impeached him because of his position on the various Constitutional Amendments proposed during Reconstruction.

8. This term, which has remained in the American vocabulary, refers to the suitcases used by travelers during this time. These soft bags were easy to pack and simple to store during traveling. Many of them were floral and reminded one of the cloth and texture of a carpet. Northerners (sometimes called "do-gooders") who were interested in advancing the cause of the ex-slave traditionally used this travel case because of its popularity.

9. Paul Johnson, *A History of the American People* (New York: Harper Collins, 1997), 507.

10. Both Brenham and Brownsville were burned. In both of these cases, rumors spread that Northern White officers refused to discipline their troops to the extent they issued no arrest warrants.

11. T. R. Fehrenbach, *Lone Star: a History of Texas and the Texans* (New York: American Legacy Press,1983), 396.

12. During the height of the Civil War, slave owners from Arkansas and Louisiana sent their slaves to Texas for safekeeping. Treating the slaves as financial "assets," slave owners believed if they "banked" their slaves in Texas they would be happy to return home after the war.

13. T. R. Fehrenbach, *Lone Star,* 395. This date is celebrated as a holiday, Juneteenth.

14. Carl H. Moneyhon, "Black Codes," *Texas Online* (tsha.utexas.edu/handbook/online/). Moneyhon discusses how this piece of legislation was strongly attacked by General Joseph B. Kiddoo of the Freemen's Bureau. While he was successful in preventing its enforcement, the damage had been done. In fact, this act became the central pillar that governed Black-White relations in Texas from the end of Reconstruction to *Brown v. Board of Education.*

15. Ibid.

16. Ibid.

17. Of course, Blacks were not allowed to succeed because of the social ballet called segregation and White identification of Blacks as a race-class of laborers who had such a rudimentary understanding of work, they had to be taught by White employers its "finer points."

18. Grace Elizabeth Hale, *Making Whiteness,* 23. Hale makes the argument that *Plessy v. Ferguson* is significant because of the question, "What is race?" Her response is that Plessy's lawyer, Albion Tourgee, argued the case on the point governments do not have the right to classify persons according to race. The United States Supreme Court's ruling was that color is not something humans decide—it was beyond the law (or divinely created?). Human agencies, such as the Louisiana public transportation system, could only reflect that truth or reality. Therefore, the Court argued, Homer Plessy could not be both Black and White. He was "colored" even if he had one drop of Black blood. Hale contends, like Albert Murray's incontestably "mulatto"of present society that this is the lie upon which society sits. Hale's, Murray's, and Tourgee's observations are similar to those of South African writers such as Alan Paton prior to the collapse of apartheid and South Africa.

19. Booker T. Washington, *Up from Slavery* (1901: reprinted, New York: University Books, 1993) 221–222. Undoubtedly influencing this period was Booker T. Washington's 1895 opening speech at the Atlanta Fair in which he said, "In all things that are purely social we can be as separate as fingers, yet one as the hand in all things essential to mutual

progress." Washington gave credit to the Black Codes such as those in Texas which confirmed that the bottom run in America's class ladder belonged to Blacks.

20. The *Separate Car Act* allowed Blacks to ride in "White Only" passenger cars as long as they were in the employment of a White passenger and were required to perform essential service for their employers during the trip. Therefore, nannies and servants usually traveled with their "mistresses." However, a Black handyman who was traveling with his employer would ride in the "Colored Only" car and join his White employer at the end of the trip.

21. William E. Segall and Anna V. Wilson, *Introduction to Education: Teaching in a Diverse Society* (Columbus: Prentice-Hall/Merrill, 1998), 71-72.

22. John David Smith, *An Old Creed for the New South: Proslavery Ideology and Historiography, 1865–1918.* (Athens: The University of Georgia Press,1991), 285–289. Smith argues that during this period the argument between proslavery and antislavery ideologies was intense. Proslavery, says Smith easily won partly because of biblical, ethnological, educational, and racial explanations of slavery. Defenders of slavery says Smith continually talked about the moral decline of Blacks after the Civil War.

23. "Grandfather" is a unique term used by White legislators during this period. Many states judged voting and other activities according to the individual's family heritage. For example, Blacks might lose their right to vote if their grandfathers were slaves or placed in some menial position. Through legal gymnastics state legislation allowed Whites to vote based on what their grandfathers did. Of course, Whites understood the idea of "grandfathering" and Blacks did not. See footnote 24.

24. Because the military was segregated, Blacks served in special military units designated with the world "color" or "colored." This practice had started in the Civil War and continued until the last phases of World War II in which these exclusionary laws were declared unconstitutional in *Smith v. Allwright* (1944) and a supporting decision in *Terry v. Adams* (1953).

25. John S. D. Eisenhower, *Intervention! The United States and the Mexican Revolution, 1913–1917* (New York: W. W. Norton & Company, 1993). Eisenhower points out that White commanding officers quickly learned that Black First Sergeants held considerable influence with the men. As a consequence, the First Sergeants traditionally were given responsibilities about day-to-day activities.

26. Ibid.

27. Anthony J. Lukas, *Big Trouble* (New York: Simon & Schuster, 1997), 131, 135–136. Lukas describes in detail a spectacular example of Jim Crowism against the Twenty Fourth in the military during the 1898 Spanish-American War. After the regiment's participation in the Battles of Kettle Hill and San Juan Hill, it was force marched to the military hospital at Siboney to act as nurses to six hundred White soldiers suffering from various stages of Yellow Fever. Of the 456 Black soldiers who had survived the battles and the forced march, only twenty-four were alive after Siboney. Lukas reports the spontaneous recognition of Whites that was immediately followed by the silence of official White written military history.

28. The ideals of the Ku Klux Klan have not lessened during the century. Former Ku Klux Klansman David Duke announced that he was starting a new group called the National Organization for European American Rights. Its purpose is to defend European values which are presently, he says maligned in favor of Blacks, Hispanics, Jews, and

homosexuals. The group's headquarters is in Louisiana. "David Duke forms white rights group," Oklahoma City *Daily Oklahoman,* January 22, 2000, A, 8.

29. Fehrenbach, *Lone Star,* 682. Fehrenbach points out that in comparison with other Southern states, Texas was very violent. In this regard he positions Texas with Oklahoma, which had an extremely violent history. Of course, Black Texans were continuing to emigrate from Texas while White and Hispanic populations were increasing. As a consequence, Black percentage of the population continued to decline.

30. Ibid., 258–259. It was not until the Lamar Presidency that European nations began to take Texas seriously. In England, the Palmerston government signed three commercial treaties with Texas. Belgium and France also signed diplomatic treaties.

31. David C. Humphrey "untitled," *Texas Online* (www.tsha.utexas.edu/ web_evaluate). Twenty percent of Austin's 34,876 residents were Black in1920. Historically, Austin was the fourth largest city in the state, although in 1920 was tenth. Other reasons why Austin may have been a "safe haven" is that White-instigated riots were coming to an end in the 1920s. Another is that the Black percentage of the population decreased and fewer Whites felt threatened by Black involvement (see footnote 29). Also, Blacks performed important services for White Austinites. State government offices and the university campus needed workers who performed low-paying menial chores, such as chambermaids, gardeners, cleaners, street sweepers, and others.

32. It was not unthinkable for a White person to be lynched. They were usually people at the bottom of the social ladder who had offended Protestant religious values or European morals to such an extent that it was impossible for the community to forgive them.

33. The "color line," W. E. B. Du Bois insisted, would be the major problem of the twentieth century. There is a history of accommodation or "peeking over the line" by both sides, however. Hale retells the story Booker T. Washington wrote in his 1909 text, *The Story of the Negro: the Rise of the Race from Slavery.* A Black, fearing he would be late catching a train, flagged a hack (that is, a horsedrawn taxi) to take him to the station. Unfortunately, the hackman was White and therefore was not allowed to have Black customers. The segregation problem was solved when the Black suggested the White hackman sit in the passenger seat of the cab and the Black "passenger" would "drive." When the hack arrived at the train station, the "driver" got out of the front seat and paid the "passenger." The Black was able to catch his train and the White gained a fare. Hale, *Making Whiteness.*

34. William D. Rogosin, "Willie Wells," *Texas On Line* (www.tsha.utexas.edu/handbook/ online). Perhaps the greatest baseball player in the United States not commemorated by the Baseball Hall of Fame is Willie (Devil) Wells. Born in Austin in 1905, Wells played in the Negro League as well as in integrated Cuban and Mexican professional leagues. In every league he performed better than White players. His lifetime batting average is .358. Wells played with his friend Jackie Robinson during the Negro League championship games. In 1945 Wells played second base for the West and Robinson shortstop for the East. Wells was selected eight times for the East-West Classic. Wells was player-manager of the top ranked Black League Newark Eagles in the 1940s. Some Newark players he helped send to the major leagues were Monte Irvin, Larry Doby, and Don Newcombe. Willie Wells died in Austin in 1989.

35. Sports, like life, was segregated. Blacks and Whites seldom played together, therefore, college and professional sports teams were composed solely of Whites. Blacks were marginalized in sports conferences as well. Playing in communities throughout Texas, for example, most of their history is lost because of White unconsciousness. Who knows the

number and names of those who were seldom able to show their talents? An example of Black athletic talent was usually demonstrated by Satchel Paige's All-Star team. He selected outstanding Black sports talent such as Willie Wells to play against White major league players after the World Series.

36. Nat King Cole, the first Black musician to host a network television program, tells the story of being the lead entertainer at hotels, yet not being allowed to stay at the hotel that hired him. He also affirmed the story in which several Whites who physically threatened him later were seen sitting in the audience wildly applauding his act.

37. Lisa C. Maxwell, "Deep Ellum" *Texas Online* (www. tsha.utexas.edu/handbook/online). Elm is pronounced as a two syllable word ("El-lum") in Dallas. Ellum Street originally was reserved for Blacks. Called Deep Ellum, located close to train tracks east of downtown Dallas, the area continued to grow. Through the years Ellum Street has changed. Because of freeway construction the area is smaller than the original. Its focus presently is on arts and crafts.

38. Anthony Lewis, "A badge of inferiority," Tulsa *Tribune,* January 23, 2000, A19. Mr. Lewis wrote this article as a tribute to his friend, Philip Elman. Elman's legal brief is extraordinary. Sixty-six pages long, it attacks the very core of *Plessey v. Ferguson.* Elman advanced Albion Tourgee's 1896 legal argument when he defended Homer Plessy. Lewis allows readers to assume Elman was White and typical of Washingtonian "bureaucrats." He points out that it was only after the Henderson case that the Supreme Court became interested in segregation. The Supreme Court "did not then face the constitutionality of segregation. But on the day they decided the Henderson case, they began striking down state rules that made [B]lacks go to a separate law school or be segregated in university classrooms." In the meantime, Lewis points out, bureaucrats in the Justice Department continued to be involved in similar cases "—right up to Brown Vs. Board of Education, decided on May17, 1954, 12 years to the day from Elmer Henderson's train ride."

39. William E. Segall, and Anna V. Wilson, "Mary McLeod Bethune," in *Historical Dictionary of Women's Education in the United States,* ed. Linda Eisenmann (Westport, CT: Greenwood Publishing Group, 1998), 42–43.

40. William E. Segall and Anna V. Wilson, "National Association of College Women," in *Historical Dictionary of Women's Education in the United States,* 290–291. Bethune was a major influence on President Roosevelt during the 1940 Ford-union conflicts. Her memo to the President, delivered by her friend Eleanor Roosevelt, averted a race war and educated him to the importance of civil rights. Doris Kearns Goodwin, *No Ordinary Time: Franklin and Eleanor Roosevelt: the Home Front in World War II* (New York: Simon & Schuster, 1994), 227–230.

41. Fehrenbach, *Lone Star.* Fehrenback paints a realistic view of official apathy about the education of Black Texans. Texas organized schools for Blacks in 1870 during Reconstruction. Buildings were poorly constructed, few books were purchased, and teachers generally had little or no college experiences. They were paid accordingly. As a consequence many schools were built by Black parents who wanted their children to learn how to read and write. This "double taxation" of Black communities by Blacks bought supplies and books and paid teacher salaries. In post–World War II years Texas attempted to validate its "separate but equal" educational policies, but the monies were so inadequate and the task so great, education still suffered even with two state institutions of higher education and the eight independent colleges.

42. Fehrenbach, *Lone Star,* 654. Fehrenbach, a White historian, is a good example of how some historians reflected on that postwar period, placing the "separate but equal" doctrine akin to Nazi Germany's social policies. Said he, "Texans neither understood nor approved Hitler's bloody rancor against the Jews, which was subtly different from their own determination to subordinate internal groups considered inferior. The Texan attitude toward . . . races, probably, was closer to the Nazi view of eastern Europeans, who seemed to provide a ready-made laboring mass." Of course, Fehrenbach is only defining "separate but equal" in this instance as a class problem and less a race problem.

43. *Brown v. Board of Education,* 1954 United States Supreme Court. The drama of this Supreme Court case equals that of *Dred Scott v. Sanford.* Unlike that case, which was polluted with political intrigue, *Brown v. Board of Education* was the product of the National Association for the Advancement of Colored People. *Brown* was the concluding step in a series of United States Supreme Court cases argued by its chief attorney Thurgood Marshall. Marshall later sat on the Court. Goodwin, *No Ordinary Time,* 320–322. Goodwin recounts how Chief Justice Earl B. Warren, as attorney general of California during World War II, actively supported, along with Governor Culbert Olson, Executive Order 9066 requiring Japanese Americans to be forcefully removed from California as a war measures act. As a consequence, Japanese Americans lost property, fortunes, and their Constitutional rights. They were "interned" in "camps" until the end of the war.

CHAPTER THREE
OH, I DO REMEMBER!

1. Taylor Interview, OHC.

2. See note 1 in chapter 1.

3. Taylor Interview, OHC. The initial Supreme Court decision was handed down in 1954 and the second, or follow-up decision, occurred the following year, 1955. The two decisions are commonly known as *Brown I* and *Brown II. Brown v. Board of Education of Topeka, Kansas,* 347 U.S. 483 (1954) and 355 U.S. 294 (1955).

4. Oral History Interview with W. Charles Akins, October to December 1996, at his office in Austin, Texas. Mr. Akins, the Associate Superintendent for Austin Independent School District, lives in Austin, Texas. He taught secondary social studies before, during, and after school desegregation. The interview tapes are deposited at the Oral History Collection, Center for the History of Education, The University of Texas at Austin. Hereinafter referenced Akins Interview, OHC.

5. The *Austin Statesman* interviewed numerous people about their reactions to the *Brown* decision and published those interviews in a lengthy article on the date cited. All comments taken from this source are cited as "Non Segregation Finds Austin Widely Divided on Outcome," *The Austin Statesman,* May 18, 1954, 13.

6. Ibid.

7. Ibid.

8. Ibid.

9. Ibid.

10. The doctrine of interposition focused on the rights of individual states to "interpose" themselves between the federal government and the citizens of the states when the

state identified a federal law or court decision deemed as either (1) harmful to the state's citizens, or (2) contrary to the Constitution. For more information regarding interposition, see Robert Mann, *The Walls of Jericho: Lyndon Johnson, Hubert Humphrey, Richard Russell, and the Struggle for Civil Rights* (New York: Harcourt Brace and Company, 1996), 160; United States Constitution, Tenth Amendment; Robert Brisbane, "Interposition: Theory and Fact," *Phylon* 17 (1956): 12–16; Reed Sarratt, *The Ordeal of Desegregation: The First Decade* (New York: Harper and Row, 1966), 38–39; report on Interposition (no author, title, or date), LBJ Papers, United States Senate Files, 1949–1961, Office Files of George Reedy, 1956–1957, Reedy: Convention 1956, Box 418, LBJ Library.

11. "Non Segregation Finds Austin Widely Divided on Outcome," 13.

12. Ibid.

13. Ibid.

14. Ibid.

15. R. Ray McCain, "Reactions to the U. S. Supreme Court Decision of 1954," *Georgia Historical Quarterly* 52 (December 1968): 373.

16. *De jure* segregation was segregation by law while *de facto* segregation occurred through housing segregation but not by legal statute.

17. Richard Kluger, *Simple Justice: The History of Brown v. Board of Education and Black America's Struggle for Equality* (New York: Random House, 1975).

18. W. G. Stephan and J. R. Feagin, *School Desegregation: Past, Present, and Future* (New York: Plenum, 1980); Kluger, *Simple Justice;* R. Wolters, *The Burden of Brown: Thirty Years of School Desegregation* (Knoxville, TN: University of Tennessee Press, 1984).

19. Freedom of choice plans refer to each student's having the unrestricted opportunity to attend the school of his/her choice. These plans were initially used throughout the South as a method to achieve token school desegregation. For a detailed discussion of southern states use of the freedom-of-choice plans, see Wolters, *The Burden of Brown.*

20. The term *segregation* means "to separate on the basis of race." Thus, *desegregation* means to remove separation on the basis of race. The terms *segregation* and *desegregation* are inextricably bound together, one with the other. Over time, integration has been used interchangeably with desegregation. This usage is incorrect and, most often, represents a Northern view of the elimination of segregation.

21. The *Dred Scott* decision announced that Blacks were neither citizens of the United States nor could they become citizens in the future. Furthermore, Blacks had no legal rights that Whites were bound to respect. For example, immediately prior to the Civil War, most southerners claimed that Negroes and Whites belonged to different species. This decision by the Supreme Court had as far reaching social and political consequences as the later *Brown* decision. The Supreme Court found "[Negroes had] for more than [a] century before been regarded as beings of an inferior order, and altogether unfit to associate with the White race, either in social or political relations; and so far inferior that they had no rights which the White man was bound to repeat" (*Dred Scott v Sanford,* 60 U. S. [19 How.] 393, 407 [1857]).

22. Woodward stated, "The determination of the Negro's 'place' took shape gradually under the influence of economic and political conflicts among divided White people—conflicts that were eventually resolved in part at the expense of the Negro. In the early years of the twentieth century, it was becoming clear that the Negro would be effectively disfranchised throughout the South, that he would be firmly relegated to the lower rungs of the

economic ladder, and that neither equality nor aspirations for equality in any department of life were for him. Woodward, *The Strange Career of Jim Crow,* 7.

23. Stephan and Feagin, *School Desegregation;* Kluger, *The History of Brown v. Board of Education;* Wolters, *The Burden of Brown;* Davison M. Douglas, *Reading, Writing, and Race, The Desegregation of the Charlotte Schools* (Chapel Hill: University of North Carolina Press, 1996); Sarratt, *The Ordeal of Desegregation;* Mann, *The Walls of Jericho.*

24. James D. Anderson, *The Education of Blacks in the South, 1860–1935* (Chapel Hill: The University of North Carolina Press, 1988). Kluger, *Simple Justice;* Anderson, *Education of Blacks* Press.

25. The rebel states were Alabama, Arkansas, Florida, Georgia, Louisiana, Mississippi, North Carolina, South Carolina, Tennessee, Texas, and Virginia. The border states included Delaware, Kentucky, Maryland, Missouri, West Virginia, and the District of Columbia.

26. Lerone Bennett Jr., *Before the Mayflower: A History of Black America,* 6th edition (New York: Penguin Books, 1988); Alwyn Barr, *Black Texans: A History of African Americans in Texas 1528–1995,* 2nd edition (Norman: University of Oklahoma Press, 1996). See chapter 2.

27. In 1865, the Thirteenth Amendment to the United States Constitution abolished slavery: "Neither slavery nor involuntary servitude, except as a punishment for crime whereof the party shall have been duly convicted, shall exist within the United States, or any place subject to their jurisdiction" (United States Constitution).

28. The Fourteenth Amendment to the United States Constitution, ratified July 21, 1868, granted citizenship to former slaves and mandated equal protection for all: "No State shall make or enforce any law which shall abridge the privileges or immunities of citizens of the United States, nor shall any State deprive any person of life, liberty or property without due process of law, nor deny to any person within its jurisdiction the equal protection of the laws" (United States Constitution).

29. In 1870, the Fifteenth Amendment to the United States Constitution further delineated the rights of all male citizens of the nation, and in particular Blacks: "The rights of the citizens of the United States to vote shall not be denied or abridged by the United States or by any State on account of race, color, or previous condition of servitude" (United States Constitution).

30. However, to some a loophole appeared in this amendment with the phrase "equal protection of the laws." They argued that equality could be separate. Using this argument, a railroad company that forced blacks and Whites to ride in separate railroad cars maintained that "equal protection of laws did not require exact equality, but only theoretical equality, or, at most only substantial equality." In 1873, the Supreme Court disagreed with this argument and found, "[T]his discrimination must cease, and the colored and White race, in the use of the cars, be placed on an equal basis" (*Railroad Company v. Brown,* 84 U. S. [17 Wall.] 445, 452–453 [1873]). Woodward argued, "Law has a special importance in the history of segregation, more importance than some sociologists would allow, and that the emphasis on legal history is justified. At the same time [he wanted] to stress that was not the whole story. Segregation often anticipated and frequently exceeded the law. Sometimes law merely sanctioned what had become erratically practiced by custom. And sometimes reform of the law merely registered the disturbed consciences and pious hopes of remote regional majorities essentially unaffected by the law's demands and not vitally concerned about its enforcement." (Woodward, *Strange Career of Jim Crow,* xiii).

31. In 1890, Louisiana, following Florida's, Mississippi's, and Texas' lead, passed a law requiring public carriers to segregate its passengers on the basis of race. Two years later, a very light- skinned [classified as seven-eighths White] Negro—Homer A. Plessy boarded an East Louisiana Railway car in New Orleans reserved for Whites. By pre-arrangement he was told to move to the "colored" car. He refused to do so and was promptly arrested. The New Orleans District Court ruled against Plessy's argument that the segregation law violated the Fourteenth Amendment. The ruling was appealed directly to the U. S. Supreme Court. Four years later, the Supreme Court handed down its decision. See chapter 2.

32. In *Plessy v. Ferguson,* Judge Harry Billings Brown wrote the majority opinion for the Court: "The most common instance of this [state-sanctioned separation of the races] is connected with the establishment of separate schools for White and colored children, which has been held to be a valid exercise of the legislative power even by courts of States where the political rights of the colored race have been longest and most earnestly enforced . . . we cannot say that a law which authorizes or even requires the separation of the two races in public conveyances is unreasonable . . . we consider the underlying fallacy of the plaintiff's argument to consist in the assumption that the enforced separation of the two races stamps the colored race with a badge of inferiority. If this be so, it is not by reason of anything found in the act, but solely because the colored race chooses to put that construction upon it" (*Plessy v. Ferguson,* 163 U. S. 537 [1896]).

33. C. Vann Woodward, 1974.

34. These states were [South] Alabama, Arkansas, Florida, Georgia, Louisiana, Mississippi, North Carolina, South Carolina, Tennessee, Texas, Virginia, [Border] Delaware, Kentucky, Maryland, Missouri, Oklahoma, West Virginia, and the District of Columbia.

35. *Texas Constitution,* art. 7, § 7, enacted in 1876.

36. *Texas Revised Civil Statute Annotated,* art. 2900, enacted in 1905.

37. Anderson's *Education of Blacks* discusses in detail Blacks' view of education as liberation and freedom. Anderson stated, "there developed in the slave community a fundamental belief in learning and self-improvement and a shared belief in universal education as a necessary basis for freedom and citizenship. . . . [E]ducation was fundamentally linked to freedom and dignity. . . . Blacks' motivation for intellectual achievement . . . persisted into the twentieth century and into our own present. . . . There was nothing naive about a belief in learning and self-improvement as a means to individual and collective dignity. It was not the end of their struggle for freedom and justice; only a means toward that end" (Anderson, *Education of Blacks,* 284–285).

38. Because school funds were separate at the state level, local school administrators maintained they received less funding for Black schools than for White schools. Many believed funding for White schools included monies originally identified for Black schools. Funding issues were difficult, if not impossible, to track from beginning to end of a school year in a school district.

39. For a detailed discussion of public school funding, see J. W. Alvord, *Schools and Finances of Freedom,* January 1, 1866, reprinted from 1868 copy by Washington Government Printing Office (New York: AMS Press, Inc, 1980); Anderson, *Education of Blacks;* Henry A. Bullock, *A History of Negro Education in the South: From 1619 to the Present* (Cambridge: Harvard University Press, 1867).

40. Anderson, *Education of Blacks;* Bullock, *History of Negro Education.*

41. Roger L. Ransom and Richard Sutch, *One Kind of Freedom: The Economic Consequences of Emancipation* (Cambridge: Cambridge University Press, 1977); 67; Bullock, *A History of Negro Education,* 44–52; Anderson. *Education of Blacks,* 23; Horace Mann Bond, *The Education of the Negro in the American Social Order* (New York: Prentice Hall, 1934): 115.

42. Anderson, *Education of Blacks,* 23; Bullock, *History of Negro Education,* 44–52.

43. According to Anderson, "[P]roponents of southern industrialization increasingly viewed mass schooling as a means to produce efficient and contented labor and as a socialization process to instill in black and white children an acceptance of the southern racial hierarchy" (Anderson, *Education of Blacks,* 27). Anderson also noted, "[T]his model of education reflected both market interests and the interests of maintaining the existing racial hierarchy" (James D. Anderson, "Education as a vehicle for the manipulation of black workers," in *Work, Technology, and Education: Dissenting Essays in the Intellectual Foundations of American Education,* ed. W. Feinberg and H. J. Rosemont, [Urbana: University of Illinois Press, 1975], 15–40). See also, James D. Anderson, "Northern foundations and southern rural black education, 1921–1935," *History of Education Quarterly* 18, (Winter 1978): 371–396.

44. Anderson argued that the "oppression of black schoolchildren during the critical stage of the transformation of American secondary education seriously affected the long-term development of education in the black community and was one of the fundamental reasons that the education of Black Americans lagged far behind that of other Americans"(Anderson, *Education of Blacks,* 113).

45. Anderson. *Education of Blacks,* 111.

46. Anderson, *Education of Blacks,* 114; Bullock, *History of Negro Education,* 48.

47. One of the colleges that successfully resisted this pressure was Tillotson College in Austin, Texas.

48. Anderson, *Education of Blacks,* 112; Bullock, *History of Negro Education,* 54.

49. Indeed, Hearne, Texas, where Iola Taylor was born and raised, was noted for its school that emphasized classical and higher education. Taylor Interview, OHC.

50. Anderson, *Education of Blacks,* 181–182.

51. Taylor Interview, OHC.

52. Bernard I. Miller, "Some Anticipated Problems Incident to Racial Integration in the Public Schools and Some Suggested Approaches to the Problems," *Journal of Negro Education* 21 (1955): 285–292.

53. Several of the Black teachers recalled their aunts, uncles, or other family members describing how they, as teachers, had to pay a "kickback" to the White school administrators to keep their teaching positions prior to the mid-1940s.

54. Kluger, *Simple Justice,* 1975.

55. Kluger, *Simple Justice,* 1975; Gunnar Myrdal, *An American Dilemma* (New York: Harper & Bros., 1944; McGraw-Hill paperback, 1964); Bennett Jr. *Before the Mayflower,* 260.

56. Dubois and other Black leaders believed that education should provide training for direct political empowerment along with an intellectual curriculum, especially at the college level. By 1905 DuBois and the Black leaders organized the Niagara Movement, which advocated direct action to achieve civil rights for Blacks. By 1910 the Niagara Movement had organized the National Association for the Advancement of Colored People. Carol D. Lee and Diana T. Slaughter-Defoe, "Historical and sociocultural influences on African American education," in *Handbook of Research on Multicultural Education,* ed.

James A. Banks and Cherry A. McGee Banks (New York: Macmillan Publishing, 1995), 348–371.

57. Until the end of the Civil War, White ownership of African Americans was legally protected throughout the South. Although the Emancipation Proclamation promised freedom to slaves, that promise proved hypocritical. A system of enforced racial separation throughout both public and private life emerged during the latter half of the nineteenth century and the first half of the twentieth century. The legacy of segregation left the nation divided along economic, cultural, and geographic racial lines.

58. *Brown v. Board of Education of Topeka, Kansas,* 347 U.S. 483 (1954) and 355 U.S. 294 (1955).

59. Davison M. Douglas, *Reading, Writing, and Race: The Desegregation of the Charlotte Schools* (Chapel Hill: The University of North Carolina Press, 1995); Kluger, *Simple Justice*; Mann, *The Walls of Jericho,* 463.

60. Robin M. Williams Jr., and Margaret W. Ryan, *Schools in Transition* (Chapel Hill: The University of North Carolina Press, 1954), 247.

61. On Monday, May 17, 1954, the U. S. Supreme Court declared segregation to be unconstitutional. Chief Justice Earl B. Warren: "Does segregation of children in public schools solely on the basis of race, even though the physical facilities and other 'tangible' factors may be equal, deprive the children of the minority group of equal educational opportunities? We believe it does. We cannot turn the clock back to 1868 when the Fourteenth Amendment was adopted, or even to 1896, when Plessey versus Ferguson was written. . . . We conclude that in the field of public education the doctrine of 'separate but equal' has no place." A year later the Court ordered public school desegregation "with all deliberate speed." *Brown v. Board of Education of Topeka, Kansas,* 347 U.S. 483 (1954). In fact, most public schools in the Southern states remained segregated until the mid–1970s.

62. Each regional area within the United States argued they belonged to a unique, cultural area. However, segregationists within the South used this argument as a justification for segregation, in particular during the decade following the *Brown* decision.

63. Guy B. Johnson, "Freedom, Equality, and Segregation," in *Integration versus Segregation,* ed. Hubert H. Humphrey (New York: Thomas Y. Crowell, 1964), 100.

64. For a fuller discussion of the concept of "Southern State of Mind," see James M. Dabbs, *The Southern Heritage* (New York: Alfred A. Knopf, 1958), 68–131; James J. Jackson, *The Southern Case for School Segregation* (New York: Crowell-Collier, 1962), 20–21; Albert Blaustein and Clarence C. Ferguson, Jr., *Desegregation and the Law: The Meaning and Effect of the School Segregation Cases* (New Brunswick: Rutgers University Press, 1957), 211. Please note that these books, written shortly after the *Brown* decision, depict numerous people's reactions to that decision. This state of mind was not restricted to the South during the 1950s and early 1960s. In fact, these feelings were common among many citizens of the United States.

65. McCain, "Reactions to the U. S. Supreme Court Decision of 1954": 373.

66. Harold C. Fleming, "Resistance Movements and Racial Desegregation," *Annals of the American Academy* 304 (1956): 46–50; Frederick B. Routh and Paul Anthony, "Southern Resistance Forces," *Phylon* 18 (1957): 50–58; Lyndon Baines Johnson Papers (hereafter referred to as LBJ papers), United States Senate Files, 1949–1961, 1956 General Files—Civil Rights, Box 567, Lyndon Baines Johnson Library, University of Texas, Austin (hereafter referred to as LBJ Library).

67. United States Constitution, Tenth Amendment; Robert Brisbane, "Interposition: Theory and Fact," *Phylon* 17 (1956): 12–16; Reed Sarratt, *The Ordeal of Desegregation: The First Decade* (New York: Harper and Row, 1966), 38–39; report on Interposition (no author, title, or date), LBJ Papers, United States Senate Files, 1949–1961, Office Files of George Reedy, 1956–1957, Reedy: Convention 1956, Box 418, LBJ Library; Mann, *The Walls of Jericho,*160.

68. Mann, *The Walls of Jericho,*163; Congressional Record 3/12/56, 4460–4464, Office Files of George Reedy, Box 423, LBJ Library.

69. Marvin Brooks Norfleet, *Forced School Integration in the U. S. A.* (New York: Carlton Press, 1961); 51, 55.

70. David J. Garrow, *Bearing the Cross: Martin Luther King, Jr., and the Southern Christian Leadership Conference* (New York: Vintage Books, 1986); Taylor Branch, *Parting the Waters: America in the King Years 1954–63* (New York: Simon and Schuster, 1988); Kluger, *Simple Justice,* 1975.

71. Garrow, *Bearing the Cross;* Branch, *Parting the Waters;* Kluger, *Simple Justice.*

72. The other states were Florida, North Carolina, and Tennessee.

73. The Alabama law specified criteria for assignment that included available room, teaching capacity, available transportation, adequacy of a student's scholastic aptitude and preparation, psychological qualifications of the pupil, possibility or threat of friction or disorder, home environment, and morals. Wilson, "Stranger in a Strange Land": 150–155; Sarratt, *Ordeal of Desegregation, 32.*

74. Kluger, *Simple Justice;* Garrow, *Bearing the Cross;* Sarratt, *Ordeal of Desegregation.*

75. This comment is a consensus of the oral history interviews of all the teachers.

76. Beginning in 1948, Mexican American students were classified as White for purposes of residence.

77. In 1955, Austin Independent School District Board of Trustees initiated the school desegregation process at the high school level, grades ten through twelve. At this time, Austin had expanded the high school system by opening A. N. McCallum and W. B. Travis High Schools in addition to the S. F. Austin and L. C. Anderson High Schools. Five years later, 1960, a fifth high school was opened, A. S. Johnston High School. Despite the *Brown* decision, Austin, McCallum, and Travis High Schools remained all-White, Johnston was predominantly Mexican American and Anderson was the Black high school.

78. Between 1955 and 1968, numerous articles appeared in Austin's newspapers claiming that Austin's schools were "integrated." For example, "Austin Faculty Integrated" appeared the day of the transfer of the first three cross-over teachers in 1964. In 1970, the League of Women Votes issued a report that stated all the public schools in Austin were integrated. However, Austin was in the midst of a lawsuit that charged AISD was out of compliance with the federal guidelines regarding desegregated schools.

CHAPTER FOUR
MOVING FROM THE SHADOWS INTO THE SUNLIGHT

1. Myrdal, *The American Dilemma,* cited in Woodward, *The Strange Career of Jim Crow,* 118.

2. Patterson Interview, OHC.

3. R. W. Irvine and J. J. Irvine, "The Impact of the Desegregation Process on the Education of Black Students: Key Variables," *Journal of Negro Education* 52 (4): 419.

4. "In every aspect of the child's life a trusted elder, neighbor, Sunday school teachers, school teacher, or other community member might instruct, discipline, assist, or otherwise guide the young of a given family. Second, as role models, community members show an example to and interest in the young people. Third, as advocates they actively intercede with major segments of society (a responsibility assumed by professional educators) to help young members of particular families find opportunities which otherwise would be closed to them. Fourth, as supportive figures, they simply inquire about the progress of the young, take a special interest in them. Fifth, in the formal roles of teacher, leader, elder, they serve youth generally as part of the general role or occupation" (A. Billingsley, *Black Families in White America* [Englewood Cliffs, NJ: Prentice Hall, 1968], 99).

5. Akins Interview, OHC.

6. Akins, Patterson, and Chambers Interviews, OHC.

7. Oral History Interviews with Melvin Chambers between January and February 1997, in Austin, Texas. The interview tapes are deposited at the Oral History Collection, Center for the History of Education, The University of Texas at Austin. Hereinafter referenced Chambers Interview, OHC.

8. Taylor Interview, OHC. Her brother has a doctorate in constitutional law from the University of Indiana. He is currently the chairperson of the Department of Political Science at San Diego State University.

9. Ibid.

10. Ibid.

11. Ibid.

12. Ibid.

13. Ibid.

14. The separate law school was to have "substantially equal facilities" as the University of Oklahoma law school. (Kluger, *Simple Justice*, 258).

15. Marshall's brief declared, "[Cl]assification and distinctions based on race or color have no moral or legal validity in our society. Segregation in public education helps to preserve a caste system which is based upon race and color. It is designed and intended to perpetuate the slave tradition. . . . Equality, even if the term be limited to a comparison of physical facilities, is and can never be achieved . . . the terms 'separate' and 'equal' can not be used conjunctively in a situation of this kind; there can be no separate equality" (Kluger, *Simple Justice*, 259).

16. The United States Supreme Court held that "Oklahoma had to provide Ada Sipuel with a legal education in conformity with the equal protection clause of the 14th Amendment and provide it as soon as it does for applicants of any other group" *(Sipuel v. Oklahoma State Board of Regents,* 332 U. S. 631 [1948]).

17. One law school professor said: "It is a fake, it is a fraud, and . . . I think it is indecent" (Kluger, *Simple Justice*, 258–261).

18. Kluger, *Simple Justice*, 260.

19. Ibid., 261.

20. Marshall challenged the constitutionality of Texas laws by showing "that segregation's statutes in the state of Texas . . . have no line of reasonableness. There is no under-

standable factual basis for classification by race, and under a long line of decisions by the Supreme Court, not on the question of Negroes, but on the Fourteenth Amendment, all courts agree that if there is no rational basis for the classification, it is flat in the teeth of the Fourteenth Amendment" (Kluger, *Simple Justice,* 264).

21. *McLaurin v. Oklahoma State Regents for Higher Education,* 339 U. S. 637 (1950); Kluger, *Simple Justice,* 265.

22. Kluger, *Simple Justice,* 267; Willis D. Hawley, ed., *Effective School Desegregation: Equity, Quality, and Feasibility* (Beverly Hills: Sage Publications: 1981); James H. Laue, ed., *Direct Action and Desegregation, 1960–1962: Toward a Theory of the Rationalization of Protest* (New York: Carlson Publishing: 1989); Wolters, *The Burden of Brown;* Stephan and Feagin, eds., *School Desegregation.*

23. For the first time, the U. S. Supreme Court asserted that "Our society grows increasingly complex, and our need for trained leaders increases correspondingly. Appellant's case represents, perhaps, the epitome of that need, for he is attempting to obtain an advanced degree in education, to become, by definition, a leader and trainer of others. Those who will come under his guidance and influence must be directly affected by the education he receives. Their own education and development will necessarily suffer to the extent that his training is unequal to that of his classmates. State-imposed restricts which produce such inequalities cannot be sustained. . . . There is a vast difference—a Constitutional difference—between restrictions imposed by the state which prohibit the intellectual commingling of students, and the refusal of individuals to commingle where the state presents no such bar. . . . The removal of the state restrictions will not necessarily abate individual and group predilections and choices. But at the very least, the state will not be depriving appellant of the opportunity to secure acceptance by his fellow students on his own merits"(Kluger, *Simple Justice,* 282; *McLaurin v. Oklahoma State Regents for Higher Education,* 339 U. S. 637 [1950]).

24. Finding VIII from *Brown v. Board of Education,* 98 F. Supp. 797 (1951) cited in Kluger, *Simple Justice,* 424.

25. *Brown v. Board of Education,* United States Supreme Court, May 31, 1955, 349 U.S. 294, 75 S. Ct. 753.

26. *Report of the United States Commission on Civil Rights, 1959* (Washington, DC: Government Printing Office, 1959): 201; William H. Jones, "Desegregation of Public Education in Texas—One Year Afterward," *Journal of Negro Education* 24 (1955): 350–351; Jimmy Banks, *Money, Marbles, and Chalk: The Wondrous World of Texas Politics* (Austin: Texas Publishing Company, 1971).

27. Allan Shivers to Dwight D. Eisenhower, July 16, 1953, in James C. Duram, *A Moderate among Extremists: Dwight D. Eisenhower and the School Desegregation Crisis* (Chicago: Nelson-Hall, 1981), 60.

28. *Austin American,* May 18, 1954, n. p. Jones, "Desegregation of Public Education in Texas—One Year Afterward": 352.

29. Jones, "Desegregation of Public Education in Texas—One Year Afterward."

30. *Southern School News,* October 1954.

31. Kluger, *Simple Justice,* 734.

32. Five Black students eventually attended the previously all-White elementary school. There were no Black high school students.

33. Lorene Barbee, "Big Spring Independent School District Desegregation, 1955," *The Permian Historical Annual XXVII* (1987): 61–72.

34. In particular, Citizens' Councils were organized in Arlington, Beaumont, Dallas, Forth Worth, Galena Park, Houston, Kilgore, LaGrange, Mansfield, Marshall, Orange, Texarkana, and Waco. In November 1955, 250 members from twelve chapters organized the Associated Citizens' Council of Texas. The chairman, Ross Carlton of Dallas, claimed, "Negroes have . . . become unwitting and dumb tools of the Communistic propagandists in the NAACP" (*Dallas Morning News,* July 23, 29, November 12, 13, 1955. Cited in Robyn Duff Ladino, *Desegregating Texas Schools: Eisenhower, Shivers and the Crisis at Mansfield High* [Austin: University of Texas Press, 1996], 41).

35. There were fewer than five black families living in Big Springs at this time.

36. Barbee, "Big Spring Independent School District Desegregation, 1955": 61–72.

37. Ibid., 63.

38. The Citizens' Council lawsuit was based on the Texas statute prohibiting commingling of public school funds for Black and White children. In 1905, Texas mandated separation of public funds for schooling of White and Black children: "All available public school funds of this State shall be appropriated in each county for the education alike of white and colored children, and impartial provisions shall be made for both races. No white children shall attend schools supported for colored children, nor shall colored children attend schools supported for white children. The terms 'colored race' and 'colored children,' as used in this title, include all persons of mixed blood descended from Negro ancestry" (*Texas Revised Civil Statute Annotated,* art. 2900, enacted in 1905).

39. Arguments of Attorney General John Ben Sheppard of Texas before the Supreme Court of Texas in *McKinney et al. v. Blankenship et al.*, Supreme Court of Texas, 282 S. W. 2nd 691, October 12, 1955.

40. *McKinney et al. v. Blankenship et al.,* Supreme Court of Texas, 282 S. W. 2nd 691, October 12, 1955.

41. Barbee, "Big Spring Independent School District Desegregation, 1955," 61–72.

42. United Press Release, April 19, 1955, *Archives of Moorehead Papers,* Center for American History, The University of Texas at Austin. Hereinafter referenced *Moorehead Papers.*

43. Ladino, *Desegregating Texas Schools,* 6–7.

44. This decision is commonly referred to as *Brown v. Board of Education of Topeka, Kansas,* 355 U.S. 294 (1955).

45. Ladino, *Desegregating Texas Schools,* 75–76.

46. The NAACP sent directives to all its chapters shortly after the *Brown II* decision. The directives advised how to move school boards toward desegregation and defined anticipated difficulties arising from the decision. "The decision places a challenge on the good faith of the public officials, on the militancy of Negroes and on the integrity of the federal courts . . . we must be prepared to meet the challenge. . . . Our branches must seek to determine in each community whether the school board is prepared to make a prompt and reasonable start towards integration. . . . Promises unaccompanied by concrete action are meaningless; nor can there be concern with the attitudes of individuals towards a change in the school system. Segregated schools are illegal, . . . the Court . . . does not allow time to procrastinate, stall or evade. "The directives included eight steps" 1. Immediately file a petition with the local school board emphasizing the *Brown II* rulings and offering branch

assistance in solving problems to integration; 2. Periodically check on the school board's integration plans to ensure compliance with the Court's decision; 3. Emphasize over the summer and fall months, during all meetings and discussions within the black community, the importance of understanding the implementation and enforcement decrees of *Brown II* and the role of the lower federal courts in school integration; 4. Inform and organize black families in the community into a knowledgeable group ready to be considered plaintiffs in lawsuits if school integration does not occur; 5. Seek the support of liberal and moderate groups within the local white community, considering especially, churches, labor and civic organizations, and sympathetic individuals; 6. When the school board has prepared a plan, request the "exact text" and notify the state conference and national offices for consultation; 7. If no plans are made by the beginning of the 1955 school year, "the time for a lawsuit has arrived. At this stage court action is essential because only in this way does the mandate of the Supreme Court . . . become fully operative on the school boards in question"; and 8, the final step, the matter should be turned over to the NAACP Fund and handled in the courts ("Directives to the Branches Adopted by emergency Southwide NAACP Conference," *Crisis* 62 [June-July 1955], 339–340, 380; Ladino, *Desegregating Texas Schools,* 73–74).

47. *Jackson v. Rawdon,* United States District Court, Texas, Civ. No. 3152, November 21, 1955, 135 F. Supp. 936, United States Court of Appeals, Fifth Circuit, June 28, 1956, Civ. No. 15927

48. Fear of communism was rampant during the 1950s and allegations linking communism and the NAACP were common among segregationists. These rumors were fueled by Senator Joe McCarthy and J. Edgar Hoover. *Mansfield News,* October 27, 1955; "Texas School Told to Integrate," *Texas Observer,* August 1, 1956. Cited in Ladino, *Desegregating Texas Schools,* 81–82.

49. *Mansfield News,* October 27, 1955; "Texas School Told to Integrate," *Texas Observer,* August 1, 1956. Cited in Ladino, *Desegregating Texas Schools,* 82.

50. *Southern School News,* August 1956; *Moorehead Papers,* Box 4Ze233; Ladino, *Desegregating Texas Schools,* 88–89.

51. Ladino, *Desegregating Texas Schools,* 90.

52. Davis's telegram read "A valid order from a United States court has been entered directing admission of Negro students to the High School at Mansfield, Texas. I understand the Board will enroll them in good faith and the students want to enroll. This morning a mob of 300 men gathered at the school to prevent their enrollment. The sheriff of this county has been diligent, but advises me his force is inadequate to control a mob of such proportion. Violence is almost certain to occur when these students attempt to enroll on Friday unless additional law enforcement officers are dispatched to this area. These Negro students are exercising a constitutional right and the full strength of law enforcement agencies of the state should protect them if law and order is to prevail in our great state. I call upon you as Governor to cause to be dispatched additional law enforcement officers to Mansfield to assure that law and order will be maintained and that these students will be protected in their right to attend Mansfield High School. I respectfully request answer will contact you tomorrow if necessary" (Ladino, *Desegregating Texas Schools,* 98–99).

53. Shivers issued two press memoranda from his office in Austin on August 31, 1956: "Law and order must be maintained in Mansfield, as in the rest of Texas. Neither the Governor's Office nor the Department of Public Safety has received any request from the

Tarrant County sheriff for assistance. When and if such a request is made, it will be honored. I am certainly not inclined to move state officers into Mansfield at the call of a lawyer affiliated with the National Association for Advancement of Colored People, whose premature and unwise efforts have created this unfortunate situation at Mansfield. [He then outlined a three step plan] 1. Under the general powers of the Governor to enforce the laws and see that order is kept in Texas, I have instructed Colonel Garrison to send Texas Rangers to Mansfield to cooperate with local authorities in preserving peace. 2. I have talked by telephone with R. L. Huffman, superintendent . . . and have wired O. C. Rawdon, . . . urging that the Board go ahead and transfer out of the district any scholastics, white or colored, whose attendance or attempts to attend Mansfield High School would reasonably be calculated to incite violence. These transfers should be for the general welfare, to preserve peace and orderly conduct, and not for any other reason. This action would be in line with the U. S. Supreme Court decision in the Lucy Case in Alabama. 3. I have asked Colonel Garrison to instruct his men to arrest anyone, white or colored, whose actions are such as to represent a threat to the peace at Mansfield" (Ladino, *Desegregating Texas Schools,* 102).

54. Angela Roberts and Kelly Nichols, "Harlem School Built on Site in Historic Black Community," *The Baytown Sun* (nd, np).

55. Notes of interview with Beth McPhail (1987). *Moorehead Papers.*

56. Notes of interview with Chris Richard (1987). *Moorehead Papers.*

57. Notes of interview with Chris Richard (1987). *Moorehead Papers.*

58. Johnella Boynton, "Trustees Hope to Integrate Harlem Through 'Enrichment,'" *The Baytown Sun,* February 25, 1964; 1–2. Chris Pendergrass, "Majority of Trustees are for Action," *The Baytown Sun,* May 29, 1964; 1–2. One year later, the Goose Creek Consolidated Independent School District spent $90,000 to build the new Pumphrey Elementary School, in the middle of an all-White neighborhood, which could house three times the number of students that Harlem Elementary could.

59. "Compliance with Civil rights Act Voted," *The Baytown Sun,* May 11, 1965, 1; "Here is Complete Text of School Board's Desegregation Order," *The Baytown Sun,* May 11, 1965, 2.

60. "Faculty Desegregation Starts in School Here," *The Baytown Sun,* June 16, 1966, 1; Notes of interview with Arthur Coltharp (1987). *Moorehead Papers.*

61. Notes of interview with Arthur Coltharp (1987). *Moorehead Papers.*

62. "Compliance with Civil rights Act Voted," *The Baytown Sun,* May 11, 1965, 1; "Here is Complete Text of School Board's Desegregation Order," *The Baytown Sun,* May 11, 1965, 2; "More Integration Due in Schools Here," *The Baytown Sun,* August 30, 1965, 1.

63. "Compliance with Civil Rights Act Voted," *The Baytown Sun,* May 11, 1965, 1; "Here is Complete Text of School Board's Desegregation Order," *The Baytown Sun,* May 11, 1965, 2; "More Integration Due in Schools Here," *The Baytown Sun,* August 30, 1965, 1.

64. Four of these were small, one-room schools with enrollments ranging from twenty-eight to fifty-eight. One Black school had an enrollment of 198.

65. The League of Women Voters of Austin, "Austin: School Desegregation, 1954–1970," October 1, 1970: n.p.

66. With a total student population of 25,178, 66 percent were White (16,498), 20 percent were Mexican-Americans (5,042), and 14 percent were African Americans (3,638).

"Brief Background Information on Integration in Austin, Texas: June 4, 1968." (Unpublished document compiled by Austin School Board). Updated January 14, 1970: 7–8.

67. The term *east side* was commonly used to designate the area bounded by the Travis County line on the east, the Colorado River and Town Lake on the south, Congress Avenue and San Jacinto Street on the west, and east 19th Street on the north. The majority of Austin's segregated schools were located in this area.

68. *Texas Constitution,* art. 7 § 7, enacted 1876 and *Texas Revised Civil Statute Annotated,* art. 2900, enacted 1905.

69. In 1954, Austin High School was one of three Austin high schools open to enrollment by non-Black students.

70. Akins Interview, OHC.

71. The early 1900s witnessed Black men willing to die for their country and freedom returning from overseas to a nation, a state, and a city where their opportunities for jobs, educational opportunities, and residences, to name a few, were severely restricted by segregation. In Austin, as in other cities in the South, Jim Crow reigned supreme. Many Black men were unwilling to quietly return to a life limited by segregation, and in many areas of the South, including Texas, bitter race riots erupted. Although San Antonio and Houston experienced "wanton destruction of Negro life and property . . . in 1919," Austin experienced no riots. However, rumors flooded the city in the late summer of 1919. The *Austin American* reported, "Without detailing all the rumors and 'confidential tips' and many 'I know to be a fact,' the net result is that the rumors have created a certain amount of apprehension in some quarters of both whites and Negroes, but there is no special reason for alarm or uneasiness, unless of course, some excitable, harebrained person would 'start trouble.' [Plott said] I have no concrete evidence that there will be any trouble but I have made arrangements to have the city whistle give five blasts to call together all of Austin's thirty policemen and detectives in case they are needed." Fortunately, the race riots spared Austin. Many attributed Austin's lack of riots to the Black community's antipathy toward violence. Reports from the St. John's Baptist Association August 31 meeting reveal their attitudes, "We refer especially to those magazines, newspapers, and periodicals published by Negroes that magnify the wrong and minimize the good. . . . There seems to be an organized effort against the whites of the South . . . the saner cause is to strive for friendship and helpful cooperation of the southern people." Austin's Black community's conciliatory attitude surfaced many times during their quest for civil rights. (Robert L. Sangrado, *The Black Experience in America* [Austin, TX: University of Texas Press, 1970], 146; "Those Rumors of Race Current in Austin," *Austin American,* August 3, 1919, n. p.; "Austin Negroes Speak Against Agitators of Race Organization," *Austin American,* September 1, 1919, n.p. The St. John's Baptist Association had an active membership of approximately 20,000 Blacks who resided in the Austin area).

72. "Resolution on Integration." Attachment to Austin School Board Minutes, August 8, 1955.

73. "Resolution on Integration," 2

74. *Austin American,* September 1, 1955: n.p.

75. The transfer rules included: (1) continue policy of transferring pupils for reasons of health or handicap (2) allow a child to remain in his/her old school (3) allow children to transfer in event of hardship (4) maintain certain designated schools as "open schools" to which children from any residential zone could transfer, and (5) allow transfers for conve-

nience of schools in balancing building load. Of particular interest, the only "open schools" were Negro schools, Anderson high, and Kealing junior high (*Austin American,* June 15, 1955: n.p.)

76. "Other Acts Accompany Integration," *Austin-American Statesman,* August 10, 1955; "Liberalized Plan Put Before School," *Austin-American Statesman,* June 14, 1955; "Pupil Transfer System Looks to Desegregation," *Austin-American Statesman,* June 15, 1955; "School Board May Eye Integration at Meeting," *Austin-American Statesman,* July 11, 1955; "Full Integration Effect Uncertain," *Austin-American Statesman,* August 9, 1955; "Three High Schools Get 13 Negroes," *Austin-American Statesman,* September 2, 1955: n.p.

77. "Brief Background Information on Integration in Austin, Texas: June 4, 1968" (Unpublished document compiled by Austin School Board). Updated January 14, 1970: 18

78. The League of Women Voters of Austin, "Austin: School Desegregation, 1954–1970," October 1, 1970: n.p.. "Brief Background Information on Integration in Austin, Texas: June 4, 1968" (Unpublished document compiled by Austin School Board). Updated January 14, 1970: 18

79. The League of Women Voters of Austin, "Austin: School Desegregation, 1954–1970," October 1, 1970: n.p.

80. Akins Interview, OHC.

81. Taylor Interview, OHC.

82. *The Dallas Morning News,* September 5, 1963: n.p.

83. Ibid.

84. Akins and Taylor Interviews, OHC.

85. "Brief Background Information on Integration in Austin, Texas: June 4, 1968" (Unpublished document compiled by the Austin School Board and updated January 14, 1970).

CHAPTER FIVE
WITH ALL DELIBERATE SLOWNESS

1. *Austin American,* September 11, 1964: n.p.

2. Ibid.

3. Ibid.

4. Ibid.

5. Ibid.

6. Ibid.

7. Ibid.

8. Ibid.

9. Ibid.

10. Ibid.

11. Ibid.

12. Ibid.

13. Ibid.

14. Taylor Interview, OHC.

15. Ibid.

16. Ibid.

17. Ibid.

18. Ibid.

19. Ibid.

20. A letter to each parent from Irby Carruth, dated May 10, 1966, regarding school choice.

21. "TSTA Integrates," *The Texas Outlook* 48, 12 (December 1964); 15.

22. Vernon McDaniel, *The History of the Teachers State Association of Texas* (Washington, DC: National Education Association, 1977), 86-87.

23. Skimming the News," *The Texas Outlook* 49, 6 (June, 1965): 7.

24. Smither Interview, OHC.

25. Ibid.

26. Ibid.

27. Ibid.

28. Ibid.

29. Ibid.

30. Akins and Taylor Interviews, OHC.

31. Taylor Interview, OHC.

32. Akins Interview, OHC.

33. Ibid.

34. Ibid.

35. Ibid.

36. Taylor Interview, OHC.

37. Ibid.

38. Ibid.

39. Ibid.

40. Ibid.

41. Ibid.

42. Smith Interview, OHC.

43. Ibid.

44. William L. Katz, *Teachers' Guide to American Negro History* (Chicago: Quadrangle Books, 1968), 8.

45. Smith Interview, OHC.

46. Ibid.

47. Taylor Interview, OHC.

48. A consensus of the Taylor, Smith, and Akins Interviews, OHC.

49. "School board to Follow HEW Steps," *Austin American,* August 15, 1968, 1–8.

50. "The Forward Look of a Minority Teacher," Iola Taylor, *The Austin Classroom Teacher* 3, 1 (August 1968): n.p.

51. All records of TEDTAC were destroyed when the office closed in the mid-1970s.

52. Taylor Interview, OHC.

53. Ibid.

54. Ibid.

55. Ibid.

56. *Green v. Board*, 391 U. S. 430[1968], 438–439. Emphasis in original.

57. The superimposition of the Negro attendance zone guaranteed that Negro students would attend only Negro schools while White students would go to White schools.

58. Letter to Superintendent Carruth from Jerold D. Ward, chief, Dallas Educational Branch of the Office for Civil Rights, Department of Health, Education, and Welfare. August 26, 1968.

59. "School Plan 'Splits' Board," *Austin American*, December 20, 1968, 1–4.

60. Ibid.

61. Ibid.

CHAPTER SIX
NO WHITE MISSIONARIES NEED APPLY

1. The first federal advisory group proposed changing the Anderson attendance boundaries, including extending the northern edge from East 19th Street to the intersection of the Interregional Highway (IH-35) and East 49th Street. The boundary change would have brought the predominantly White Maplewood school into the Anderson district. The second federal advisory group proposed the conversion of Anderson high to a junior high (dividing the Anderson High students between Austin and Johnston High schools) and changing the all-Negro Kealing Junior High to a middle school for grades five and six. "Federal Desegregation Plans Rejected by School Board," *American Statesman*, January 10, 1969, 1, 6; "Desegregation Plan Proposals are Given," *Austin American*, February 27, 1969, 2.

2. Board president Roy Butler stated, "The result of [Austin's] plan will add approximately 68 non-Negro pupils to the Anderson High student body." When asked if the plan would be acceptable to the federal government, Butler replied, "I don't know. We will submit it and see." Several of the board members said they were willing to defend the board's actions in court. "Closing of Anderson Opposed," *Austin American*, January 9, 1969, 1, 6; "Federal Desegregation Plans Rejected by School Board," *American Statesman*, January 10, 1969, 1, 6; "Rotarians Briefed on Austin Schools," *Austin American*, January 29, 1969, 1.

3. "Austin Races School Plan Funds Cutoff," *Austin American*, February 27, 1969, 1, 6; "School Panel Plans HEW Funds Talks," *Austin American*, March 18, 1969, 1; "Letter to HEW Says School Plans 'Justified,'" *Austin American*, March 7, 1969, 1, 6.

4. "NAACP Head Chides Austin Schools," *American Statesman*, February 16, 1969, 1.

5. Patterson Interview, OHC.

6. The Austin ISD moved closer to losing $2.3 million in federal funds when HEW rejected its latest desegregation plan. "HEW Again Nixes Integration Plan," *Austin American*, May 1, 1969, 1, 2; "School board's Mission to HEW" *Austin American*, May 4, 1969, 8; "School board told to Prepare 'Proof,'" *Austin American*, May 7, 1969, 1, 3; "Third Desegregation proposal Attempt Due," *Austin American*, May 8, 1969, 1, 3; "Trustees Assume

Guarded Optimism," *Austin American,* May 9, 1969, 1, 4; "HEW Visits Austin Next Week," *Austin American,* May 17, 1969, 2; "Integration Team Due in Austin," *American Statesman,* May 22, 1969, 1; "Pickle Defends School Board on Integration Issues," *American Statesman,* May 22, 1969, 3; "School Board, HEW Will Meet Today," *American Statesman,* May 23, 1969, 1, 6; "Austin Schools to Comply, but Will Seek Own Plan," *American Statesman,* May 24, 1969, 1, 6; "Anderson High Students Petition to Retain School," *American Statesman,* May 29, 1969, 1, 6.

7. Chambers Interview, OHC.

8. Letter to parents from Roy Butler, president of AISD Board of Trustees, July 15, 1969.

9. Roy Butler Letter, July 15, 1969.

10. Oral History Interview with E. Ann Stoll, February 1997, at her home in Austin, Texas. Mrs. Stoll lives in Austin, Texas. She taught social studies during and after desegregation. The interview tapes are deposited at the Oral History Collection, Center for the History of Education, The University of Texas at Austin. Hereinafter referenced Stoll Interview, OHC.

11. Oral History Interview with Tom T. Allen, February 1997, at his office in Austin, Texas. Mr. Allen lives in Austin, Texas. He taught the sciences during and after desegregation. The interview tapes are deposited at the Oral History Collection, Center for the History of Education, The University of Texas at Austin. Hereinafter referenced Allen Interview, OHC.

12. Oral History Interview with Herbert Brown, February 1997, at author's office in Austin, Texas. Mr. Brown lives in Austin, Texas. He was a coach and taught the sciences during and after desegregation. The interview tapes are deposited at the Oral History Collection, Center for the History of Education, The University of Texas at Austin. Hereinafter referenced Brown Interview, OHC.

13. Austin school board trustees submitted another desegregation plan to HEW. This plan would close Anderson High School, Kealing Junior High, and St. John's Elementary. The plan would redraw boundary lines between seven east side elementary schools. Students displaced by the closing of Anderson High and Kealing Junior High would be bused to formerly all-White high schools. "Eastside Schools Face Shutdown," *Austin American,* June 10, 1969 1, 4; "Board Discusses Special Education," *Austin American,* June 13, 1969, 1; "Prospects Slim on Two-Way Busing; Board Meets June 23," *Austin American,* June 17, 1969, 1; "Segregation Plan to Be Discussed," *Austin American,* June 18, 1969, 1; "Citizens May Take Bus Plan to HEW," *Austin American,* June 19, 1969, 1; "East Austin Group Blocks Newsman," *Austin American,* June 20, 1969, 1, 6; 'Austin School Desegregation," *Austin American,* June 20, 1969, 1; "NAACP Supports School Plan," *American Statesman,* June 21, 1969, 1; "Bus Plan Outlined by E. Austinites," *American Statesman,* June 22, 1969, 1; "Board Will Hear Busing Opponents," *Austin American,* June 23, 1969, 1, 6; "3 School Closing, Bus Plan Dropped," *Austin American,* June 24, 1969, 1, 6; "Year of Grace to Follow Rejection of Busing Plan," *Austin American,* June 25, 1969, 1, 6; "At Crossroads on School Issue," *Austin American,* June 25, 1969, 10.

14. "Nixon Eases Rule on Desegregation," *Austin American,* July 4, 1969, 1, 6; "Austin hails 'Extra Time,'" *Austin American,* 4 July 1969, 1, 6; "Nixon Said 'Breaking the Law,'" *American Statesman,* July 4, 1969, 1; "A Chance (Slim) for School Plan," *Austin American,* July 10, 1969, 13; "Letter From HEW," *Austin American,* July 14, 1969, 12;

"Official Appeal to HEW Voted," *Austin American,* July 15, 1969, 1, 6; "Whites Ignoring School Race Plea," *Austin American,* July 25, 1969, 1.

15. "Nixon Eases Rule on Desegregation," *American Statesman,* July 4, 1969, 1.

16. "Austin Hails 'Extra Time,' " *Austin American,* July 4, 1969, 1.

17. Akins Interview, OHC.

18. Ibid.

19. "One White teacher for every Black teacher in a previously all-Negro high school. That was the goal of Austin's school trustees in their June 23 desegregation plan. At Anderson, Kealing, and several predominantly Negro elementary schools, the desegregation process is White into Black. It is the other way around at the predominantly White schools, which make up the bulk of the local schools." "Black Into White is Integration Pattern," *Austin American,* July 26, 1969, 1, 6; "Four Transfer to Anderson High Received by Board," *American Statesman,* July 31, 1969, 1.

20. "Desegregation Rules Outlined," *American Statesman,* August 22, 1969, 1, 12; "School Integration Said Going Well," *American Statesman,* September 10, 1969, 1.

21. Oral History Interview with James Dorsett, January 1997, at his home in Manor, Texas. He was a coach and taught industrial arts during and after desegregation. The interview tapes are deposited at the Oral History Collection, Center for the History of Education, The University of Texas at Austin. Hereinafter referenced Dorsett Interview, OHC.

22. Dorsett Interview, OHC.

23. Ibid.

24. Brown Interview, OHC.

25. Stoll Interview, OHC.

26. Allen Interview, OHC.

27. "Examiner to Hear Austin Plan," *American Statesman,* October 11, 1969, 1; "Local School Desegregation Hearing Jan. 20 in Dallas," *American Statesman,* December 3, 1969, 1.

28. *Morehead Papers;* Austin ISD Board of Trustees Minutes, 1964–1971 inclusive. The minutes identify new hires, transfers, retirements, leaves of absence, and resignations.

29. Oral History Interview with Clifford McPherson, January 1997, at his home in Austin, Texas. He is currently a Spanish teacher and taught Spanish during and after desegregation. The interview tapes are deposited at the Oral History Collection, Center for the History of Education, The University of Texas at Austin. Hereinafter referenced McPherson Interview, OHC.

30. Patterson Interview, OHC.

31. Allen Interview, OHC.

32. Brown Interview, OHC.

33. Stoll Interview, OHC.

34. Ibid.

35. Ibid.

36. Ibid.

37. Ibid.

38. Ibid.

39. Ibid.

40. Ibid.

41. Brown Interview, OHC.

42. Ibid.

43. Ibid.

44. Ibid.

45. Ibid.

46. Ibid.

47. Ibid.

48. Ibid.

49. Dorsett Interview, OHC.

50. Ibid.

51. Ibid.

52. Ibid.

53. Allen Interview, OHC.

54. Ibid.

55. "Minorities File on School Issue," *American Statesman*, August 15, 1970, 1; "East Austin Group Gains Agreement," *American Statesman*, September 3, 1970, 1; "Crossover Busing Discussed," *American Statesman*, September 9, 1970, 1; "Race Panel Members Announced," *Austin American*, December 2, 1970, 1; "Tri-Ethnic Group Discusses Schools," *Austin American*, December 2, 1970, 1; "School Line Deadline Extension Suggested," *Austin American*, December 4, 1970, 29.

56. Taylor Interview, OHC.

57. Patterson Interview, OHC.

58. Taylor Interview, OHC.

59. Ibid.

60. Chambers Interview, OHC.

61. Ibid.

62. Ibid.

CHAPTER SEVEN
DEATH OF A SCHOOL

1. *The Comet*, Austin High School Yearbook, 1971, 4.

2. The initial Supreme Court decision was handed down in 1954 and the second, or follow up decision, occurred the following year, 1955. The two decisions are commonly known as *Brown I* and *Brown II. Brown v. Board of Education of Topeka, Kansas,* 347 U.S. 483 (1954) and 355 U.S. 294 (1955).

3. "School Plan 'Splits' Board," *Austin American*, December 20, 1968, 1, 6.

4. "Year of Grace to Follow Rejection of Busing Plan," *Austin American*, June 25, 1969, 1 & 6.

5. "Black Into White is Integration Pattern," *Austin American*, June 24, 1969, 5–6.

6. The lawsuit had been filed the previous year by the Department of Health, Education, and Welfare. On May 14, 1971, AISD filed two desegregation plans and HEW filed an alternative desegregation plan. Each plan included some form of busing. "Battle Lines Drawn for Austin's School Suit," *Austin American,* June 13, 1971, 1, 6; "Tri-Ethnic Unit Backs School Plan," *Austin American,* May 18, 1971, 1; "League May Sue Board," *The Citizen,* May 27, 1971, 2; "School Group to Discuss Integration with Federals," *Austin American,* May 25, 1971, 1, 6.

7. "Battle Lines Drawn for Austin's School Suit," *Austin American,* June 13, 1971, 1,6; "Tri-Ethnic Unit Backs School Plan," *Austin American,* May 18, 1971, 1; "League May Sue Board," *The Citizen,* May 27, 1971, 2; "School Group to Discuss Integration with Federals," *Austin American,* May 25, 1971, 1, 6.

8. Throughout the South, White school boards closed Black schools as a direct result of lawsuits stemming from the Brown decisions and the 1964 Civil Rights Act. In no instances were White schools closed and White students bused to formerly Black schools. As in other aspects of desegregation, the Black community bore the brunt of their pursuit of equality of opportunities.

9. Charles Johnson, "Some Significant Social and Educational Implications of the U. S. Supreme Court's Decision," *Journal of Negro Education* 23, 3 (1954): 364–371.

10. Walker's *Their Highest Potential* is a historical ethnography of Caswell County Training School in North Carolina during segregation. Her study is both a reconstruction of the events and activities during the school's history and a search for understanding the events' values. Of particular importance to this study was her analysis of (1) a national memory about segregated schools, and (2) the relationship between the school and the community. V. S. Walker, *Their Highest Potential: An African American School Community in the Segregated South* (Chapel Hill: University of North Carolina Press, 1966), 3, 5.

11. Ibid.

12. Billingsley, *Black Families in White America,* 99.

13. These states were: (South) Alabama, Arkansas, Florida, Georgia, Louisiana, Mississippi, North Carolina, South Carolina, Tennessee, Texas, Virginia; (Border) Delaware, Kentucky, Maryland, Missouri, Oklahoma, West Virginia, and the District of Columbia.

14. *Texas Constitution,* art. 7, § 7, enacted in 1876.

15. Unpublished manuscript of Travis County Superintendent found in Austin Independent School District's archives.

16. *Texas Revised Civil Statute Annotated,* art. 2900, enacted in 1905.

17. Anderson's *Education of Blacks* discusses in detail Blacks' view of education as liberation and freedom. Anderson stated, "There developed in the slave community a fundamental belief in learning and self-improvement and a shared belief in universal education as a necessary basis for freedom and citizenship. . . . [E]ducation was fundamentally linked to freedom and dignity. . . . Blacks' motivation for intellectual achievement . . . persisted into the twentieth century and into our own present. . . . There was nothing naive about a belief in learning and self-improvement as a means to individual and collective dignity. It was not the end of their struggle for freedom and justice; only a means toward that end" (Anderson, *Education of Blacks,* 284–285).

18. Because school funds were separate at the state level, local school administrators maintained they received less funding for Black schools than for White schools. Many believed funding for White schools included monies originally identified as for Black schools.

Funding issues were difficult, if not impossible, to track from beginning to end of a school year in a school district.

19. For a detailed discussion of public school funding, see J. W. Alvord, *Schools and Finances of Freedom*, January 1, 1866, reprinted from 1868 copy by Washington Government Printing Office (New York: AMS Press, Inc, 1980); Anderson, *Education of Blacks;* Bullock, *History of Negro Education.*

20. Anderson, *Education of Blacks,* 181–182.

21. Patterson Interview, OHC.

22. *The Geyser,* first annual of the Anderson High School, Austin, Texas. Published June 1926. Located in the archives of the Austin Independent School District, Austin, Texas.

23. L. C. Anderson was born of slave parents in Fayette County, Tennessee, in 1853. He attended the public schools of Memphis, and with the abolition of slavery and the end of the Civil War, he resolved to prepare himself to become a leader for his people. He entered Fisk University in 1870, and after an interval of several years during which he taught school in Arkansas, he graduated in 1880. He came to Texas that same year as principal of a training school in Brenham. In 1884 he was chosen by Governor Oran M. Roberts to become principal of Prairie View Normal and Industrial College, the forerunner of Prairie View A&M College. In 1896 he came to Austin as principal of the high school, which in 1909 was named for E. H. Anderson, his brother. He served in this capacity for thirty-four years, resigning in 1929 because of poor health, but remaining on the faculty as teacher of Latin. Continued failing health forced his resignation from the faculty in January 1932.

24. A. N. McCallum, Superintendent of Schools, at the time of L. C. Anderson's death in 1938.

25. Akins Interview, OHC.

26. Ibid.

27. Ibid.

28. Taylor Interview, OHC.

29. Ibid.

30. Ibid.

31. Smith Interview, OHC.

32. Akins Interview, OHC.

33. Oral History Interview with Clifford McPherson between October and December 1996, in Austin, Texas. The tapes are deposited at the Oral History Program, Center for the History of Education, The University of Texas at Austin. Hereafter cited as McPherson Interview, OHC.

34. Patterson Interview, OHC.

35. Taylor Interview, OHC.

36. Ibid.

37. Ibid.

38. "Integration Plan Said Gives Blacks Burden," *The American Statesman,* July 13, 1971, 1.

39. Ibid.

40. Thomas J. Sergiovanni, *Building Community in Schools* (San Francisco: Jossey-Bass Publishers, 1994), xiii.

41. Sergiovanni, 1994, 4.

42. Ibid.

43. Ibid.

44. A consensus of the teachers' interviews.

CHAPTER EIGHT
REFLECTIONS AND MEMORIES

1. Segall and Wilson, *Introduction to Education,* 90–91. Segall-Wilson mention that of the 2,909 segregated school districts in 1954, only 802 had been desegregated by 1960. In fact, they report, some Southern states such as Alabama, South Carolina, and Mississippi blatantly refused to consider school integration. Other school districts simply "dragged their feet." It is in this category Austin is placed. Wilson, Anna V., "Education for African Americans," *The New Handbook of Texas, Vol 2.* Austin, TX: The Texas State Historical Society, 1996, 794–796. Wilson mentions that in 1964, 60 percent of all desegregated school districts in the South were located in Texas. She also mentions that more than half of all Black students attending Southern integrated schools were in Texas. The logic of the data is understood because of Texas' large number of school districts, most of which were very small. During the 1960s, many small districts had little difficulty integrating because Blacks represented a minuscule percentage of the district's population.

2. Lyndon Baines Johnson was a senator representing Texas prior to his vice-presidency in 1960. Johnson was born on a farm near Stonewall, Texas, not far from Austin. His knowledge of Austin was expansive in that he knew the city both as a politician and businessman. He and his wife, Lady Bird, owned several radio stations, one of which used her initials (KLBJ) as its call letters. Johnson graduated in education from Southwest Texas State Teachers College (now Southwest Texas State University). He taught school at Cotulla, a small south Texas community, for a year to make money to finish his college education. It was here he witnessed the abject poverty experienced by his Hispanic students.

3. Fehrenbach, *Lone Star,* 663–664. Fehrenbach is very specific in his evaluation of Johnson. He describes him as pragmatic. As a senator, Johnson represented the oil and mineral interests of the state. In fact, he represented the segregationist attitudes of White East Texans. By using the term the "Great Society," Johnson meant that the Federal government had the resources to identify the various ills of American society and correct them. Johnson wanted to improve the lives of all Americans, not just the poor. His aim was to improve Black Americans' ability to exercise their civil rights as well as their quality of life.

4. The election campaign was fought between the respected Republican Arizona Senator, Barry Goldwater, and Lyndon Baines Johnson, who had become president upon Kennedy's assassination in Dallas. Johnson's landslide victory was staggering as measured by Electoral College votes, 486–52.

5. Johnson's War On Poverty initiative created a plethora of legislation including the: Equal Opportunity Act (1964), Appalachian Regional Development Act (1965), Higher Education Act (1967), Water Restoration Act (1966), and the Wilderness Areas Act (1964). Agencies including the Department of Housing and Urban Development (HUD) and the Department of Transportation were inaugurated. Programs such as Volunteers in Service to America (Vista), the Jobs Corps, Upward Bound, and the Model Cities Program were also started.

6. Speech to Congress, March 16, 1964. Many give credit to Johnson for the phrase, "War On Poverty." In fact, it had been used in 1960 by Kennedy when he depicted Social Security as a weapon to help the aged. Johnson used the term to illustrate his desire to fight poverty on the national level.

7. Blacks had transferred their loyalty to the Democratic Party during the Roosevelt administration; the War On Poverty was another important factor in maintaining Black political loyalty.

8. A staggering list of legislative initiatives begun during the Johnson administration continued in succeeding years. Some major examples are seen in: early childhood education, personnel training, reading, language, and mathematics skill programs, dropout prevention, and bilingual education.

9. As early as December 1963, Johnson was calling upon Congress to complete the portions of the National Education Improvement Act with programs focused on elementary and secondary schools. In his "Annual Budget Message to Congress," Johnson spoke of it again on January 21, 1964, but did not outline his thoughts about how Congress could help disadvantaged children. Johnson, Lyndon B., *Public Papers,* 1963–64, 189–190. See, S. L. Sullivan, unpublished Ed.D. dissertation, *President Lyndon Baines Johnson and the Common School, 1963–1969,* Stillwater: Oklahoma State University, 1973, for his description of the politics of passing the Elementary and Secondary Education Act.

10. The original legislation was aimed at improving the health and educational levels of children who came to school unprepared, received a rudimentary education, and then dropped out early.

11. Head Start continues to help students today through additional Federal legislation continuing its original mandates.

12. Many of the teachers had a similar experience that teacher Lyndon Baines Johnson had at Cotulla. The Cotulla yearbook shows him as a young man, with a typical Johnson smile standing in the school doorway with his students. Poverty was so apparent that the viewer immediately understands the conditions in which his students lived.

13. Many Head Start programs also served children lunch and breakfast. Eventually, many programs served breakfast to the children's parents because they lived in the same condition as their children.

14. Fehrenbach, *Lone Star,* 708–711. Fehrenbach discusses White Texas urbanization during this period as somewhat of a family affair. While Northern urbanization constituted immigrants who might have traveled thousands of miles or come from another country to live in cities such as New York, Boston, or Chicago, Texans stayed close to home, moving on the average seventy miles. From this analysis it is easy to understand why White Austinites, who thought of themselves as Texans first, felt threatened with Washington sponsored change.

15. Odintz, Mark, "Senator Ralph Yarborough," *Texas Online,* www.tsha.utexas.edu/handbook/online. Senator Ralph Yarborough was one of only three Southern senators that voted for the Civil Rights Act. Odintz describes Yarborough as the leading influence of the liberal or progressive wing of the Texas Democratic party. Yarborough was known as a bright lawyer who was concerned about people and schools. He challenged Governor Severs in the 1952 Democratic primary and lost. Odintz speculated that the reason President Kennedy was in Dallas in 1963 was to heal the political rift between liberal Yarborough and conservative Governor Connolly.

16. Undoubtedly the Austin school board was concerned about the Civil Rights Act. It had the legislative teeth to force school districts to integrate students, regardless of local opinion. It was now possible that the Federal courts could take over management of the school district, leaving the school board powerless.

17. Johnson, *A History of the American People,* 952–955. Johnson discusses the constitutionality of the Civil Rights Act and Gunner Myrdal's theory of social engineering. Johnson is especially critical of Myrdal's 1944 text, *An American Dilemma,* which he says became Thurgood Marshall's bible. Regardless, White Texans were incensed with affirmative action. In *Griggs v. Duke Power Company* (1971) the Supreme Court interpreted the Civil Rights Act to mean that minorities were protected. That is, they could sue under an "automatic presumption" of discrimination. Yet Whites felt they were unprotected. White males discovered they were also unprotected when females were defined as "protected minorities."

18. Mike Godwin, "Daily Texan," *Handbook of Texas Online.* Godwin describes how University of Texas Regent Frank C. Erwin campaigned against the student paper, *Daily Texan,* for writing anti-Vietnam editorials. Eventually, in 1971, as the paper's charter was to be renewed, negotiations culminated in a settlement in which the *Daily Texan* lost its assets (reported by some to be as much as $600,000). In return, the *Daily Texan* was allowed to control its editorial page while a university-appointed general manager would head the rest of the paper. Erwin's pro-Vietnam position was clearly stated when the Regents developed a policy that directed University administrators *not* to negotiate with antiwar demonstrators if that became necessary. See also, Mike Godwin, "The Daily Texan Does Not Belong to You (but it used to)," Austin: *Utmost,* October 1987.

19. Henry, Kissinger, *The White House Years* (Vol. 1.) (Boston: Little, Brown and Company 1979), 230–239. Kissinger mentions in his memoirs that in October 1965, he wrote in his personal diary Vietnam could not be won. He reaffirmed his conclusions on August 18, 1966, in a letter to Henry Cabot Lodge: "Candor compels me to say that I did not find any substantial change. . . ."(233).

20. Robert Wooster, "Military History", *Handbook of Texas Online.* Wooster reports 21,000 Texans were killed during the Vietnam War. Kissinger, *The White House Years,* 235. Kissinger reports that at the height of the war, 543,000 American soldiers served in battle. He reports average death rates of two hundred soldiers per week in 1968 and cites a total of more than 31,000 lives lost during the war. Kissinger mentions that young Americans demonstrated in large Northern cities. For example, he reports college student attendance at the October 1970 Moratorium demonstrations in New York (20,000), New Haven Green (30,000), Washington (50,000), and Boston (100,000). Kissinger states that protests against the war increased when students returned to college. During that period, few Blacks attended non-Black colleges and universities.

21. Johnson, *A History of the American People,* 893. Johnson charts the process in which a Student Non-Violent Coordination Committee subcommittee composed of Bob Moses, James Forman, and Marion Barry planned student demonstrations in Mississippi and Alabama. Johnson also reasons that the disproportionate numbers of young Black soldiers in Vietnam was one of the reasons King and the President's friendship cooled. King viewed this as a change in Johnson's race relations policy.

22. Nicholas Lemann, *The Promised Land: the Great Black Migration and How it Changed America* (New York: Vintage Books, 1991), 352. Lemann defends the social and political necessity of district courts forcing integration. While he is discussing the evils of the Chicago projects, he is also commenting on integration. He states, "It has always been

the Federal government, not local government or private business, that has led the way on race relation . . . the personal involvement of the president himself has usually been necessary."

23. Nicholas, *The Promised Land,* 348–349. Lemann voices the difficulty racial change causes Southern Whites. He describes Southern White reaction by stereotyping all external change as liberal and racial. Southern Whites, Lemann says, reject the assumption that organizations and peoples who live outside the community (or state) can understand the needs of the local people.

24. Fehrenbach, *Lone Star,* 711. Fehrenbach mentions that the average number of miles Texans traveled when they moved to the city from their rural homes was seventy miles. Urban emigration would be less.

25. Austin's case was a matter of moving north and northwest from the city center. The new interstate highway system pointed the direction. Running north and south from Dallas to San Antonio, the Interstate acted like an artery, giving White Austinites access to the open land. Demanding new services, multilane roads such as Mopac, Lamar, and Research Boulevards crisscrossed north Austin. As Austin's northern suburbs grew, services and businesses followed. Small shopping centers, theaters, banks, and entertainment centers quickly dotted the neighborhoods. Austin, like most cities in the Southwest, was built for the automobile. Partly because most Texas cities did not truly begin growing until World War II. Unlike their eastern counterparts, Texas cities, including Austin, grew outward. As a consequence, while Austin has a skyline, it is small and compact. Residential areas, shopping centers, and entertainment areas are beyond the city center. This allowed Whites to continue to live in Austin but away from East Austin and the African American community. In fact, this did not create a hardship on working White Austinites. Seventy percent of those who were employed used cars to get to work.

26. Mopac is an abbreviation for Missouri-Pacific Railroad. The highway follows the Missouri-Pacific tracks on a north-south axis. Because of land requirements, the northern traffic lanes were built on the east side of the tracks and the southern traffic lanes on the west.

27. Clara Stearns Scarbrough, "Round Rock, Texas," *Texas Online.* Scarbrough mentions that the original name of the settlement was Brushy Creek. In 1854, when postal officials asked Thomas C. Oatts , the first postmaster, to rename the location, he chose Round Rock. It seems, says Scarbrough, the postmaster and the blacksmith were good friends who fished together in Brushy Creek near a round rock. Other than those who needed the services of Mr. Harrell and Mr. Oats, Round Rock was also known by ranchers who drove their cattle north on the Chisholm Trail to Kansas. They forded Brushy Creek next to the round rock.

28. Scarbrough, "Round Rock, Texas." Scarbrough reports that because of growth, the original site is now part of Round Rock. Several restored buildings remain.

29. Scarbrough, "Round Rock, Texas."

30. Ibid. Scarbrough states that the original Round Rock was approximately eighteen miles from downtown Austin. During the 1970s and 1980s, Round Rock and Austin would geographically merge as Austinites moved into north Austin and Round Rock continued to expand. At present, reflecting the area's economic interest in technology, Round Rock is home to several computer companies. In 1990, Round Rock's population was 30,923.

31. David K. Shipler, *A Country of Strangers: Blacks and Whites in America* (New York: Alfred A. Knopf, 1997), 34–35. Shipler defines integration as the "blending of the parts into a unified whole." Blacks, he says, think of integration as assimilating to a White culture which demands they give up their personal and cultural histories. Because Blacks do not feel they will be allowed to share power equally with Whites, Blacks, says Shipler, turn inward to "black friendships, black institutions, and black culture."

32. Shipler, 34. Shipler quotes from W. E. B. Du Bois's *The Souls of Black Folk* in which he writes about an experience that happened to him one day when he and his fellow elementary students were to exchange cards. When one student, with a sneer, refused his card, it was then he knew he was different. Reflecting on that experience and others he had during his life, Du Bois is quoted: "Why did God make me an outcast and a stranger in mine own house? The shades of the prison-house closed round about us all: walls strait and stubborn to the whitest, but relentlessly narrow, tall, and unscalable to sons of night who must plod darkly on in resignation, . . ." (34). Shipler argues that this is the description of contemporary Black-White relations.

33. Shipler, 79–80. Shipler discusses Thomas Kochmann's concept of "Strip Mining" as told to him by Blacks as they discussed their feelings about being divested of their culture. In order to accommodate Whites in the marketplace, Blacks must remove their "Blackness" so Whites may feel more comfortable. He states that Whites may lose their individuality but will gain an identity. Blacks, on the other hand, lose both.

34. Carol Korn, "I used to be very smart: Children talk about immigration," *Education and Culture: The Journal of the John Dewey Society,* University of Iowa, John Dewey Society (1997): 17–24. Although not using the term, Korn identifies the consequences of fronting from the perspective of children of immigrants who are taught in school a new loyalty to the United States. She quotes Lisette, an elementary student, who describes her confusion about loyalty as, "This was my flag and this was me. . . . I am not there and I have to pledge allegiance to the American's flag every day. Sometimes Santo Domingo seems so far. . . ." (22).

35. Perhaps the best metaphor one can use to explain Black students' attitudes is to recall those happy feelings you may have had when you returned to the United States from a foreign country where you experienced different languages, music, manners, and all those other things not commonly thought about. As one returning tourist said, "It sure is nice to wake up in your own bed."

36. Shipler, 39–40. Shipler relates an experience in which a Black adult referred to his mother's reaction to a White elementary teacher's attempt to introduce him to classical music. His mother, a pianist, played for him excepts from Rachmaninoff and Liszt and told him this was European classical music. She played Billy Eckstine and Sarah Vaughan and then said, "'Understand that in our frame of reference we have our own classical art, music, literature, and if you lose that you'll be lost forever and be significantly less strong in the world than you have to be'" (40).

37. Cathi L. Cornelius, *"Village Perspectives" A Case Study Investigating the Perspectives Concerning the Oklahoma City Public Schools Neighborhood Schools Plan/student Reassignment Plan,* Oklahoma State University, unpublished Ed.D dissertation, 1999. Cornelius reports a *U.S. News & World Report* study that indicated Black acceptance of busing increased by eight percent during a twenty year period. In 1972, 55 percent of Blacks favored busing. In 1991, 63 percent agreed. Interestingly, White acceptance of busing increased during that period as well. In 1972, 14 percent of Whites believed busing was an appropriate method

to end school desegregation. In 1991, 32 percent accepted that rationale. See, D. Whitman and D. Friedman, "Busing's unheralded legacy," *U. S. News & World Report* 112, 14 (1992), 63–65 for greater detail.

38. G. Orfield, *The Growth of Segregation in American Schools: Changing Patterns of Separation and Poverty since 1968* (Cambridge: Harvard University Press, 1993). Orfield reported that two-thirds of all Black students attended a predominantly minority school in 1992. Also, White attendance at integrated schools had dropped in 1994 to an all-time low of 33.9 percent.

39. Shipler, 15–19. Shipler reports statistics that, in context, paint a sober picture of Black professionals, families, and youth. While Black and White female college graduates earn basically the same ($992 to Whites' $1,000), Black male college graduates earn $727 for every $1,000 earned by White college graduates. At best, many are destined, he says, to live on an edge that, when difficult economic periods are experienced, will cause them to fall into poverty.

CHAPTER NINE
CREATING PLACES OF ENGAGED LISTENING

1. The public history of segregated schools prior to *Brown* has focused almost entirely on an inferior education for African American students. Walker maintained that this national memory assumed, "Black children suffered immeasurably and received little of educational value until they were desegregated into superior white systems." She believed that, while the memory of inequality was correct, the historical picture was incomplete. Thus, "[the] historical recollections that recall descriptions of differences in facilities and resources of white and black schools without also providing descriptions of the black schools' and communities' dogged determination to educate African American children have failed to tell the complete story of segregated schools." Walker, *Their Highest Potential*, 3–5.

2. In 1954, Charles Johnson of Fisk University predicted that, as a result of the *Brown* decision, not only would racially separate schools cease to exist but the African American community's institutional structures would undergo dramatic changes. Johnson, "Some Significant Social and Educational Implications": 364–371.

3. Throughout the South, White school boards closed African American schools as a direct result of lawsuits stemming from the *Brown* decisions and the 1964 Civil Rights Act. In no instances were White schools closed and White students bused to formerly African American schools. As in other aspects of desegregation, the African American community bore the brunt of their pursuit of equality of opportunities.

4. Shortly after World War II, the Southern states spent about twice as much to educate White children as Black children, White teachers' salaries were 30 percent or more higher than Black teachers and the Southern states spent $86 million dollars on higher education for Whites and only $5 million on higher education for Blacks. During this same period in Texas, salary differentials were quite marked. White high school teachers earned between $1035 to $1485 while Black high school teachers earned far less, $900 to $1125 per year. Not until the early 1950s, with the passage of the Gilmer-Akin laws, did all high school teachers, regardless of race, receive the same pay based on a salary schedule.

5. Similar to other African Americans during segregation, this teacher learned to prevail in a very hostile environment. She eloquently named the hostility as *un-selfing*. Taylor Interview, OHC.

6. In 1944, Myrdal observed that "segregation [was] becoming so complete that the White Southerner practically never [saw] a Negro except as his servant and in other standardized and formalized caste situations." Myrdal, *The American Dilemma*, 1944, cited in Woodward, *The Strange Career of Jim Crow*, 118.

7. Patterson Interview, OHC. We have highlighted individual concepts and specific comments found in previous chapters to sum up their positions.

8. Taylor Interview, OHC.

9. Johnson, "Freedom, Equality, and Segregation."

10. To illustrate the intensity of the Southern state of mind, a national poll conducted in the summer of 1954 by the American Institute of Public Opinion confirmed that only 24 percent of Southerners approved of the *Brown* decision, whereas 71 percent disapproved and only 5 percent were undecided. McCain, "Reactions to the U. S. Supreme Court Decision of 1954."

11. Chambers interview, OHC.

12. Oral History Interview with Clara Luper, October 15, 1995. Mrs. Luper, an African American teacher now retired, continues to be active in Oklahoma racial affairs and lives in Oklahoma City. She taught U.S. History and American Government before, during, and after desegregation. The tapes are on deposit at the Oral History Program, Center for the History of Education, The University of Texas at Austin.

13. Norfleet, *Forced School Integration in the U. S. A.*, 51, 55.

14. William Doll, *A Post-Modern Perspective on Curriculum* (New York: Teachers College Press, 1993), 3

15. Walker, *Their Highest Potential*, 3.

16. Ibid.

17. Billingsley, *Black Families in White America*, 99.

18. Akins Interview, OHC.

19. Miller, "Some Anticipated Problems."

20. Irvine and Irvine. "The Impact of the Desegregation Process."

21. "In every aspect of the child's life a trusted elder, neighbor, Sunday school teachers, school teacher, or other community member might instruct, discipline, assist, or otherwise guide the young of a given family. Second, as role models, community members show an example to and interest in the young people. Third, as advocates they actively intercede with major segments of society (a responsibility assumed by professional educators) to help young members of particular families find opportunities which otherwise would be closed to them. Fourth, as supportive figures, they simply inquire about the progress of the young, take a special interest in them. Fifth, in the formal roles of teacher, leader, elder, they serve youth generally as part of the general role or occupation." (Billingsley, *Black Families in White America*, 99).

22. Akins Interview, OHC.

23. Ibid.

24. Luper Interview, OHC.

25. Taylor Interview, OHC.

26. Smith Interview, OHC.

27. Van Dempsey and George W. Noblit, "Cultural Ignorance and School Desegregation: Reconstructing a Silenced Narrative," in George W. Noblit *Particularities: Collected Essays on Ethnography and Education* (New York: Peter Lang, 1999), 181–204.

28. Community is the tie that binds students and teachers together in special ways, to something more significant than themselves: shared values and ideals. It lifts both teachers and students to higher levels of self-understanding, commitment, and performance—beyond the reaches of the shortcomings and difficulties they face in their everyday lives. Community can help teachers and students be transformed from a collection of *I*'s to a collective *We*, thus providing them with a unique and enduring sense of identity, belonging, and place.

29. Ideologies are the means by which people make sense of their lives.

30. Dempsey and Noblit.

31. Ibid., 182.

32. Consensus of teachers' interviews.

33. Consensus of teachers' interviews.

34. See J. H. Franklin and J. H. Franklin, eds., *My Life and an Era: The Autobiography of Buck Colbert Franklin* (Baton Rouge: Louisiana State University Press,1997) for a discussion of how and why Blacks valued schools.

35. Blacks and Whites agreed with each other about busing. Neither side wanted their children to leave the comforts of their neighborhood schools. White parents voiced their concern that their children would not be safe attending formerly Black schools, nor would they benefit from the quality facilities their children and teachers were used to. On the other hand, Black parents knew they would be separated from their children's education. Used to talking to teachers about their children's educational experiences, Black parents knew that would not happen in White schools simply because many of them did not have the money to travel across town. Nor did many feel free to talk to White teachers. Regardless, Black students left their neighborhoods to attend White schools. See: Cornelius, *"Village perspectives."*

36. Cornelius, *"Village perspectives,"* Forward, iv–ix. Cornelius, in her January 19, 1999, conversation with Dr. A. L. Dowell asked him to describe the events before and after the 1991 Supreme Court case, *Oklahoma City Board of Education v. Dowell.* Dr. Dowell envisioned the tradeoffs Blacks would be required to make if they wanted integration. He said, "Many Negroes got angry with me because they had to bus their children across town. Many said to me, 'You are destroying a good relationship between the good Whites and the Colored.' My response to them was what did they think about all these Blacks going without. Finally, Judge Bohannan passed an order that the district had to comply with the Finger Plan [to bus Black students to White schools]."

37. Chapter 8, n. 31.

38. Chapter 8, n. 32.

39. bell hooks, *Yearning: Race, Gender, and Cultural Politics* (Boston: South End Press, 1990).

40. Ibid.

41. Dennis Sumara and Brent Davis, "History, Memory, Curriculum," *Journal of Curriculum Theorizing* (Summer, 1997): 2–3.

42. Maxine Greene, "Curriculum and Cultural Transformation: A Humanistic View," *Cross Currents* 25(2): 175–186.

Bibliography

BOOKS AND CHAPTERS

Ahmann, Mathew H., ed. *The New Negro.* Notre Dame, IN: Fides Publishers, 1961.

Alvord, John W. *Freedmen's Schools and Textbooks, Volume I.* New York: AMS Press, Inc. Reprint of 1868.

Alvord, John W. *Schools and Finances of Freedom,* January 1, 1866, reprinted from 1868 copy by Washington Government Printing Office (New York: AMS Press, Inc., 1980).

Anderson, James D. *The Education of Blacks in the South, 1860–1935.* Chapel Hill: University of North Carolina Press, 1988.

Banks, James A. and Cherry McGee Banks, eds. *Handbook of Research on Multicultural Education.* New York: Macmillan, 1995.

Banks, Jimmy. *Money, Marbles, and Chalk: The Wondrous World of Texas Politics* (Austin: Texas Publishing Company, 1971).

Barkan, Steven E. *Protesters on Trial: Criminal Justice in the Southern Civil Rights and Vietnam Antiwar Movements.* New Brunswick, NJ: Rutgers University Press, 1985.

Barnes, Catherine A. *Journey From Jim Crow: The Desegregation of Southern Transportation.* New York: Columbia University Press, 1983.

Barr, Alwin. *Black Texans: A History of African Americans in Texas 1528–1995,* 2nd edition. Norman: University of Oklahoma Press, 1996.

Bass, Jack. *Unlikely Heroes.* New York: Simon and Schuster, 1981.

Beardslee, William R. *The Way Out Must Lead In: Life Histories in the Civil Rights Movement.* Atlanta: Center for Research in Social Change, Emory University, 1977.

Bennett, Lerone Jr. *Before the Mayflower: A History of Black America,* 6th edition. New York: Penguin Books, 1988.

———. *The Negro Mood and Other Essays.* Chicago: Johnson Publishing Co., 1964.

Berman, Daniel M. *A Bill Becomes Law: Congress Enacts Civil Rights Legislation.* New York: Macmillan, 1966.

———. *It is So Ordered: The Supreme Court Rules of School Segregation.* New York: W. W. Norton, 1966.

Bianchi, Eugene C. *The Religious Experience of Revolutionaries.* Garden City, NY: Doubleday, 1972.

Billingsley, A. *Black Families in White America.* Englewood Cliffs, NJ: PrenticeHall, 1968,

Blaustein, Albert, and Clarence C. Ferguson Jr. *Desegregation and the Law: The Meaning and Effect of the School Segregation Cases.* New Brunswick: Rutgers University Press, 1957.

Blumberg, Rhoda L. *Civil Rights: The 1960s Freedom Struggle.* Boston: Twayne Publishers, 1984.

Bond, Horace Mann. *The Education of the Negro in the American Social Order.* New York: Prentice Hall, 1934.

Booth, William D. *The Progressive Story: New Baptist Roots.* St. Paul: Braun Press, 1981.

Branch, Taylor. *Parting the Waters: America in the King Years 1954–63.* New York: Simon and Schuster, 1988.

Brauer, Carl M. *John F. Kennedy and the Second Reconstruction.* New York: Columbia University Press, 1977.

Brickman, William W., and Stanley Lehrer, eds. *The Countdown on Segregated Education.* New York: Society for Advancement of Education, 1960.

Brink, William, and Louis Harris. *The Negro Revolution in America.* New York: Simon and Schuster, 1964.

———. *Black and White.* New York: Simon and Schuster, 1967.

Bullock, Henry A. *A History of Negro Education in the South: From 1619 to the Present.* Cambridge: Harvard University Press, 1967.

Burke, Peter, ed. *New Perspectives on Historical Writing.* University Park, PA: The Pennsylvania State University Press, 1991.

Carawan, Guy and Candie. *Freedom is a Constant Struggle.* New York: Oak Publications, 1968.

Carmichael, Stokely, and Charles V. Hamilton. *Black Power: The Politics of Liberation in America.* New York: Random House, 1967.

Chafe, William H. *Civilities and Civil Rights.* New York: Oxford University Press, 1980.

Christopher, Nehemiah M. *The History of Negro Public Education in Texas, 1865-1900.* Austin: University of Texas Press, 1940.

Culbertson, Manie. *May I Speak: Diary of a Crossover Teacher.* Gretna, LA: Pelican Publishing Company, 1972.

Dabbs, James M. *The Southern Heritage.* New York: Alfred A. Knopf, 1958.

Davis, O. L. Jr. "Historical Inquiry: Telling Real Stories." In *Forms of Curriculum Inquiry,* ed. Edmund C. Short. Albany: State University of New York Press, 1991.

Davison, James W., and Mark Lytle. *After the Fact: The Art of Historical Detection, 3rd Edition, Volume III.* New York: McGraw-Hill, 1992.

Dempsey, Van, and George W. Noblit. "Cultural Ignorance and School Desegregation: Reconstructing a Silenced Narrative." In George W. Noblit, *Particularities: Collected Essays on Ethnography and Education.* New York: Peter Lang, 1999.

Denzin, Norman K., and Yvonna S. Lincoln, eds. *Handbook of Qualitative Research.* Thousand Oaks, CA: Sage Publications, 1994.

Doll, William. *A Post-Modern Perspective on Curriculum.* New York: Teachers College Press, 1993)

Dorman, Michael.. *We Shall Overcome.* New York: Delacorte press, 1964.

Douglas, Davison M. *Reading, Writing, and Race: The Desegregation of the Charlotte Schools.* Chapel Hill: The University of North Carolina Press, 1995.

Duke, Daniel L. *The School that Refused to Die: Continuity and Change at Thomas Jefferson High School.* Albany: State University of New York Press, 1995.

Dulles, Foster Rhea. *The Civil Rights Commission: 1957–1965.* Lansing: Michigan State University Press, 1968.

Duram, James C. *A Moderate among Extremists: Dwight D. Eisenhower and the School Desegregation Crisis.* Chicago: Nelson-Hall, 1981.

Egerton, John. *Speak Now Against the Day: The Generation Before the Civil Rights Movement in the South.* New York: Alfred A. Knopf, 1994.

Eisenhower, John S. D. *Intervention! The United States and the Mexican Revolution, 1913–1917.* New York: W. W. Norton & Company, 1993.

Fager, Charles E. *White Reflections on Black Power.* Grand Rapids: William B. Eerdmans, 1967.

Farmer, James. *Freedom—When?* New York: Random House, 1965.

———. *Lay Bare the Heart.* New York: Arbor House, 1985.

Feinberg, W., and H. J. Rosemont, eds. *Work, Technology, and Education: Dissenting Essays in the Intellectual Foundations of American Education.* Urbana: University of Illinois Press, 1975.

Fenderson, Lewis H. *Thurgood Marshall: Fighter for Justice.* McGraw-Hill/Rutledge Books, 1969.

Fehrenbach, T. R. *Lone Star: a History of Texas and the Texans.* New York: American Legacy Press, 1983.

Fine, Michelle. "Working with the Hyphens: Reinventing Self and Other in Qualitative Research." In *Handbook of Qualitative Research,* eds. Norman K. Denzin and Yvonna S. Lincoln. Thousand Oaks, CA: Sage Publications, 1994.

Forman, James. *The Making of Black Revolutionaries.* New York: Macmillan, 1972.

Foster, Michele. *Black Teachers on Teaching.* New York: The Free Press, 1997.

Franklin, J. H., and J. H. Franklin, eds. *My Life and an Era: the Autobiography of Buck Colbert Franklin.* Baton Rouge: Louisiana State University Press, 1997.

Garrow, David J. *Bearing the Cross: Martin Luther King, Jr., and the Southern Christian Leadership Conference.* New York: Vintage Books, 1988.

Goldman, Peter. *Report from Black America.* New York: Simon and Schuster, 1970.

Goodwin, Doris Kearns. *No Ordinary Time: Franklin and Eleanor Roosevelt: the Home Front in World War II.* New York: Simon & Schuster, 1994.

Grant, Joanne, ed. *Black Protest.* Greenwich, CT: Fawcett Books, 1968.

Hale, Grace Elizabeth. *Making Whiteness: the Culture of Segregation in the South, 1890–1940.* New York: Pantheon Books, 1998.

Harvey, James C. *Black Civil Rights During the Johnson Administration.* Jackson: University and College Press of Mississippi, 1973.

Hawley, Willis D., ed. *Effective School Desegregation: Equity, Quality, and Feasibility.* Beverly Hills: Sage Publications, 1981.

Holmes, Madelyn. "A White Teacher in Alexandria, Virginia: Cora Kelly (1868–1953). In *Lives of Women Public Schoolteachers: Scenes from American Educational History,* eds. M. Holmes and B. J. Weiss. New York: Garland Publishing, Inc., 1995.

Holmes, Madelyn, and Beverly J. Weiss, eds. *Lives of Women Public Schoolteachers: Scenes from American Educational History.* New York: Garland Publishing, Inc., 1995.

hooks, bell. *Yearning: Race, Gender, and Cultural Politics.* Boston: South End Press,1990.

Jackson, James J. *The Southern Case for School Segregation.* New York: Crowell-Collier, 1962.

Jacoway, Elizabeth, and David R. Colburn, eds. *Southern Businessmen and Desegregation.* Baton Rouge: Louisiana State University Press, 1982.

Johnson, Guy B. "Freedom, Equality, and Segregation." In *Integration versus Segregation,* ed. Hubert H. Humphrey. New York: Thomas Y. Crowell, 1964.

Johnson, Paul. *A History of the American People.* New York: Harper Collins, 1997.

Joseph, Peter. *Good Times: An Oral History of America in the Nineteen Sixties.* New York: Charterhouse, 1973.

Katz, William L. *Teachers' Guide to American Negro History, revised edition.* Chicago: Quadrangle Books, 1971.

Kendall, Robert. *White Teacher in a Black School.* New York: Devin-Adair Company, 1964.

King, Martin Luther Jr. *Why We Can't Wait.* New York: New American Library, 1964.

Kissinger, Henry. *The White House Years,* Vol. 1. Boston: Little, Brown and Company, 1979.

Kluger, Richard. *Simple Justice: The History of Brown v. Board of Education and Black America's Struggle for Equality.* New York: Random House, 1975. Vintage, 1977.

Kotz, Nick and Mary Lynn. *A Passion for Equality.* New York: W. W. Norton, 1977.

Kyvig, David, and Myron A. Marty. *Nearby History: Exploring the Past Around You.* Walnut Creek, CA: AltaMira Press, 1996.

Ladino, Robyn Duff. *Desegregating Texas Schools: Eisenhower, Shivers, and the Crisis at Mansfield High.* Austin: University of Texas Press, 1996.

Laue, James H., ed. *Direct Action and Desegregation, 1960–1962: Toward a Theory of the Rationalization of Protest.* New York: Carlson Publishing, 1989.

Lawson, Steven F. *Black Ballots: Voting Rights in the South, 1944–1969.* New York: Columbia University Press, 1976.

———. *In Pursuit of Power: Southern Blacks and Electoral Politics 1965–1982.* New York: Columbia University Press, 1985.

———. "Civil Rights." In *Exploring the Johnson Years,* Robert A. Divine, ed. Austin: University of Texas Press, 1981, 93–125.

Lee, Carol D., and Diana T. Slaughter-Defoe. "Historical and Sociocultural Influences on African American Education." In *Handbook of Research on Multicultural Education,* eds. James A. Banks and Cherry McGee Banks. New York: Macmillan, 1995.

Lee, Eugene, ed. *School Desegregation: Retrospect and Prospect.* Atlanta: SNPA Foundation Seminar Books, 1970.

Lemann, Nicholas. *The Promised Land: the Great Black Migration and How it Changed America.* New York: Vintage Books, 1991.

Linden, Glenn, M. *Desegregating Schools in Dallas: Four Decades in the Federal Courts.* Dallas: Three Forks Press, 1995.

Lomas, Louis. *The Negro Revolt.* New York: Harper and Brothers, 1962.

———. *To Kill a Black Man.* New York: Harper and Brothers, 1968.

Lukas, J. Anthony. *Big Trouble.* New York: Simon & Schuster, 1997.

Lynd, Staughton, ed. *Nonviolence in America*. Indianapolis: Bobbs-Merrill, 1966.

Mann, Robert. *The Walls of Jericho: Lyndon Johnson, Hubert Humphrey, Richard Russell, and the Struggle for Civil Rights*. New York: Harcourt Brace & Company, 1996.

Manning, Diane. *Hill Country Teacher: Oral Histories From the One-Room School and Beyond*. Boston: Twayne Publishers, 1990.

Marable, Manning. *Race, Reform, and Rebellion: The Second Reconstruction in Black America, 1945–1982*. Jackson: University Press of Mississippi, 1984.

Marshall, Burke. *Federalism and Civil Rights*. New York: Columbia University Press. 1964.

Marius, Richard. *A Short Guide to Writing About History*, 2nd edition. New York: Harper Collins, 1995.

McDaniel, Vernon. *The History of the Teachers State Association of Texas*. Washington, DC: National Education Association, 1977.

Mitchell, Glenford E., and William H. Peace III, eds. *The Angry Black South*. New York: Corinth Books, 1962.

Morgan, Harry. *Historical Perspectives on the Education of Black Children*. Westport, CT: Praeger, 1995.

Morris, Aldon D. *The Origins of the Civil Rights Movement*. New York: Free Press, 1984.

Muse, Benjamin. *The American Negro Revolution*. Bloomington: Indiana University Press, 1968.

Myrdal, Gunnar. *An American Dilemma*. New York: Harper & Bros., 1944; McGraw-Hill paperback, 1964.

Niebuhr, Reinhold. *Moral Man and Immoral Society*. New York: Charles Scribner's Sons, 1932.

Nixon, Richard M. *Six Crises*. Garden City, NY: Doubleday, 1962.

Noar, Gertrude. *The Teacher and Integration, revised edition*. Washington, DC: National Education Association, 1974.

Norfleet, Marvin B. *Forced School Integration in the U.S.A*. New York: Carlton Press, 1961.

Orfield, Gary. *The Reconstruction of Southern Education, the Schools, and the 1964 Civil Rights Act*. New York: Wiley-Interscience, 1969.

Orfield, Gary, Susan E. Eaton, and the Harvard Project on School Desegregation. *Dismantling Desegregation: The Quiet Reversal of Brown v. Board of Education*. New York: the New Press, 1996.

Powledge, Fred. *Black Power—White Resistance*. Cleveland: World Publishing, 1967.

Ransom, Roger L., and Richard Sutch. *One Kind of Freedom: The Economic Consequences of Emancipation*. Cambridge: Cambridge University Press, 1977.

Ritchie, Donald A. *Doing Oral History*. New York: Twayne Publishers, 1995.

Robinson, Jackie. *I Never Had It Made*. New York: G. P. Putnam's Sons, 1972.

Rowan, Carl T. *Go South to Sorrow*. New York: Random House, 1957.

Rustin, Bayard. *Down the Line*. Chicago: Quadrangle Books, 1971.

———. *Strategies for Freedom*. New York: Columbia University Press, 1976.

Sangrado, Robert L. *The Black Experience in America*. Austin: University of Texas Press, 1970.

Sarratt, Reed. *The Ordeal of Desegregation: The First Decade*. New York: Harper & Row, 1966.

Schlesinger, Arthur M., Jr. *A Thousand Days*. Boston: Houghton Mifflin, 1965.

School Desegregation in Texas Policy Research Project. *School Desegregation in Texas: The Implementation of United States v. State of Texas*. Lyndon B. Johnson School of Public Affairs: The University of Texas at Austin, 1982.

Schultz, Michael J. Jr. *The National Education Association and the Black Teacher: the Integration of a Professional Organization*. Carol Gables, FL: University of Miami Press, 1970.

Segall, William E., and Anna V. Wilson. "National Association of College Women." In *Historical Dictionary of Women's Education*, ed. Linda Eisenmann. Westport, CT: Greenwood Publishing Group, 1998.

———. "Mary McLeod Bethune." In *Historical Dictionary of Women's Education in the United States*, ed. Linda Eisenmann. Westport, CT: Greenwood Publishing Group, 1998.

———. *Introduction to Education: Teaching in a Diverse Society*. Columbus: Prentice-Hall/Merrill, 1998.

Seidman, I. E. *Interviewing as Qualitative Research: A Guide for Researchers in Education and the Social Sciences*. New York: Teachers College Press, 1991.

Selby, Earl and Miriam. *Odyssey: Journey Through Black America*. New York: G. P. Putnam's Sons, 1971.

Sergiovanni, Thomas J. *Building Community in Schools*. San Francisco: Jossey-Bass Publishers, 1994.

Shipler, David K. *A Country of Strangers: Blacks and Whites in America*. New York: Alfred A. Knopf, 1997.

Shoemaker, Don. *With All Deliberate Speed: Segregation—Desegregation in Southern Schools*. New York: Harper & Brothers, 1957.

Smith, John David. *An Old Creed for the New South: Proslavery Ideology and Historiography, 1865–1918*. Athens: The University of Georgia Press, 1991.

Southern Regional Council, *School Desegregation 1966: The Slow Undoing*. Atlanta: December 1966.

Stampp, Kenneth M. *The Peculiar Institution: Slavery in the Ante-Bellum South*. New York: Vintage Books, 1956.

Stanfield, John H. II. "Ethnic Modeling in Qualitative Research." In *Handbook of Qualitative Research*, eds. Norman K. Denzin and Yvonna S. Lincoln. Thousand Oaks, CA: Sage Publications, 1994.

Stephan, Walter G., and Joe R. Feagin. *School Desegregation: Past, Present, and Future*. New York: Plenum Press, 1980.

Suggs, Henry L., ed. *The Black Press in the South, 1865–1979*. Westport, CT: Greenwood Press, 1983.

Tuchman, Gayle. "Historical Social Science: Methodologies, Methods, and Meanings." In *Handbook of Qualitative Research*, eds. Norman K. Denzin and Yvonna S. Lindoln. Thousand Oaks, CA: Sage Publications, 1994.

Tushnet, Mark V. *The NAACP's Legal Strategy Against Segregated Education, 1925–1950*. Chapel Hill: University of North Carolina Press, 1987.

Walker, V. S. *Their Highest Potential: An African American School Community in the Segregated South*. Chapel Hill: University of North Carolina Press, 1996.

Walker, Wyatt T. *"Somebody's Calling My Name": Black Sacred Music and Social Change.* Valley Forge, PA: Judson Press, 1979.

Washington, Booker T. *Up from Slavery.* 1901: reprinted, New York: University Books, 1993.

Watras, Joseph. *Politics, Race, and Schools: Racial Integration, 1954–1994.* New York: Garland Publishing, 1997

Weiss, Beverly J. "An African American Teacher in Washington, D.C.: Marion P. Shadd (1856–1943. In *Lives of Women Public Schoolteachers: Scenes from American Educational History,* eds. M. Holmes and B. J. Weiss. New York: Garland Publishing, Inc., 1995.

Whalen, Charles and Barbara. *The Longest Debate: A Legislative History of the 1964 Civil Rights Act.* Cabin John, MD: Seven Locks Press, 1985.

Whitman, Mark, ed. *Removing a Badge of Slavery: The Record of Brown v. Board of Education.* Princeton: Markus Wiener Publishing,1993.

Williams, David A. *Bricks Without Straw: A History of Higher Education for Black Texans, 1872–1977.* Austin, TX: University of Texas Press, 1980.

Williams, Juan. *Eyes on the Prize: America's Civil Rights Years, 1954–65.* New York: Viking Press, 1987. Penguin, 1988.

Williams, Robin M. Jr., and Margaret W. Ryan. *Schools in Transition.* Chapel Hill: The University of North Carolina Press, 1954.

Wilson, Anna V. "Education for African Americans." In *The New Handbook of Texas, Vol. 2.* Austin: The Texas State Historical Society, 1996, 794–796.

Wilson, Anna V., and William E. Segall. "National Council of Negro Women," In *Historical Dictionary of Women's Education,* ed. Linda Eisenmann. Westport, CT: Greenwood Press, 1998.

Wolcott, Harry E. *Transforming Qualitative Data: Description, Analysis, and Interpretation.* Thousand Oaks, CA: Sage Publications, 1994.

Wolters, Raymond. *The Burden of Brown: Thirty Years of School Desegregation.* Knoxville, TN: University of Tennessee Press, 1984.

Woodward, C. Vann. *The Strange Career of Jim Crow,* 3rd edition. New York: Oxford University Press,1974.

ARTICLES

Anderson, James D. "Northern foundations and southern rural Black education, 1921–1935," *History of Education Quarterly* 18 (Winter 1978): 371–396.

———. "Education as a vehicle for the manipulation of Black workers," in *Work, Technology and Education: Dissenting Essays in the Intellectual Foundations of American Education,* eds. W. Feinberg and H. J. Rosemont. Urbana: University of Illinois Press, 1925, 15–40.

Barbee, Lorene. "Big Spring Independent School District Desegregation, 1955," *The Permian Historical Annual XXVII* (1987): 61–72.

Beck, William W.,and Glenn M. Linden. "Anglo and Minority Perceptions of Success in Dallas School Desegregation," *Phi Delta Kappan* 60, 5 (Jan. 1979): 378–382.

Beck, William W. "Identifying School Desegregation Leadership Styles," *Journal of Negro Education* 49, 2 (Spring 1980): 115–133.

Bell, Derrick. "Learning from Our Losses: Is School Desegregation Still Feasible in the 1980s?" *Phi Delta Kappan* 64, 8 (April 1983): 572–575.

Bolce, Louis Henri III, and Susan H. Gray. "Blacks, Whites and 'Race Politics,' " *Public Interest* 54 (Winter 1979): 61–75.

Bosma, Boyd. "The Role of Teachers in School Desegregation," *Integrated Education* 15, 6 (1976): 106–111.

Brisbane, Robert. "Interposition: Theory and Fact," *Phylon* 17 (1956): 12–16.

Bullock, Charles S. III, and Harrell R. Rodgers Jr. "Adjusting to School Desegregation: Perceptions and Correlates of Post-Desegregation Problems," *Negro Educational Review* 29, 2 (1978): 87–96.

Buxton, Thomas H., and Keith W. Prichard. "The Power Erosion Syndrome of the Black Principal," *Integrated Education* 15, 3 (1978): 9–14.

Candoli, I. C. "An Urban Superintendent Looks at School Desegregation," *Theory Into Practice* 17, 1 (1978): 17–22.

Carter, David G. "The Case Against Separate Schools," *Clearing House* 51, 3 (1978): 125–130.

Chambers, Julius L. "Implementing 'Brown,' " *Educational Forum* 41, 4 (1977): 415–429.

Davis, O. L. Jr. "The American School Curriculum Goes to War, 1941–1945: Oversight, Neglect, and Discovery," *Journal of Curriculum and Supervision* 8, 2 (Winter 1993): 112–127.

Dickinson, George E., and Kent Freeland. "Student, Teacher, and Administrator Attitudes Toward School Desegregation," *Integrated Education* 19, 3-6 (May–December 1981): 40–43

Doughty, James J. "Black School Board Members and Desegregation," *Theory Into Practice* 17, 1 (1978): 32–38.

Edmonds, Ronald R. "Desegregation Planning and Educational Equity," *Theory Into Practice* 17, 1 (1978): 12–16.

Falk, William W. "School Desegregation and the Educational Attainment Process: Some Results from Texas Schools," *Sociology of Education* 51, 4 (1978): 282–288.

Felice, Lawrence G., and Ronald L. Richardson. "Effects of Desegregation on Minority Student Dropout Rates," *Integrated Education* 15, 6 (1976): 47–50.

Ferguson, Carol C. "The Inside-Out Curriculum," *Educational Leadership* 39, 2 (November 1981): 114–116.

Fischer, Sylvia. "The Way I See It: Reflections on School Desegregation by Teachers from Four Cities," *School Review* 84, 3 (1975/76): 481–511.

Fleming, Harold C. "Resistance Movements and Racial Desegregation," *Annals of the American Academy* 304 (1956): 46–50.

Flygare, Thomas. "Austin and Indianapolis: A New Approach to Desegregation," *Phi Delta Kappan* 58, 9 (1976/77): 709–710.

Franks, Joan C. "School Desegregation: Negative Attitudes and Coping Methods for the Black Child," *Western Journal of Black Studies* 1, 3 (September 1977): 195–198.

Gay, Geneva. *Differential Dyadic Interactions of Black and White Teachers with Black and White Pupils in Recently Desegregated Social Studies Classrooms: A Function of Teacher and Pupil Ethnicity.* Final Report to U. S. Department of Health, Education and Welfare. Project No. 2F113, January 1974.

Gerard, Harold B. "School Desegregation: The Social Science Role," *American Psychologist* 38, 8 (August 1983): 869–877.

Gill, Robert Lewis. "*Brown II vs Board of Education of Topeka*: Its Human Advances and Human Tragedies, 1955–1980," *Negro Educational Review* 32, 1 (January 1981): 15–55.

Greene, Maxine. "Curriculum and Cultural Transformation: A Humanistic View," *Cross Currents* 25, 2 175–186.

Griffore, Robert J. "Factors Associated with Black Parent Participation and Non-Participation in Voluntary School Desegregation," *Educational Research Quarterly* 4, 4 (Winter 1979): 25–33.

Harper, Frederick. "Self-Actualization and Three Black Protesters," *Journal of Afro-American Issues 2* (Fall 1974): 303–319.

Harris, J. John III. "Education, Society, and the *Brown* Decision: Historical Principles versus Legal Mandates," *Journal of Black Studies* 13, 2 (December 1982): 141–154.

———. "Historical and Legal Antecedents of Public School Desegregation," *Planning and Changing—A Journal for School Administrators* 10, 1 (Spring 1979): 20–36.

———. "Desegregation Since *Brown v. Board of Education*: A Critical Assessment," *Journal of Thought* 12, 3: 217–227.

Hart, John. "Kennedy, Congress, and Civil Rights," *Journal of American Studies* 13 (August 1979): 165–178.

Hawley, Willis D. "The New Mythology of School Desegregation," *Law & Contemporary Problems* 42, 4 (Fall 1978): 214–233.

———. "Getting the Facts Straight About the Effects of School Desegregation," *Educational Leadership* 36, 5 (February 1979): 314–321.

Henderson, Thelton. "The Law and Civil Rights: The Justice Department in the South," *New University Thought* 3 (1963): 36–45.

Hunsaker, David M. "The Rhetoric of *Brown v. Board of Education*: Paradigm for Contemporary Social Protest," *Southern Speech Communication Journal* 43, 2: 91–109.

Irvine, R. W., and J. J. Irvine. "The Impact of the Desegregation Process on the Education of Black Students: Key Variables," *Journal of Negro Education 52* (4): 419.

Johnson, Charles. "Some Significant Social and Educational Implications of the U. S. Supreme Court's Decision," *Journal of Negro Education* 23, 3 (1954): 364–371.

Jones, William H. "Desegregation of Public Education in Texas—One Year Afterward," *Journal of Negro Education* 24 (1955): 352.

Kahn, Tom, and August Meier. "Recent Trends in the Civil Rights Movement," *New Politics* 3 (Spring 1964): 34–53.

Killian, Lewis M. "Organization, Rationality, and Spontaneity in the Civil Rights Movement," *American Sociological Review* 49 (December 1984): 770–783.

Korn, Carol. "I used to be very smart: Children talk about immigration," *Education and Culture: The Journal of the John Dewey Society* 1997.

Levin, Betsy. "School Desegregation Remedies and the Role of Social Science Research," *Law & Contemporary Problems* 42, 4 (Fall 1978): 1–36.

Levine, Daniel U., and Nolan Estes. "Desegregation and Educational Reconstruction in the Dallas Public Schools," *Phi Delta Kappan* 59, 3 (1977/78): 163–167.

Lieske, Joel A. "Group Disorders in Urban Schools: The Effects of Racial Desegregation and Social Emancipation," *Urban Affairs Quarterly* 14, 1 (September 1978): 79–101.

Love, Barbara J. "Desegregation in Your School: Behavior Patterns That Get in the Way," *Phi Delta Kappan* 59, 3 (1977/78): 168–170.

Macekura, Joseph. "Building Discipline in a 'Tough' School," *Social Education* 42, 2 (1978): 100–104.

McCain, R. Ray. "Reactions to the U. S. Supreme Court Decision of 1954," *Georgia Historical Quarterly* 52 (December 1968): 373.

McIntire, Ronald G. "Houston's Successful Desegregation Plan," *Phi Delta Kappan* 63, 8 (April 1982): 536–538.

Meier, August. "New Currents in the Civil Rights Movement," *New Politics* 2, 9 (Summer 1963): 7–32.

———. "The Dilemmas of Negro Protest Strategy," *New South* 21 (Spring 1966): 1–18.

Miller, Bernard I. "Some Anticipated Problems Incident to Racial Integration in the Public Schools and Some Suggested Approaches to the Problems," *Journal of Negro Education* 21 (1955): 285–292.

Monti, Daniel J. "Examining the Desegregation Process," *Integrated Education* 15, 6 (1976): 41–46.

———. "Desegregation as *Couvade*," *Integrated Education* 18, (1980): 1–4, 21–25.

Monti, Daniel J., and James H. Laue. "Implementing Desegregation Plans: The Social Scientist as Intervenor," *Education and Urban Society* (1977) 9, 3: 369–384.

Nelson, William E. Jr. "School Desegregation and the Black Community," *Theory Into Practice* 17, 2 (1978): 122–130.

Newby, Robert G. "Desegregation — Its Inequities and Paradoxes," *Black Scholar* 11, 1,(September–October 1979): 17-28, 67–68.

Payne, Essie K. "Student perceptions: The Value of Desegregation," *Theory Into Practice,* 17, 2 (1978): 172–178.

Poussaint, Alvin F., and Toye Brown Lewis. "School Desegregation: A Synonym for Racial Equality," *School Review* 84, 3 (1975/76): 326–336.

Pulliam, Roger L. "Historical Review of Black Education: Chicago," *Negro Educational Review* 29, 1 (1978): 22–32.

Rabinow, Kathryn L. E., and James M. Cooper. "A Case Study of the Historical Attempts of Two Colleges of Education to Prepare Teachers to Teach in a Desegregated Society," *Integrated Education* 18, (1980): 1–4, 128–133.

Rist, Ray C. "Sorting Out the Issues: The Current Status of School Desegregation," *Civil Rights Digest* 10, 2 (1978): 40–43.

Robinson, Sharon P. "Desegregation: A Bibliographic Review of Teacher Attitudes and Black Students," *Negro Educational Review* 31, 2 (April 1980): 48–59.

Rossell, Christine H. "School Desegregation and Community Social Change," *Law & Contemporary Problems* 42, 3 (Summer 1978): 133–183.

———. "The Effect of School Integration on Community Integration," *Journal of Education* 160, 2 (1977): 46–62.

Routh, Frederick B., and Paul Anthony. "Southern Resistance Forces," *Phylon* 18 (1957): 50–58.

Russell, Dorothy S., and Joseph F. Rogus. "Exploring Desegregation Through a Case Study Approach," *Social Studies* 69, 1 (1977): 25–30.

Rustin, Bayard. "A Prospectus for Civil Rights: The New Phase," *New America* (September 24, 1963): 6–7.

———. "From Protest to Politics: The Future of the Civil Rights Movement," *Commentary* 39 (February 1965): 25–31.

Sampson, William A., and Ben Williams. "School Desegregation—The Non-Traditional Sociological Perspective," *Journal of Negro Education* 47, 1 (1978): 72–80.

Serow, Robert C., and Daniel Solomon. "Parents' Attitudes Toward Desegregation: The Proximity Hypothesis," *Phi Delta Kappan* 60, 10 (June 1979): 752–753.

Simun, Patricia Bates. "Exploding the Myths of School Integration," *Integrated Education* 15, 6 (1976): 59–85.

Slawski, Edward J., and Jacqueline Scherer. "The Rhetoric of Concern: Trust and Control in an Urban Desegregated School," *Anthropology and Education Quarterly* 9, 4 (Winter 1978): 258–271.

Sly, David F., and Louis G. Pol. "The Demographic Context of School Segregation and Desegregation," *Social Forces* 56, 4 (1977): 1072–1086.

Smith, Marzell. "Level and Remedy in School Desegregation Research," *Theory into Practice* 17, 2 (1978): 187–194.

Smith, A. Wade. "Racial Tolerance as a Function of Group Position," *American Sociological Review* 46, 5 (October 1981): 558–573.

———. "Tolerance of School Desegregation, 1954–1977," *Social Forces* 59, 4 (June 1981): 1256–1274.

Southern Regional Council. *The South and Her Children: School Desegregation 1970–1971.* Atlanta: March 1971.

Stephan, Walter G. "School Desegregation: An Evaluation of Predictions Made in *Brown v. Board of Education*," *Psychological Bulletin* 85, 2 (1977): 217–238.

Stephan, Walter G., and David Rosenfield. "Effects of Desegregation on Racial Attitudes," *Journal of Personality and Social Psychology* 36, 8 (1976): 795–804.

Sullivan, Marcer L. "Desegregation, Culture Contact, and the Social Organization of Schools," *Research Bulletin* (*Horace Mann-Lincoln Institute*) 18, 4 (1976): 1–13.

Sumara, Dennis, and Brent Davis. "History, Memory, Curriculum," *Journal of Curriculum Theorizing* (Summer 1997): 2–3.

Texas Advisory Committee on Segregation in the Public Schools—Legal and Legislative Subcommittee. *Report of the Legal and Legislative Subcommittee of the Texas Advisory Committee on Segregation in the Public Schools, September 1, 1956.* Austin: Texas State Docs. No. L1836.54 Se38.

Thomas, Gail E., and Frank Brown. "What Does Educational Research Tell Us About School Desegregation Effects?" *Journal of Black Studies* 13, 2 (December 1982): 155–174.

Trombly, William. "Houston," *Integrated Education* 15, 6 (1976): 92–94.

Venditti, Fred P. "Major School Desegregation Problems: A Status Report," *Integrated Education* 19, (May–December 1981): 3–6, 35–39.

Washington, Valora. "The Role of Teacher Behavior in School Desegregation," *Educational Horizons* 57, 3 (Spring 1979): 145–151.

Wilson, Anna V. "Stranger in a Strange Land: One Black Student's Experience of Desegregation of a Birmingham, Alabama High School," *Midwest History of Education Society Journal* 23 (1996):117–123.

Wilson, Anna V., and William E. Segall. "Moving from the Shadows into the Sunlight: African American Teachers Incorporating Black History into the Curriculum before Desegregation," *Midwest History of Education Journal* 24 (1997): 172–174.

———. "Staying Alive in an Alien Land: Cognitive Dissonance, African American Teachers, and Desegregation," *Midwest History of Education Society Journal* 23 (1996): 61–64.

———. "With All Deliberate Slowness: The Role of Cross-Over Teachers in Desegregation," *Midwest History of Education Journal* 24 (1997): 64–68.

Wise, Michael B. "Desegregation in Education: A Legal Bibliography," *Notre Dame Lawyer* 52, 4 (1978): 733–790.

THESES, DISSERTATIONS, AND ESSAYS

Akin, Charles. *A Study of School Boundaries in East Austin, Texas.* Unpublished master's thesis, University of Texas at Austin, 1951.

Busacca, Richard L. *Social Movements and the Construction of Reality: A Study of the Civil Rights Movement and Its role in the Transformation of American Politics, 1954–1968.* Ph.D. dissertation, University of California, Berkeley, 1976.

Chote, James. *Desegregation of the Austin Independent School District: A Question of Balance.* Master's Thesis, University of Texas at Austin, 1991.

Cornelius, Cathi L., *"Village Perspectives" A Case Study Investigating the Perspectives Concerning the Oklahoma City Public Schools Neighborhood Schools Plan/student Reassignment Plan.* Unpublished Ed.D dissertation, Oklahoma State University, 1999.

Elms, James E. *Attendance of Mexican and Anglo Students in Two Austin, Texas, Schools.* Unpublished master's thesis, University of Texas at Austin, 1950.

Herd, Patricia. *Equal Educational Opportunity in the Austin Elementary Schools.* Unpublished master's thesis, University of Texas at Austin, 1975.

Knisely, Colette. *The Influence of Federal, State, and Local Policies on School Desegregation in the Austin, Texas, Independent School District.* Master's Thesis, University of Texas at Austin, 1978.

Kuhr, Nancy. *Segregated Public Schools in Texas.* Unpublished master's thesis, University of Texas at Austin, 1971

Leavitt, Urban James. *Desegregation and Attendance Zoning in Austin.* Unpublished master's thesis, University of Texas at Austin, 1956.

League of Women Voters of Austin. *Austin: School Desegregation 1954–1970.* Austin, 1970.

Mangold, Lana C. *Pupil-Teacher Dyadic Interaction in Desegregated Elementary School Classrooms.* Ph.D. Dissertation, University of Texas at Austin, 1974.

Marty, William R. *Recent Negro Protest Thought: Theories of Nonviolence and "Black Power."* Ph.D. dissertation, Duke University, 1968.

Stubbs, Janine L. *Social Stratification in a Desegregated High School.* Master's Thesis, University of Texas at Austin, 1983.

Sullivan, Donald F. *The Civil Rights Programs of the Kennedy Administration: A Political Analysis.* Ph.D. dissertation, University of Oklahoma, 1965.

Sullivan, S. L. *President Lyndon Baines Johnson and the Common School, 1963–1969.* Unpublished Ed.D. dissertation, Oklahoma State University, 1973.

Wise, Charlotte Anne. *The Treatment of Blacks in Selected American History Textbooks.* Master's thesis, University of Texas at Austin, 1973.

Witt, Sharon K. *School Integration and Racial Prejudice.* Master's thesis, University of Texas at Austin, 1970.

Wright, Harry K. *Civil Rights U. S. A.: Public Schools, Southern States, 1963, Texas. Staff Report Submitted to the United States Commission on Civil Rights.* Washington, DC, 1964.

Young, Roy. *Presidential Leadership and Civil Rights Legislation, 1963–1964.* Ph.D. dissertation, University of Texas at Austin, 1969.

COURT CASES

Dred Scott v. Sanford, 60 U.S. (19 Howard) 393, 407 (1857), 393.

Green v. Board, 391 U.S. 430 (1968), 438–439.

Jackson v. Rawdon, U.S. District Court, Texas, Civ. no. 3152, November 21, 1955, 135 F. Supp. 936, U.S. Court of Appeals, Fifth Circut, June 28, 1956, Civ. No. 15927.

Plessy v. Ferguson, 163 U. S. 537 (1896).

Railroad Company v. Brown, 84 U.S. (17 Wall.) 445, 452–453 (1873).

Sipuel v. Oklahoma State Board of Regents, 332 U.S. 631 (1948).

Sweatt v. Painter, 1948.

Sweatt v. Painter, 339 U.S. 629 (1950).

McLaurin v. Oklahoma State Regents for Higher Education, 339 U.S. 637 (1950).

Brown v. Board of Education of Topeka, Kansas, 347 U.S. 483 (1954).

Brown v. Board of Education of Topeka, Kansas, 355 U. 294 (1955).

McKinney et al. v. Blankenship et. al., Supreme Court of Texas, 282 S. W. 2nd 691 (October 12, 1955).

Texas Constitution, art. 7, § 7 enacted in 1876.

Texas Revised Civil Statute Annotated, art. 2900, enacted in 1905.

United States v. Texas Education Agency et. al., (1970).

ORAL HISTORIES

Oral histories collected on audiotape for this dissertation are deposited in the Oral History in Education Collection at The University of Texas at Austin (UTOHE).

Oral history interviews of William Charles Akins with Anna V. Wilson (October to December, 1996).

Oral history interviews of Iola Taylor with Anna V. Wilson (October to December, 1996).

Oral history interviews of Vernice T. Smith with Anna V. Wilson (October to December, 1996).

Oral history interviews of Alvin Patterson with Anna V. Wilson (January to February, 1997).

Oral history interviews of Hertha Webb Glenn with Anna V. Wilson (January to March, 1997).

Oral history interviews of Will Davis with Anna V. Wilson (April 1997).

Oral history interviews of Wilhelmina Delco with Anna V. Wilson (April 1997).

Oral history interviews of Clifford McPherson with Anna V. Wilson (January 1997).

Oral history interviews of Tom T. Allen with Anna V. Wilson (January to February, 1997).

Oral history interviews of Herbert Brown with Anna V. Wilson (January to February, 1997).

Oral history interviews of James Dorsett with Anna V. Wilson (January 1997).

Oral history interviews of Elizabeth Ann Stoll with Anna V. Wilson (January to February, 1997).

Oral history interviews of Jimmy Raines with Anna V. Wilson (November to December, 1997).

Oral history interviews of Melvin Chambers with Anna V. Wilson (January to February, 1997).

NEWSPAPERS

Austin American
American Statesman
Austin Capital City
Austin Citizen
Chicago Defender
Christian Science Monitor
Dallas Morning News
Houston Informer
New York Times
Oklahoma City Daily Oklahoman
The Texas Outlook
Tulsa Tribune
Washington Post

PERIODICALS

Ebony
Jet

Negro Digest
New America
Newsweek
North and South
SCLC Newsletter
Southern Courier
Southern Education Reporting Service
Southern School News
The Austin Classroom Teacher
Time
U.S. News & World Report
Utmost

PAPERS AND ARCHIVAL COLLECTIONS

Austin Independent School District Archives, Lucy Read School, Austin, TX.

Austin Independent School District Board Minutes, Administration Building, Austin, TX.

Austin Desegregation Papers, Austin History Center, Austin, TX.

Lyndon B. Johnson Vice-Presidential Papers, Johnson Library, Austin, TX.

Lyndon B. Johnson Presidential Papers, White House Central Files, Johnson Library, Austin, TX.

Moorhead Papers, Center for American History, Austin, TX.

National Association for the Advancement of Colored People Papers, Library of Congress, Washington, DC.

George Sanchéz Papers, Benton Latin American Center, Austin, TX.

Texas Education Agency Archives, Austin TX.

Texas State Teacher's Association Archives, Austin, TX.

WEB RESOURCES

Humphrey, David C. "untitled," *Texas Online, www.tsha.utexas.edu/web_evaluate*

Maxwell, Lisa C. "Deep Ellum," *Texas Online, www.tsha.utexas.edu/handbook/online*

Moneyhon, Carl H. "Black Codes," *Texas Online, www.tsha.utexas.edu/handbook/online*

Odintz, Mark. "Senator Ralph Yarborough," *Texas Online, www.tsha.utexas.edu/handbook/online*

Rogosin, William D. "Willie Wells," *Texas Online, www.tsha.utexas.edu/handbook/online*

Scarbrough, Clara S. "Round Rock, Texas," *Texas, Online, www.tsha.utexas.edu/handbook/online*

Index